PEACEMAKING, POWER-SHARING AND INTERNATIONAL LAW: IMPERFECT PEACE

This monograph provides a contemporary analysis of the frictions between peacemaking and international human rights law based on the cases of post-conflict power-sharing in Lebanon and Bosnia-Herzegovina. In this context it evaluates the long-standing debate in the United Nations and human rights bodies about the 'imperfect peace'. Written from a practitioner–scholarly viewpoint and drawing from new authentic sources, the book describes the mechanisms used in peace agreements and post-conflict constitutions for managing ethnic or religious diversity, explains their legal limits under international human rights law, and provides a conceptual framework for analysing the nexus between law and peacemaking. The book argues that the relationship between the content of peace agreements and post-conflict constitutions, their negotiation process and the element of time, needs to be untangled to better understand the legal limits of statebuilding in the aftermath of armed conflict. It is a key resource for scholars in human rights law and peace and conflict studies, advisers in peace processes, constitution-makers, and peace mediators.

Peacemaking, Power-sharing and International Law

Imperfect Peace

Martin Wählisch

•HART•
OXFORD • LONDON • NEW YORK • NEW DELHI • SYDNEY

HART PUBLISHING

Bloomsbury Publishing Plc

Kemp House, Chawley Park, Cumnor Hill, Oxford, OX2 9PH, UK

HART PUBLISHING, the Hart/Stag logo, BLOOMSBURY and the Diana logo are trademarks of Bloomsbury Publishing Plc

First published in Great Britain 2019

A catalogue record for this book is available from the British Library.

Library of Congress Cataloging-in-Publication data

Names: Wählisch, Martin, 1982-, author.

Title: Peacemaking, power-sharing and international law : imperfect peace / Martin Wählisch.

Description: Chicago : Hart Publishing, 2019. | Includes bibliographical references and index.

Identifiers: LCCN 2019021082 (print) | LCCN 2019021934 (ebook) | ISBN 9781509914234 (EPub) | ISBN 9781509914258 (hardback)

Subjects: LCSH: Pacific settlement of international disputes. | Mediation, International. | International human rights. | Humanitarian law. | Peace. | BISAC: LAW / International. | POLITICAL SCIENCE / Peace.

Classification: LCC KZ6045 (ebook) | LCC KZ6045 .W34 2019 (print) | DDC 341.5/2—dc23

LC record available at https://lccn.loc.gov/2019021082

ISBN: HB: 978-1-50991-425-8
ePDF: 978-1-50991-422-7
ePub: 978-1-50991-423-4

Typeset by Compuscript Ltd, Shannon
Printed and bound in Great Britain by CPI Group (UK) Ltd, Croydon CR0 4YY

FSC www.fsc.org MIX Paper from responsible sources FSC® C013604

PREFACE

When I started the research for this book, I was working for the German Embassy in Kosovo nearly ten years ago. We were following the appointments for the Supreme Court and the establishment of other state institutions after the country's independence. Their composition was supposed to mirror the multi-ethnic composition of the country, but the realities made it clear that peace remained imperfect. There was much talk in Pristina about the Dayton Peace Accords that posed similar challenges in Bosnia-Herzegovina. After the Balkans, I moved to Lebanon, a place with a multi-confessional social fabric and a complex post-civil war path. I arrived some years after the adoption of the Doha Agreement that ended a political crisis in the country through a layered power-sharing formula. The political and legal debate centered on the quasi constitutional character of the agreement and how it relates to early power-sharing provisions in the Taif Peace Agreement that marked the end of the Lebanese Civil War in 1989. I was eager to better understand why it is so difficult to turn war into peace and what the legal baseline for peace is. Going through the archives at the United Nations as a doctoral student, I stumbled upon the debate about the 'imperfect peace'; and things started to make more sense. This book is the result of this research journey.

I am thankful for the inspiring research environments that allowed me to think openly and critically about law in the context of peacemaking. First and foremost, I owe gratitude to my doctoral supervisor Professor Dr George Nolte. He has been nothing but supportive in nurturing my curiosity in law and diligent in challenging my conclusions. I am also thankful for the constructive advice and comments on the manuscript from the Examination Committee members Professor Dr Dr hc Christian Tomuschat and Professor Dr Alexander Blankenagel at the Humboldt University of Berlin. My research at the Lauterpacht Center for International Law at the University of Cambridge, the Issam Fares Institute for Public Policy and International Affairs at the American University of Beirut, the Harriman Institute at Columbia University, the Institute for Global Law and Policy at New York Law School, and the Faculty of Law at Durham Law School was invaluable for this project. I am very grateful to all my mentors, colleagues, friends, and family for their patience, above all to my wife Maureen. The German Academic Foundation (Studienstiftung des deutschen Volkes) generously supported the research for this book.

I finished the manuscript in 2014 and included updates but could not capture all new published research and case law since then. Eventually, the book is a piece of the larger puzzle of the literature on peacemaking and law. As the topic and content of this book, the monograph is imperfect and an invitation for a conversation. Unsurprisingly, most addressed conflicts in this book are still unresolved and more questions have emerged since the answers to the research of this monograph were written.

When it was time to pick a cover for this book, I chose the mural 'Guerra e Paz', as it reminds me in my current work at the United Nations Headquarters in New York of the dilemmas of humanity in its struggle with conflict. There are two parts of the painting that are placed in opposite side to each other at the entrance of the General Assembly: one exhibits peace in bright colors, and the other one in grey depicts the grim impact of war. The Brazilian artist Cândido Portinari painted it and said it was meant as an encouragement for diplomats to turn armed conflict into peace. It contrasts the fluctuating experiences societies live through and stands symbol for the call to the international community for joint efforts to turn evil into good. In between both parts of the mural in the delegates entrance of the UN building there is space where people meet, discuss, agree or depart – maybe this is what the imperfect peace is about …

CONTENTS

LIST OF ABBREVIATIONS

App	Application
ArCHR	Arab Charter on Human Rights
Art	Article
AU	African Union
BiH	Bosnia and Herzegovina
CEDAW	Convention on the Elimination of all Forms of Discrimination Against Women
CERD	Committee on the Elimination of Racial Discrimination
Ch	Chapter
CPA	Comprehensive Peace Accord/ Agreement
Dec	Decision
Def	Definition
ECHR	European Convention on Human Rights
ECRI	European Commission against Racism and Intolerance
ECtHR	European Court of Human Rights
ETS	European Treaty Series
EU	European Union
FBiH	Federation Bosnia and Herzegovina
Fn	Footnote
GA	General Assembly
HRC	Human Rights Council
IACHR	Inter-American Commission on Human Rights
ICC	International Criminal Court
ICCPR	International Covenant on Civil and Political Rights

ICERD	International Convention on Elimination of All Forms of Racial Discrimination
ICESCR	International Covenant on Economic, Social and Cultural Rights
ICJ	International Court of Justice
IFOR	Implementation Force
ILC	International Law Commission
ODIHR	Office for Democratic Institutions and Human Rights
OSCE	Organization for Security and Co-operation in Europe
R2P	Responsibility to Protect
Res	Resolution
RS	Republika Srpska
RUF/SL	Revolutionary United Front of Sierra Leone
SAA	Stabilisation and Association Agreement
SC	Security Council
UN	United Nations
UDHR	Universal Declaration of Human Rights
UNDM	United Nations Declaration on the Rights of Persons Belonging to National or Ethnic, Religious and Linguistic Minorities
UNDRIP	United Nations Declaration on the Rights of Indigenous Peoples
UNTS	United Nations Treaty Series
VCLT	Vienna Convention of the Law on Treaties

TABLE OF CASES

ICJ judgments and advisory opinions

ECtHR cases

Human Rights Committee communications

Constitutional Court of Bosnia-Herzegovina

Other cases, awards and judgments

TABLE OF INTERNATIONAL CONVENTIONS, TREATIES, PEACE AGREEMENTS, DOCUMENTS AND REPORTS

Conventions, covenants and declarations

Constitutions, statutes and laws

Peace agreements and other agreements

UN General Assembly resolutions

UN Security Council resolutions

UN Security Council reports and notes

UN Security Council presidential statements

UN meeting records

UN human rights monitoring bodies reports and resolutions

CERD General Recommendations

CCPR General Comments

ILC reports and draft articles

Reports of the UN Secretary General

UN guidance notes

Opinions of the Venice Commission

African Union documents

Speeches, statements and press releases

Other reports and documents

LIST OF FIGURES AND TABLES

1

Introduction

I. State Transitions, Power-Sharing and International Law

In 2011, a series of uprisings hit the Middle East and Northern Africa. Like the Balkans in the 1990s, the Arab world has been facing the challenge of transformation, all while trying to manage confessional and ethnic diversity. Issues such as the political participation of minorities, the containment of extremism, as well as sectarian tensions continue to bear the potential of conflict in the region.

In 2012, in a keynote address in Beirut on reform and transition to democracy, the UN Secretary-General responded to the change in the region by calling for 'a fair share of political power' to balance interests.[1] Yet, decisions by the European Court of Human Rights (ECtHR) and recommendations by the UN human rights monitoring bodies have affirmed that certain power-sharing systems can also infringe upon human rights.[2] While consociational constitutions and peace settlements can bring about a pause in civil strife, enhance rights and state stability, they can lay the ground for renewed injustice, which can eventually lead to a relapse into armed conflict.[3]

In such cases of state transitions, international law is confronted with normative collisions between the right of self-determination, the right to life, the prohibition of discrimination and the prerogative of peace. The result has been described as 'imperfect peace', whose legal limits and necessity are the focus of this book.[4]

A. Peacemaking and Power-Sharing

Aiming to accommodate pluralism, power-sharing is globally a frequent element of peace agreements and constitutional frameworks, creating opportunities but also entailing shortcomings.

[1] Keynote Address at High-level Meeting on Reform and Transitions to Democracy, Speech by UN Secretary-General Ban Ki-moon, Beirut, 15 January 2012.

[2] On Bosnia and Herzegovina, see *Sejdic and Finci v Bosnia and Herzegovina*, ECtHR Judgment, App Nos 27996/06 and 34836/06, 22 December 2009, para 42. A further case on Bosnia and Herzegovina is still pending at the ECtHR, see *Ilijaz Pilav v Bosnia and Herzegovina*, ECtHR Application, App No 41939/07, lodged on 24 September 2007. On Lebanon, see, eg, UN Doc CERD/C/64/CO/3, 28 April 2004, para 10; UN Doc CEDAW/C/LBN/CO/3, 8 April 2008, para 44.

[3] For details, see Ch 2.

[4] On the term *imperfect peace* and its usage in international practice, see Part I.B. below.

In the Balkans, the Dayton Peace Accords introduced a multi-layered state system based on ethnicity that ended one of Europe's most ruthless civil wars at the end of the twentieth century while regenerating an unresolved cycle of conflict.[5] Meanwhile, a secession of the mainly Serb-dominated Republika Srpska from Bosnia and Herzegovina is still under debate.[6] A similar situation can be seen in Kosovo, where a split of constitutional power between the Albanian majority, the Serbian minority and other minorities did not fully calm down tension.[7]

In the Middle East, Lebanon is an example of the success but also the downsides of a consensus-driven democracy. Although the Taif Peace Agreement formally ended 15 years of civil war, the political stability and balance in the country is fragile, and remains to be affected by regional dynamics.[8] Over the last years, there have been public demonstrations against the confessionalism system; yet formal and informal entrenched sectarian structures makes it difficult to overcome the conflict-prone past.[9] At the same time, Lebanon has been considered as an exemplary model to guarantee some type of rough equity and communal security in the Arab region.[10]

On the African continent, new political arrangements appear on an ongoing basis, either to prevent or react to *coups d'état*.[11] Power-sharing deals continue to be at the centre of peace talks and post-electoral contestations.[12] In parallel, the African Union has responded by outlawing 'unconstitutional changes of

[5] For a comprehensive critical analysis, see Florian Bieber, *Post-War Bosnia: Ethnicity, Inequality and Public Sector Governance* (New York, Palgrave Macmillan, 2006) 1. Also see Julian Borger, 'Bosnian War 20 Years on: Peace Holds but Conflict Continues to Haunt' *The Guardian* (4 April 2012).

[6] 'Is Another Conflict Looming in the Balkans?' *Al Jazeera English* (6 January 2013). 'Milorad Dodik: Republika Srpska is fully prepared for Secession from Bosnia and Herzegovina' *Sarajevo Times* (25 January 2019).

[7] Bekim Baliqi, 'Promoting Multi-Ethnicity or Maintaining a Divided Society: Dilemmas of Power-Sharing in Kosovo' (2018) 17(1) *Journal on Ethnopolitics and Minority Issues in Europe* 49. See also Kosovo 2010 Progress Report, European Commission Doc SEC(2011) 1207 final, 12 October 2011, para 1.2.

[8] Faten Ghosn and Amal Khoury, 'Lebanon after the Civil War: Peace or the Illusion of Peace?' (2011) 65(3) *Middle East Journal* 381. See also Karam Karam, 'Post-Syria Lebanon: Internal and External Determinants of a Crisis' (2006) 41(2) *The International Spectator* 51.

[9] John Nagle, 'Beyond Ethnic Entrenchment and Amelioration: An Analysis of Non-sectarian Social Movements and Lebanon's Consociationalism' (2018) 41(7) *Ethnic and Racial Studies* 1370. See also 'Lebanese Protest Against Confessionalism' *AFP* (6 May 2012); Rana Moussaoui, 'Lebanon Youths Revolt Against Confessional System' *AFP* (23 February 2011).

[10] Stephan Rosiny, 'Power Sharing in Syria: Lessons from Lebanon's Taif Experience' (2013) 20(3) *Middle East Policy* 41. For the debate, see also Rami G Khouri, 'The Islamist-Secular Battle is Under Way' *The Daily Star (Lebanon)* (31 March 2012).

[11] For a systematic overview see Andreas Mehler, 'Introduction: Power-Sharing in Africa' (2009) 44(3) *Africa Spectrum* 2.

[12] 'Central African Republic: Amnesty and Power-sharing at the Center of Peace Talks' *African Daily Voice* (29 January 2019). See also Rowland JV Cole, 'Power-sharing, Post-electoral Contestations and the Dismemberment of the Right to Democracy in Africa' (2013) 17(2) *International Journal of Human Rights* 256.

governments' to counter the legitimization of unconstitutional seizure of power under the pretext of power-sharing.[13]

In South and Central Asia, a forthcoming endeavour will be a power-sharing pact in Afghanistan, now that there is growing support for negotiations with the Taliban.[14] The political and legal modalities have been contested for a long time in this context.[15] Eventually, such an agreement could erode what little trust there is in constitutional procedures.[16]

B. Imperfect Peace

Despite the precious moment of achieving an end to hostilities, peace accords and post-conflict constitutional solutions are frequently inadequate, facing unfulfilled demands and legal implications. Those participating in peace negotiations have characterised this fundamental dilemma in peacemaking as 'imperfect peace'.

i. The Dayton Peace Agreement and Imperfect Peace

The topos 'imperfect peace' has been particularly present in the context of peace-making and peacebuilding in the former Yugoslavia.[17] US Ambassador Richard Holbrooke noted about the Dayton Peace Conference that when it 'came down to the last few hours', one 'had to choose between an imperfect peace and a resumption of the war'.[18] Tono Eitel, then Permanent Representative of Germany to the UN, commented that the Dayton Agreement came with 'painful concessions' for 'all sides', but has nevertheless been 'a major achievement and an important step forward'.[19] 'Imperfect as it may be', it represented 'the best chance in a long time for

[13] For a summary, see Pacifique Manirakizaa, 'The African Commission on Human and Peoples' Rights' Perspective on Power-sharing Arrangements' (2013) 17(2) *International Journal of Human Rights* 238. See also Pacifique Manirakiza, 'Insecurity Implications of Unconstitutional Changes of Government in Africa: From Military to Constitutional Coups' (2016) 17(2) *Journal of Military and Strategic Studies* 86.

[14] 'US and Taliban edge Toward Deal to End America's Longest War' *The New York Times* (26 January 2019). See previously Ali M Latifi, 'Taliban Talks in Doha Drag on Endlessly' *Al Jazeera English* (26 February 2013).

[15] Harmonie Toros, '"We Don't Negotiate with Terrorists!": Legitimacy and Complexity in Terrorist Conflicts' (2008) 39(4) *Security Dialogue* 407.

[16] International Crisis Group, *Talking About Talks: Toward a Political Settlement in Afghanistan*, Report No 221 (26 March 2012) 24.

[17] For an introduction to the concept of external state-building in Bosnia and Herzegovina, see Marc Weller and Stefan Wolff, 'Bosnia and Herzegovina Ten Years after Dayton: Lessons for Internationalized State Building' (2006) 5(1) *Ethnopolitics* 1. See also Richard Caplan, 'Assessing Dayton: The Structural Weaknesses of the General Framework Agreement for Peace in Bosnia and Herzegovina' (2000) 11(2) *Diplomacy & Statecraft* 213.

[18] 'In Memoriam: Richard Holbrooke on Dayton Agreement', *Dayton Council of World Affairs*, Speech by Richard Holbrooke, 17 November 2005

[19] UN Doc S/PV.3595, 22 November 1995.

a durable peace in the region', he concluded.[20] Nobody has been 'entirely satisfied with the outcome', but that 'is a sign that the Agreement as a whole has a realistic basis', remarked Eitel.[21]

The same thoughts were shared by other diplomats. The Malaysian Ambassador Razali stated that 'the international community must stand behind President Izetbegovic and the Bosnians' in order to 'give peace, however imperfect or fragile, a chance to take root'.[22] The Turkish UN Representative Baykal added later in a General Assembly debate:

> Ending conflict and human suffering and then achieving peace without sacrificing justice constitute the most fundamental objective of humankind. Although the signing of the Dayton Peace Agreement and its imperfect implementation brought about peace and ended human suffering in the territory of former Yugoslavia, justice has not prevailed fully.[23]

In November 1995, Yugoslavia's then Foreign Minister, Vladislav Jovanović, summarised in a hearing in the UN Security Council the day after the Dayton Peace Agreement was initialled:

> This Peace Agreement is not a perfect one, something that can, indeed, be said of a great majority of the peace agreements concluded throughout history. It is a result of necessary and reasonable – although at times painful and difficult – compromises. All parties to the civil war and the Bosnian crisis have come to realize that an imperfect peace is better than a protracted and uncertain war and that only in peace can just goals be best achieved.[24]

Alija Izetbegović, the first President of Bosnia and Herzegovina, concluded later:

> We who signed the Dayton/Paris Peace Agreement to establish peace have always understood it to be imperfect … In Dayton, our priority was to stop the killing, because there had been too much death. We believed that an imperfect peace would be better than a just war and that the natural integration of Bosnia and Herzegovina into the Euro-Atlantic family would help to overcome the shortcomings of such an initially unjust, as well as imperfect, peace.[25]

Since then, state representatives have increasingly referred to the term 'imperfect peace' when describing human rights compromises in peacemaking.

[20] ibid.

[21] ibid.

[22] ibid.

[23] UN Doc A/53/PV.62, 19 November 1998. See also the comment by the Special Representative of the Secretary-General and Principal Deputy High Representative for Bosnia and Herzegovina, Jacques Paul Klein: 'To be very candid, Dayton was a less than perfect peace to end a horrible war. We know that. But Dayton created a construct where post, telephone, telegraph, commerce, taxation, regulation, police and military are under two entities', UN Doc S/PV.4330, 15 June 2001.

[24] UN Doc S/PV.3595, above n 19.

[25] UN Doc A/55/PV.4, 6 September 2003.

ii. Imperfection and the 'Culture of Peace'

The matter of imperfection runs as a general theme through UN discussions. In a plenary session of the General Assembly, the President of Honduras, Carlos Roberto Flores Facussé, eloquently stated that:

> The world's age-old desire for a new world order based on peace, cooperation and fraternity between all countries rather than on a balance of arms between powerful and hegemonic States has already come to pass … That is why we must indeed acknowledge that, despite all its imperfections, the world has brought in a new world order at the end of this century and the dawn of the new, an order led by the United Nations …[26]

The Italian Foreign Minister Lamberto Dini joined in with the chorus by declaring that the Cold War 'brought a precarious, imperfect peace'.[27] In 1999, the UN Secretary-General described times of imperfect peace as a challenge for countries that 'are caught in the grey and unpredictable zone between peace and war because of protracted conflicts or prolonged transitions to peace'.[28] At the UN Millennium Summit in September 2000, Portugal's Prime Minister António Guterres called on the international community to 'perfect international law and the means for its implementation in order to protect, ever more effectively, the sovereignty of the individual and to frame properly the right of humanitarian intervention'.[29]

Similarly, the question of imperfect peace formed part of the discussion in the General Assembly about the 'culture of peace'.[30] In a session of the Security Council on post-conflict peace-building, the Slovenian Ambassador Danilo Türk made the following telling remark:

> Making peace usually implies difficult choices, a fact of which the United Nations is intensely aware today … However, we should keep in mind the wisdom of the great European philosopher Erasmus, who explained in 1508 that 'the most disadvantageous peace is better than the most just war'. This maxim is relevant to many contemporary conflicts and has a specific meaning: peace is a challenge. It can be disadvantageous from the standpoint of the basic values of humanity, but the real struggle for those values is given a chance when the war is ended …[31]

[26] Address of the President of Honduras, Carlos Roberto Flores Facussé, UN Doc A/54/PV.8, 22 September 1999.

[27] ibid.

[28] UN Doc A/54/430, 1 October 1999, para 100 ('Even in situations of "imperfect peace", opportunities and space often exist for addressing the needs of children with regard to the provision of health care, education, resettlement and rehabilitation. To meet those needs, however, will require adjustment in the prevailing theory and policy of development assistance …').

[29] UN Doc A/55/PV.4, 6 September 2000.

[30] UN Doc A/56/PV.29, 22 October 2001 (Comment by Archbishop Martino: 'It is indeed appropriate that today the General Assembly is addressing the topic of a culture of peace. The imperfect peace in which our world had been dwelling has suddenly been shattered by violent and senseless attacks against innocent human beings …').

[31] See UN Doc S/PV.4020, 8 July 1999, Comment by Mr Türk.

The debate shows that peace sometimes leaves much to be desired: post-conflict situations often begin on the basis of an imperfect peace, which can be an opportunity for change and a starting point for development.

iii. Imperfect Peace versus Illegal Peace?

In his book *Illegal Peace in Africa*, Jeremy Levitt wrote that states with internal conflicts face the need to 'legaliz[e] peace'.[32] Describing the utility of law in peacemaking, he explored the tension between legal order versus legal realism in Africa, questioning the 'legality of power-sharing' with warlords, rebels, and juntas.[33] Levitt concluded that law 'provides a framework or blueprint for peacemaking that constrains the political ambitions and shenanigans of embattled politicians and *pirates de la loi*, respectively'.[34] 'Illegal peace', he noted, 'occurs when political edicts or mandates prescribe unlawfully derived rules more weight than lawfully derived ones'.[35] Levitt asked whether political leaders should accept 'illegal peace' and whether 'individual responsibility for repression [should] be excused for the perceived collective good'.[36]

Yet, does peace become 'unlawful' just because of a legally flawed peace settlement? Do discriminatory constitutional systems, which might indeed contradict international law, change the legal status of peace, or are they instead an acceptable compromise within an imperfect system? This study will show that Levitt's conclusions appear incomplete in their disregard for the factual circumstances of peace. International judicial bodies have analogously emphasised that the 'factual situation' is conclusive for the status of armed conflict and not the signing of a legally valid peace treaty.[37] As Myres McDougal convincingly phrased it in his contribution to an intense scholarly debate about this issue in international law after the World War II, peace and war are a 'factual continuum with multiple legal consequences'.[38] The debate about imperfect peace expresses that there are impasses in peacemaking. Indeed, international law faces the paradox that peace agreements might settle one area of human rights demands, while entailing other human rights implications. Nonetheless, labelling peace as 'illegal' could stigmatise and

[32] Jeremy I Levitt, *Illegal Peace in Africa: An Inquiry into the Legality of Power Sharing with Warlords, Rebels, and Junta* (Cambridge, Cambridge University Press, 2012) 24.

[33] ibid, 29.

[34] ibid, 24–25.

[35] On the other hand, according to Levitt, '[a] *legal peace* is one that is made in accordance with or sanctioned by lawful law or law that is lawfully derived (eg, from a democratic constitution)': ibid, 19 (fn 59).

[36] ibid, 19.

[37] See *Military and Paramilitary Activities in and against Nicaragua (Nicaragua v US)*, Merits, 27 June 1986, ICJ Reports 1986, 14, para 58; *Prosecutor v Tadic, Interlocutory Appeal on Jurisdiction, ICTY*, Case No IT-94-1-AR72, 2 October 1995, para 30.

[38] Myres S McDougal, 'Peace and War: Factual Continuum with Multiple Legal Consequences' (1955) 49 *American Journal of International Law* 63.

diminish genuine peacemaking efforts, and possibly fail to acknowledge the relation between peace and law as a highly complex nexus.

C. Nexus between Law and Peace

The link between law and peace has been an enigma for centuries. Scholars and practitioners have tried to grasp how international law justifies war but also guarantees peace, as well as how peace is a condition for the rule of law.

Over 300 years ago, witnessing the times of the Eighty Years' War between Spain and the Netherlands and the Thirty Years' War between Catholic and Protestant European nations, the Dutch jurist Hugo Grotius developed rights of war and peace in his three books entitled *De Jure Belli Ac Pacis* ['On the Law of War and Peace'].[39] The German jurist Samuel Pufendorf declared in his treatise *De Officio Hominis et Civis* ['On the Duty of Man and Citizen'] that 'every peace is perpetual' while 'war is permitted, and sometimes necessary'.[40] Eméric de Vattel, a Swiss diplomat and legal scholar, realised that international law needs to differentiate between 'perfect' and 'imperfect obligations', the latter occurring in external judgments.[41] Vattel concluded that 'the right is always imperfect, when the correspondent obligation depends on the judgment of the party'.[42] He argued:

> The perfect right is that which is accompanied by the right of compelling those who refuse to fulfil the correspondent obligation; the imperfect right is unaccompanied by that right of compulsion. The perfect obligation is that which gives to the opposite party the right of compulsion; the imperfect gives him only a right to ask … Our obligation is always imperfect with respect to other people, while we possess the liberty of judging how we are to act: and we retain that liberty on all occasions where we ought to be free …[43]

Vattel stressed that nations that live together need to follow laws in order 'to maintain order and peace in their society'.[44] As this retrospective reflects, peace and law have always promised permanent stability, despite their limitations.[45]

[39] Hugo Grotius, *The Rights of War and Peace: Including the Law of Nature and of Nations* (first published 1624, Indianapolis, Liberty Fund, 2005) 1, 389, 1185.

[40] Samuel Pufendorf, *De Jure Naturae et Gentium Libri Octo* (first published 1673, New York, Oceana Publications Inc, 1964) 138 ('License in war goes so far that, although in killing, devastating and plundering a man may have overstepped the limits of humanity, still in the general opinion of nations he is not regarded as infamous, and a man whom good men should avoid …').

[41] Emmerich de Vattel, *The Law of Nations or the Principles of Natural Law* (first published 1758, Philadelphia, T & JW Johnson, 1854) 17.

[42] ibid.

[43] ibid.

[44] ibid, 214.

[45] For the most idealistic formulation of this viewpoint, see Immanuel Kant, 'Zum ewigen Frieden: Ein philosophischer Entwurf' in Wilhelm Weischedel (ed), *Immanuel Kant: Werke in Zwölf Bänden* vol 11 (Frankfurt am Main, Suhrkamp Verlag, 1977) 212–13.

i. *Intersection of Responsibility, Human Rights and Peace*

In recent scholarly debate, the intersection of responsibility, human rights and peace has increasingly been scrutinised.

Exploring the changing role of law in the international arena, Ruti Teitel highlighted in her book *Humanity's Law* that there has been a paradigm shift away from inter-state international law towards human-centred politics and law.[46] Teitel explained that evolving laws of war, international human rights law and international criminal law have been reshaping the discourse of international relations. The number of actors and rights has expanded over the course of history.[47] The development of the International Criminal Court (ICC) and the concept of universal jurisdiction, as well as the development of universal norms (*jus cogens* and *erga omnes*) have been changing rules of responsibility and accountability.[48] The law of war and the law of peace have been steadily overlapping: legal orders at international and domestic level have been gradually intersecting, making international law a central focal point for humanity.[49] As Teitel described, international law tended previously to be an instrument which worked 'hand-in-glove with statism to reinforce modern nation-building', but worldwide interventions have showed that sovereignty is 'no longer a self-evident foundation for international law'.[50]

The discourse merges with the parallel reflection about an explicit 'right to peace'.[51] In response to the intertwining of human rights law, the right to war (*jus ad bellum*) and international humanitarian law (*jus in bello*), calls for a human right to peace are rising.[52] This discussion highlights that contemporary peace operations transform the societies in which they intervene, through programmes relating to security sector reform, democratisation, power-sharing and the rule of law.[53] A critique has been that peacebuilding attempted to replicate the 'liberal, Western-style model' in states 'that were not necessarily ready to absorb it'.[54]

ii. *Post-Conflict Interventions and Jus Post Bellum*

Another attempt to address the legal implications of state transitions has been the promotion of *jus post bellum*. Rooted in *just war theory*, legal scholarship

[46] Ruti Teitel, *Humanity's Law* (Oxford, Oxford University Press, 2011) x.
[47] ibid, 4.
[48] ibid, 5.
[49] ibid, 6.
[50] ibid, 9–10.
[51] See Report of the Open-ended Inter-Governmental Working Group on the Draft United Nations Declaration on the Right to Peace, UN Doc A/HRC/WG.13/1/2, 21 February 2013; UN Doc A/HRC/14/38, 17 March 2010; The Human Right to Peace, Declaration by the UNESCO Director-General, UNESCO Doc SHS-97/WS/6, January 1997; GA Res 39/11, 12 November 1984.
[52] For the scholarly debate, see Carlos Villán Durán, *International Law for Humankind: Towards a New Jus Gentium* (The Hague, Martinus Nijhoff Publishers, 2010) 353.
[53] UN Doc A/HRC/14/38, para 19, above n 51.
[54] ibid, para 21.

has been arguing that international law needs a clarification of the rules or at least a deeper deliberation about external state-building and post-war justice.[55] Considering human rights violations by peacekeepers during UN post-conflict administrations in Bosnia and Herzegovina and Kosovo, as well as questionable counter-insurgency and detention practices as a part of the stabilisation efforts in Afghanistan, legal scholars have been advocating for adjusted normative frameworks for foreign interventions.[56]

This approach emphasises that international law has a role in post-conflict constitution-making and legislative reforms concerning the protection of minorities and other vulnerable groups, but must also be careful not to override the right of self-determination.[57] Scholars suggest that the responsibility of interveners in the post-conflict aftermath must be made explicit as a distinct obligation of international law, instead of solely being seen as a moral duty.[58] In addition to *jus ad bellum* and *jus in bello*, a supplementary *jus post bellum* is envisaged to complete the architecture of international law.[59]

Critics against the *jus post bellum* idea argue that the concept merely re-labels existing standards.[60] They suggest that post-conflict responsibility might only require the reassembling of pertinent parts of international law, instead of inventing a genuinely new body of law.[61] Other opponents reason from a philosophical and ethical perspective that *jus post bellum* could retroactively affect the legality of interventions; consequently, 'rectificatory post-war policies would lead to crippling burdens on both just and unjust belligerents'.[62] Advocates for *jus post bellum* admit that it is often practically impossible to make a clear distinction between the end of armed hostilities, post-conflict settings and conflict terminations.[63]

This quest for legal precision proves that the impact of foreign interventions and the role of international law for the restoration of peace after conflict is still insufficiently assessed.[64] Even critics of the *jus post bellum* idea agree that

[55] Brian Orend, 'Jus Post Bellum: A Just War Theory Perspective' in Carsten Stahn and Jann K Kleffner (eds), *Towards a Law of Transition from Conflict to Peace* (The Hague, TMC Asser Press, 2008) 31.

[56] Carsten Stahn, 'The Future of Jus Post Bellum' in Stahn and Kleffner, ibid, 231.

[57] John L Cohen, 'The Role of International Law in Post-Conflict Constitution-Making: Toward a Jus Post Bellum for "Interim Occupations"' (2006/07) 51 *New York Law School* 497.

[58] Carsten Stahn, 'Jus Post Bellum: Mapping the Discipline(s)' in Stahn and Kleffner, above n 55, 103–104.

[59] Michael Pugh, 'Challenges of Post-Conflict Intercession: Three Issues in International Politics' in Stahn and Kleffner, above n 55, 115.

[60] Inger Österdahl and Esther van Zadel, 'What Will Jus Post Bellum Mean?: Of New Wine and Old Bottles' (2009) 14.2 *Journal of Conflict and Security Law* 207.

[61] ibid.

[62] Seth Lazar, 'Skepticism about jus post bellum' in Larry May and Andrew Forcehimes (eds), *Morality, Jus Post Bellum, and International Law* (Cambridge, Cambridge University Press, 2012) 207.

[63] Carsten Stahn, '"Jus ad bellum", "Jus in bello" … "Jus post bellum"?: Rethinking the Conception of the Law of Armed Force' (2006) 17 *European Journal of International Law* 926.

[64] ibid.

a shepherded post-conflict phase is fundamental for a state's stability and the freedom of its people.[65] As these are aims of international law, clarity is required about how international law can promote or impede peace.

iii. Towards 'Lex Pacificatoria'?

As an attempt to frame the dilemma of peacemaking in a legal concept, Christine Bell proposed to recognise *lex pacificatoria*, as the 'law of peacemakers', which she describes metaphorically as a 'marriage of heaven and hell'.[66] In reference to Christine Chinkins, she states that this 'law of the peacemaker potentially forms part of a broader "law of peace"'.[67] Bell advocates that the law of peacemakers moves beyond the traditional concept of the law of peace, which, in her opinion, is currently seen merely as '"the rest of international law' once the laws of war are subtracted'.[68]

Bell argues that there is a dual dynamic between peace agreements and international law: peace agreements are restricted by international law but also take part in shaping international human rights. As she explains, peace accords 'take the abstract moral baseline of international human rights standards and build around them practical institutions aimed at mediating between the legacy of the past and a new future', and 'in doing so they impact on the evolutionary direction of international law'.[69] This relationship is understood as a 'dialectical evolution', where 'international law and practice draw on the arrangement in peace agreements, even while adjudicating on the human rights performance of the institutions established herein'.[70] Touching on the imperfection of peace, Bell concludes:

> It is difficult for international law to tolerate a process of conflict resolution that appears to violate norms relating to the quality of processes, or human rights baselines, that

[65] Österdahl and van Zadel, above n 60, 207.

[66] Christine Bell, *On the Law of Peace: Peace Agreements and the Lex Pacificatoria* (Oxford, Oxford University Press, 2008) 22, 285. The term *lex pacificatoria* is drawn from the notion of *lex mercatoria* ('merchant law'), understanding how law is shaped by customs and practices. Although Christine Bell asserts that her 'term lex pacific[a]toria is the author's own', it has been used previously to emphasise the nexus between law and peace: ibid, 5 (fn 1). See the writings by Sir James Dyer, who served as a judge and Speaker of the House of Commons in the sixteenth century, during the reign of Edward VI of England. For a collection of his lost writings, see John H Baker (ed), *Reports from the Lost Notebooks of Sir James Dyer* vol 109 (London, Selden Society, 1994) 159 ('[N]e per expres parolles de lestattut ne per lequitie ne conscience, quia stattut … de finibus es lex pacificatoria …'). The term was also mentioned in clerical treatises about public law, see *Disquisitio Iuris Publici De Bonis Ecclesiasticis Eorumque, Ex Alieno Territorio Debitis, Reditibus, Inter Protestantes Imperii Status Controversis* (Francofurti, Ilsnerus, 1687) 39 ('De qua ita Lex Pacificatoria: Si qua vero dubia circa interpretationem Constitutionum ac Recessuum Imperii publicorum occurrunt …'). The *law of peace* has been reflected upon extensively, see Cornelis van Vollenhoven, *The Law of Peace* (London, MacMillian and Co, 1936) 1.

[67] Bell, above n 66, 5.

[68] ibid.

[69] ibid, 319–20.

[70] ibid, 320.

> themselves claim to be part of a universal law of peace. Through these dilemmas, law starkly encounters the politics of the gun. The length, devastation, and almost interminable quality of intrastate conflict provide the most compelling moral and political argument in favour of negotiating its end. Even if only an 'imperfect peace' is realized, this is often the only alternative to a 'perfect war'. Or is it? …[71]

Bell's observation of the reciprocal effect of peace accords is not completely unfamiliar. Throughout history, inter-state peace agreements have created new orders marking momentous developments of international law. The Peace of Westphalia, for instance, which ended the Thirty Years' War (1618–1648) during Grotius' time, established a treaty-based system of multi-state diplomacy in Europe, establishing religious toleration and reconfiguring the boundaries of the Holy Roman Empire.[72] As one of the central documents of international law in the last centuries, the final Act of the Vienna Congress (1815) determined maritime navigation rights, condemned slavery and redistributed state control and power over different territories of the European continent and beyond.[73] A difference from past developments is, indeed, that the majority of contemporary peace settlements are agreed between state and non-state actors. Postulating that intra-state settlements have an impact on the shape of international law challenges the role of the 'masters of public international law', which have predominantly been states.

That there is a substantive separate section in international law for a *lex pacificatoria* is questionable. Critics have argued that Bell's approach 'relegates peace agreements to a distinct, somewhat self-contained category of transnational law' excluding them 'from the existing set of rules, practices, and institutions provided by the international legal system that is crucial to compliance'.[74] Others have rightly stated that '[p]eace agreement formation cannot be calcified into static law', as peace negotiations require flexibility.[75] Declaring a law of peacemaking could risk being 'prescriptive about what must come about in a peace agreement'.[76] Nevertheless, the *lex pacificatoria* concept adds to the trend of establishing categories to capture customs and challenges of peacemaking in the twenty-first century.

[71] ibid, 6.

[72] Randall Lesaffer, *Peace Treaties and International Law in European History: From the Late Middle Ages to World War One* (Cambridge, Cambridge University Press, 2006) 342.

[73] Anselm Doering-Manteuffel, *Vom Wiener Kongreß zur Pariser Konferenz: England, die deutsche Frage und das Mächtesystem 1815–1856* (Göttingen, Vandenhoeck und Ruprecht, 1991) 271. See also Paul Morgan Ogilvie, *International Waterways* (New York, MacMillan, 1920) 190.

[74] Andrej Lang, '"Modus operandi," "Lex pacificatoria" and the ICJ's appraisal of the Lusaka Ceasefire Agreement in the Armed Activities on the Territory of the Congo Case More than just Latin Lessons: The Role of Peace Agreements in International Conflict Resolution' (2007) 2 *Institute for International Law and Justice Emerging Scholars Paper, NYU* 22.

[75] Illan Rua Wall, 'On the Threshold of Law: A Review of "On the Law of Peace" by Christine Bell' (2008) *Irish Yearbook of International Law* 210.

[76] ibid.

iv. Peacemaking and International Law

The academic discourse reveals that there is a shortage of concrete legal guidance for international peacemakers.[77] In 1999, the UN Secretary-General issued general guidelines for envoys and representatives involved in peace negotiations.[78] These guidelines had a rather narrow focus on international criminal law and post-conflict justice, which resulted from the debate at the time about the then newly adopted Rome Statute of the ICC.[79] In 2009, the UN Secretary-General issued two essential reports, one on enhancing mediation and the other on peacebuilding in the immediate aftermath of conflict and its support activities.[80] These were belated milestones acknowledging the extensive work of the UN in the field of peace support, state building and military stabilisation in the post-Cold War era.

Both reports are cautious and vague regarding legal limitations. The report on enhancing mediation solely mentions that UN mediation 'takes place within the normative standards set by the Charter of the United Nations and international law' and highlights that mediators need the expertise to 'offer advice on legal matters'.[81] The Report on Peacebuilding in the Immediate Aftermath of Conflict states merely that '[m]aintaining flexibility and adaptability' is necessary, 'while at the same time respecting fundamental principles of international law and human rights is essential'.[82] The report shows that UN peace efforts aim for efficiency and speed:

> '[R]especting fundamental principles of international law and human rights is essential. This cannot come, however, at the expense of predictability and speed. At the very least, we need to be ready to provide support in these recurring priority areas. In the past, our response has been slow and piecemeal, reflecting inadequate organization, a resistance to prioritization and common assessment and planning approaches, a lack of capacity in several priority areas and considerable deployment delays in others, and insufficient financing delivered through poorly suited funding mechanisms …'[83]

Whether this objective can appropriately accommodate the right to self-determination is an open question. Ultimately, the UN approach is driven by pragmatism, which uncovers another cause for the imperfection of peace.

[77] For details, see Ch 5, section I.A.iii.

[78] Guidelines for UN Representatives on Certain Aspects of Negotiations for Conflict Resolution, United Nations, Department of Political Affairs, 1999 (updated 2006), printed in (2006) *United Nations Juridical Yearbook* Ch 6, 495. See also 'Secretary-General Comments on Guidelines Issued to Envoys', UN Press Release SG/SM/7257, 10 December 1999.

[79] The updated 2006 version included aspects on women and children in armed conflict, on disarmament, demobilisation and reintegration (DDR) and vetting, but also emphasised limits under international criminal law.

[80] Report of the Secretary-General on Peacebuilding in the Immediate Aftermath of Conflict, UN Doc A/63/881-S/2009/304, 11 June 2009; Report of the Secretary-General on Enhancing Mediation and its Support Activities, UN Doc S/2009/189, 8 April 2009.

[81] UN Doc S/2009/189, paras 2, 17, above n 80.

[82] UN Doc A/63/881-S/2009/304, para 22, above n 80.

[83] ibid.

II. Closing the Gap

The dichotomy of law and peace is often puzzling. It is perplexing that wars may conform more meticulously to standards of international humanitarian law than their aftermath with human rights, which puts the maxim of 'the rule of law' into perspective. The aim of achieving order through law is a Sisyphean undertaking in post-conflict situations, as fresh disorder may result if the new state system is perceived to be unjust.[84] To what extent these practical challenges in peacemaking conflict or concur with potential normative limitations by international law will be in the focus of this book.

A. Challenges of Peacemaking and International Law

Negotiations for peace agreements and constitutional transitions regularly take place in restricted settings. In 1992, UN Secretary-General Boutros Boutros-Ghali flagged in the *Agenda for Peace* that if 'conflicts have gone unresolved, it is not because techniques for peaceful settlement were unknown or inadequate'.[85] The practical challenges are enormous, particularly with regard to time, space and the capacities of peace processes.

International organisations such as the United Nations aim to settle internal conflicts and enable post-conflict transitions of states in a 'timely manner'.[86] This often leads to pressure on peace processes by rigorous benchmarks and tight time frames for the completion of transitions, while the conflict might not be 'ripe' for resolution.[87] Some scholars advise waiting for a 'hurting stalemate' to develop; others suggest that a delay may turn 'out to be costly for all concerned' as 'opportunities for early resolution' can get lost and a stalemate may, instead, lead 'to intractability'.[88] International law has its own rules about time, temporality and transitions, as will be shown in this book.[89]

[84] For the complementarity of law and justice, see Alf Ross, *On Law and Justice* (Berkeley, University of California Press, 1959) 285.

[85] Report of the UN Secretary-General, 'Agenda for Peace', UN Doc A/47/277-S/24111, 17 June 1992, para 34. The aspects mentioned will only serve as introductory examples; for furthers details about practical challenges in peacemaking, see John Paul Lederach, *The Moral Imagination: The Art and Soul of Building Peace* (Oxford, Oxford University Press, 2004) 31. See also Susan Allen Nan, Zachariah Cherian Mampilly and Andrea Bartoli (eds), *Peacemaking: From Practice to Theory* (Westport, CT, Praeger, 2011) xv.

[86] UN Doc S/2009/189, para 10, above n 80.

[87] ibid, para 11. On the matter of ripeness, see also I William Zartman, 'The Timing of Peace Initiatives: Hurting Stalemates and Ripe Moments' (2001) 1(1) *The Global Review of Ethnopolitics* 8.

[88] UN Doc S/2009/189, para 11, above n 80. On the matter of intractability, see Peter Coleman, *The Five Percent: Finding Solutions to Seemingly Impossible Conflicts* (New York, Public Affairs, 2011) 26 ('It is estimated that only 5 percent of international conflicts since 1816 were considered intractable … That means … that 95 percent of conflicts are considered resolvable …').

[89] About the matter of temporality and international law, see also Michael Hamilton and Antoine Buyse, 'Introduction' in Michael Hamilton and Antoine Buyse (eds), *Transitional Jurisprudence and the ECHR: Justice, Politics and Rights* (Cambridge, Cambridge University Press, 2011) 1.

Another challenge can be the fragmentation of conflict parties.[90] In general, peace mediators demand that processes 'be as inclusive as possible', since 'excluded parties have greater motivation to act as spoilers'.[91] At the same time, mediation is perceived 'to become more complicated' when there is an expanded number of participating actors.[92] While the Security Council called in resolutions for greater inclusion of women in peace processes, the assumption that international law provides a right to sit at the negotiation table for certain groups is debatable.[93]

Lastly, even the presence of mediating third parties can be harmful, as they might influence or pressure parties in the peace process.[94] This can result in a peace agreement and constitutional design that stop a war, but in the long-run only imperfectly tackle the root causes of conflict.[95] Moreover, the active participation of third parties can risk an imposition of values, based on their own understanding of democracy and governance.[96]

B. Focus and Research Questions

Though much has been written from a socio-political perspective about peace-making, legal challenges have not yet been adequately addressed.[97] While the incorporation of human rights guarantees in post-conflict arrangements seems to have become customary, decisions by the ECtHR and UN human rights monitoring bodies reveal that the issue of limitations to transitional and permanent power-sharing pacts is in flux.[98] This study restricts the core of its analysis to a normative assessment through the lenses of international law: to what extent are provisions in peace agreements limited by international law? What international human rights standards might be endangered? What are the absolute limitations

[90] UN Doc S/2009/189, para 10, above n 80.

[91] ibid, para 22. On the matter of inclusivity, see Allen Buchanan, *Justice, Legitimacy, and Self-Determination: Moral Foundations for International Law* (Oxford, Oxford University Press) 236.

[92] UN Doc S/2009/189, para 22, above n 80.

[93] On the issue of women and peace and security, see SC Res 1820, 19 June 2008; SC Res 1325, 31 October 2000.

[94] UN Doc S/2009/189, para 27, above n 80. For an in-depth analysis of the role of third parties in conflict mediation, see Lars Kirchhoff, *Constructive Interventions: Paradigms, Process and Practice of International Mediation* (The Hague, Kluwer Law International, 2008) 87.

[95] On the need for national ownership, see UN Doc A/63/881-S/2009/304, para 8, above n 80. For further insights, see Simon Chesterman, 'Ownership in Theory and in Practice: Transfer of Authority in UN Statebuilding Operations' (2007) 1(1) *Journal of Intervention and Statebuilding* 3.

[96] For a comprehensive assessment of failures and successes of peace mediation, see Jacob Bercovitch and Jeffrey Langley, 'The Nature of the Dispute and the Effectiveness of International Mediation' (1993) 37 *Journal of Conflict Resolution* 670. For a deeper analysis, see Herbert C Kelman, 'Building Trust among Enemies: The Central Challenge for International Conflict Resolution' (2005) 29(6) *International Journal of Intercultural Relations* 639.

[97] For a mapping of previous legal research onto power-sharing, peace agreements and international law, see Ch 2.

[98] See above n 2. On the role of human rights provisions in peace agreements, see Christine Bell, *Peace Agreements and Human Rights* (Oxford, Oxford University Press, 2000) 1.

in international law for peacemaking? In order to keep a sharp legal focus, the study examines norms and practices in international law. Accordingly, the study probes what kind of peace settlements are impermissible and what types have been accepted by state practice despite their human rights implications.

C. Lines of Argument

As this study will demonstrate, international law provides clear rules for peacemaking efforts. Although their application might entail disagreements about factual circumstances, human rights and minority protections imply unambiguous instructions for transitional post-conflict periods and constitutional designs. The study emphasises that international law contains the possibility for states to justify human rights restrictions, leading precisely to what has been described as 'imperfect peace'.

In this regard, this study issues a series of reminders about human rights principles, while highlighting areas where there are inconclusive arguments for or against legal limits. As Hart put it: 'We can then simply say, "Such is the standard case of what is meant by 'law' and 'legal system'"; remember that besides these standards you will also find arrangements in social life which … lack others of them'.[99] International law can only provide a framework for common values and procedures for enforcing them, but not substitute the action of those who need to apply them.

As Edwin Dickinson wrote in his book *Law and Peace* over half a century ago, there are 'paradoxes of action and inaction, of boldness in preachment and timidity in practice, of one step forward and two to the rear' in international law, which provide another reason for the imperfection of peace.[100] However, this paradox should not encourage a capitulation to the real-world challenges of peacemaking, but motivate to uphold legal boundaries and defend human rights safeguards.

This study stresses that the legality of peace pacts under international law needs to be assessed case by case, while applying universal human rights law. Conflict settlements have to take the rights of individuals into account, but also the obligation to maintain peace as a 'public good'.[101] International law neither prescribes nor restrains peacemaking solutions, as long as human rights are guaranteed or restrictions are justified. As the practice in the implementation of human rights conventions shows, restrictions are permissible if they are proportional. This requires a careful assessment of alternatives. What is essential is that peremptory norms (*jus cogens*) are respected.

[99] HLA Hart, *The Concept of Law* (Oxford, Clarendon Press, 1961) 5.

[100] Edwin D Dickinson, *Law and Peace* (Philadelphia, University of Pennsylvania Press, 1951) 135.

[101] Ruben P Mendez, 'Peace as a Global Public Good' in Inge Kaul, Isabelle Grunberg and Marc A Stern (eds), *Global Public Goods: International Cooperation in the 21st Century* (Oxford, Oxford University Press, 1999) 382.

III. Methodology and Scope

A. Methodology

Randall Lesaffer noted in his critique of Christine Bell's book *On the Law of Peace* that it 'does not offer a detailed and profound study of the substance of the laws of conflict resolution and constitutional formation', beyond creating an 'analytical framework'.[102] Bell has chosen 'not to go into the substance of the law of peace-making, but remains at the level of their external characteristics'.[103] This study aims to fill this gap.

The analysis looks at regional and international human rights obligations, evaluating the fragmented universality of international human rights law.[104] Ruti Teitel observed that courts, tribunals, other international bodies, and political actors draw from the various elements of international law, 'in assessing the rights and wrongs of conflict; determining whether and how to intervene; and imposing accountability and responsibility on both state and non-state actors'.[105] However, while it is tempting to see humanitarian law, international criminal law and human rights law in sum as *humanity's law*, this approach should not lead to a blurring of each element. At close sight, human rights have distinct features: they are often the reason for conflict and their solution; and they are significant indicators for post-war change. Whereas humanitarian law is temporally limited to the period of armed conflict and international criminal law is reactive to international crimes, human rights are intended to prevail in all those phases connecting *jus ad bellum, in bello* and *post bellum*. Their fulfilment is the ultimate objective of peace.

As there are different perspectives on issues in international law, this book applies a multi-dimensional institutional approach. As Tai-Heng Cheng argues in his analysis *When International Law Works*, international law is contingent on the respective standpoint of the decision-maker towards an international problem.[106] The methodology and arguments vary depending on whether international law is regarded from within an international court, an international law commission or governmental state entity.[107] The legal opinions of these contrasting perspectives can differ drastically or display elements of universality.

[102] Randall Lesaffer, 'Book Review: Christine Bell, On the Law of Peace: Peace Agreements and the Lex Pacificatoria' (2011) 24 *Leiden Journal of International Law* 522.

[103] ibid.

[104] Upendra Baxi, 'Voices of Suffering, Fragmented Universality, and the Future of Human Rights' in Burns H Weston and Stephen P Marks (eds), *The Future of International Human Rights* (Ardsley, NY, Transnational Publishers, 1999) 172.

[105] Teitel, above n 46, 4.

[106] Tai-Heng Cheng, *When International Law Works: Realistic Idealism After 9/11 and the Global Recession* (Oxford, Oxford University Press, 2012) 8.

[107] On the different perspectives of courts and science in international law, see also Hersch Lauterpacht, *The Function of Law in the International Community* (Oxford, Oxford University Press, 2003) 339, 442, and Robert E Keeton, *Judging* (St Paul, Minn, West Publishing Co, 1990) 15–17.

Martti Koskenniemi said provocatively that international law 'is what international lawyers do and how they think'.[108] He noted that 'legal practice enables the simultaneous justification and critique of particular normative outcomes'.[109] Koskenniemi concluded that international lawyers have 'corresponding roles', ranging between those of an adviser, judge, arbitrator, diplomat or academic: 'Each exists in and is reinforced by the different legal practices of international lawyering'.[110] Consequently, the 'routine of international law is most immediately shaped by these roles'.[111] This study tests this approach, understanding that all perspectives eventually contribute to an objective common sense of the law (*Objektivität des Rechts*).[112] Complementary to previous research, this study particularly focuses on interpretations by international human rights courts and human rights monitoring bodies.[113]

B. Case Studies

As two comparable cases, Bosnia and Herzegovina and Lebanon demonstrate the impasses of peacemaking. Despite formally signed peace accords, both countries are struggling with stepping out of the shadows of their violent past. They represent different types of power-sharing: whereas the constitutional system in Bosnia and Herzegovina is based on a quota for the former war-waging ethnic groups, Lebanon's political structures remain ingrained in sectarianism.[114]

Historically, Bosnia and Herzegovina and Lebanon share a similar path. Ethnic groups and sects used to manage their own internal and external affairs independently through immemorial custom and feudal ties forming the basis of social order.[115] In the fifteenth century, power-sharing was institutionalised by the Ottoman Empire, which conquered the Balkans and the Middle East. With their arrival followed a system of ethnic and sectarian segregation arranged in what is

[108] Martti Koskenniemi, *The Politics of International Law* (Oxford, Hart Publishing, 2011) 284.

[109] ibid, 293.

[110] Martti Koskenniemi, *From Apology to Utopia: The Structure of International Legal Argument* (Helsinki, Lakimiesliiton Kustannus Finnish Lawyers' Publishing Company, 1989) 492.

[111] ibid.

[112] Matthew Kramer, *Objectivity and the Rule of Law* (Cambridge, Cambridge University Press, 2007) 60.

[113] For a summary of previous research, see Ch 2.

[114] For an overview on Bosnia and Herzegovina, see above n 17. For an introduction on Lebanon, see Myriam Catusse and Karam Karam, 'Back to Parties?: Partisan Logics and Transformations of Politics in the Arab World' in Myriam Catusse and Karam Karam (eds), *Returning to Political Parties?: Partisan Logic and Political Transformations in the Arab World* (Sin el Fil, The Lebanese Center for Policy Studies, 2010) 19.

[115] Kamal S Salibi, *The Modern History of Lebanon* (Delmar New York, Caravan Books, 1965) xxvii. See also Peter F Sugar, *Southeastern Europe Under Ottoman Rule: 1354–1804* (Seattle, University of Washington Press, 1977) 3.

known as the *millet* system.[116] As the Lebanese historian Fawwaz Traboulsi explains, this structure established 'a two-tier hierarchy between a higher community, made up of Muslims, and a lower "protected" community, made of the "people of the book", such as Christians and Jews'.[117] Certain non-Muslim minorities (*dhimmi*) were granted special status under the Sharia law, to excuse them from specific religious duties within the Islamic Ottoman Empire, but treating them as equal regarding property, contracts and other obligations.[118] *Millets* organised their religious, culture and social life independently, and established their own schools, churches and hospitals. Being permitted to maintain separate personal status law courts for Christian Canon law and Jewish Halakha law, they were allowed to rule themselves with only minor interference from the Ottoman Empire.

In the late nineteenth century, in an attempt to modernise the Ottoman Empire along European lines by abolishing sectarian and ethnic divisions, the Balkans and parts of the Middle East were transformed into autonomous political and administrative provinces (*mutassarrifiya*). This reform gave distinct sects and ethnic groups exclusive spheres of influence. As part of a series of reforms aimed to satisfy European demands for the protection of Christian communities and secular statehood, non-Muslims and Muslims were declared equal before the law regardless of their religion. Appointments in the public sector were restricted on a sectarian basis. As Ussama Makdisi historically reconstructed:

> European and Ottoman officials engaged in a contest to win the loyalty of the local inhabitants – the French by claiming to protect the Maronites, the British, the Druze, and the Ottomans by proclaiming the sultan's benevolence toward all his religiously equal subjects.[119]

This was a moment where feudal and factional rivalries transformed into sectarian feuds.[120]

Both regions remained under foreign influence. Following the Treaty of Berlin in 1878, Bosnia and Herzegovina was annexed to the Austro-Hungarian Empire.[121] Lebanon became a part of the French Mandate within the League of

[116] On the Ottoman Empire and the function of provincial administration, see Halil Inalcik, *The Ottoman Empire: The Classical Age, 1300–1600* (London: Phoenix Press, 1973) 104. For a detailed overview about later developments, see Ussama Makdisi, 'After 1860: Debating Religion, Reform, and Nationalism in the Ottoman Empire' (2002) 34 *International Journal of Middle East Studies* 601.

[117] Fawwaz Traboulsi, *A History of Modern Lebanon* (London, Pluto Press, 2007) 3–4.

[118] Mohamed Berween, 'Non-Muslims in the Islamic State: Majority Rule and Minority Rights' (2006) 10 *International Journal of Human Rights* 95. See also Najwa Al-Qattan, 'Dhimmis in the Muslim Court: Legal Autonomy and Religious Discrimination' (1999) 31 *International Journal of Middle East Studies* 429.

[119] Ussama Makdisi, 'Corrupting the Sublime Sultanate: The Revolt of Tanyus Shahin in Nineteenth-Century Ottoman Lebanon' (2000) 42.1 *Comparative Studies in Society and History* 180.

[120] Marie-Joelle Zahar, 'Power Sharing in Lebanon: Foreign Protectors, Domestic Peace, and Democratic Failure' in Donald Rotschild and Philip Roeder (eds), *Sustainable Peace: Power and Democracy after Civil Wars* (Ithaca, Cornell University Press, 2005) 221.

[121] Robin Okey, *Taming Balkan Nationalism: The Habsburg 'Civilizing' Mission in Bosnia, 1878–1914* (Oxford, Oxford University Press, 2007) 1.

Nations system in 1922 after World War I. At the end of the twentieth century, Bosnia and Herzegovina as well as Lebanon modified their constitutional order on the basis of peace accords that ended armed conflict but also impacted on human rights.

Above all, both cases offer intriguing legal considerations from different institutional perspectives. While ethnic power-sharing provisions in the constitution of Bosnia and Herzegovina have been examined by the ECtHR, Lebanon's confessional system has been of concern in the UN human rights bodies.

C. Structure and Scope

As a prelude, the first part of this study lays the theoretical foundations of the analysis, dissecting the thinking of prior commentators about power-sharing, peace agreements and post-conflict constitutional designs. Chapter 2 explores the spectrum of institutional options, for which legal considerations are accordingly complex. The chapter maps legal challenges and explains why a case-study-driven, context-specific analysis is needed to define universal principles of legal limitations for peacemaking.

Chapter 3 focuses on Bosnia and Herzegovina and its ethnic constitutional setting introduced by the Dayton Peace Accords. This chapter reviews the ECtHR decision *Sejdić and Finci v Bosnia and Herzegovina* (2009) and related case law.[122] The chapter concludes with general lessons learnt for the burden of proof in discrimination cases and rules for post-conflict state transitions.

Chapter 4 scrutinises Lebanon's system of political confessionalism. This chapter explores arguments and concerns raised in UN human rights monitoring bodies about discriminatory aspects of the Lebanese consensus democracy. The chapter examines possible justifications of human rights constraints by states, whereby particular attention is paid to temporal limits as an aspect of proportionality.

The final chapter of the book provides a reflection on the overall quest for absolute limitations and their consequences for peacemaking. Returning to the challenges of post-conflict state transition, power-sharing and international law, this concluding chapter assesses the function between law and peace from an academic and practitioner perspective. The chapter closes with an agenda for future research. The final remarks shed light on the opportunities which imperfect peace provides, bridging the divide between normative limits of international law and realism in peacemaking.

[122] See above n 2.

2

Power-Sharing in Theory and Practice

Concepts, Mechanisms and Legal Challenges

I. Ethnic and Religious Diversity as a Challenge for International Law

One of the central questions for peacemakers and constitutional lawyers has been how to achieve stability in fragile states with pluralistic societies.[1] Following decolonialisation, the dissolution of the Soviet Union and the former Yugoslavia, emerging intra-state conflicts required a revision of conceptual designs for internal state order. *Power-sharing* has been praised as a panacea for reducing inter-religious or inter-ethnic rivalries; yet, it has also been the reason for continuing tension. In this context, international guarantees such those for human rights and minority rights have been seen as a blessing or a burden, as they enhance but can also hinder peacemaking efforts.

This chapter links the different understandings of power-sharing in democracy scholarship with aspects of international law. The chapter shows that there has been a lively debate in international human rights law about peace arrangements, particularly those which are discriminatory. The first part of the chapter gives a brief introduction to the concepts of power-sharing, and how it serves or hinders the cause of conflict resolution. The second part outlines the spectrum of mechanisms used in peace agreements and constitutions. As a preface to the in-depth case studies in the next two chapters, an overview about the post-war constitutional systems of Bosnia and Herzegovina and Lebanon is provided. The third part of this chapter maps areas of legal concern as well as existing blind spots in the scholarly debate.

[1] Katharine Belmont, Scott Mainwaring, and Andrew Reynolds, 'Introduction: Institutional Design, Conflict Management, and Democracy in Divided Societies' in Andrew Reynolds (ed), *The Architecture of Democracy: Constitutional Design, Conflict Management, and Democracy* (Oxford, Oxford University Press, 2002) 1.

II. Democracy Theory and the Perspective of Conflict Resolution

Alternating between euphoria and scepticism, practitioners and scholars view power-sharing arrangements ambivalently. The UN Secretary-General frequently applauds and welcomes them as transitional steps necessary to overcome political impasses on the road to peace.[2] They are critical for breaking political stalemates and paving the way towards stability during post-conflict interim periods. However, whether power-sharing can end deep-rooted conflict is disputed. Experts disagree about which mechanisms are the most effective for consolidating democracy. Empirical research in conflict resolution about the durability of peace agreements points in contradictory directions.

A. Conceptual Foundations of 'Consociationalism'

At the end of the 1960s, work by Arend Lijphart and other political scientists fundamentally shaped the academic field of power-sharing.[3] Lijphart developed the concept of 'consociationalism' based on previous academic writings on pluralism.[4] He defined 'consociational democracy' as 'a government by elite cartel designed to turn democracy with fragmented culture into a stable democracy'.[5] Comparing the two basic models of democracy, majoritarianism and consensus, Lijphart derived four mechanisms for consociationalism: grand coalitions; minority vetoes; proportional representation; and group autonomy. Lijphart argued that consociationalism would essentially help to avoid secession, bringing more stable solutions to conflicts of segmented societies. In Lijphart's view, majority-rule systems do not

[2] 'Secretary-General Welcomes Regional Initiatives to Hold Talks on Zimbabwe Power-sharing Government', UN Press Release, UN Doc SG/SM/11887, 27 October 2008; 'Secretary-General Applauds Formation of Northern Ireland Power-sharing Government', UN Press Release, UN Doc SG/SM/10982, 8 May 2007; 'Secretary-General Welcomes Sudan Political, Power-Sharing Agreements as "Major Step Forward", Urges Progress on Darfur', UN Press Release, UN Doc SG/SM/9332, 26 May 2004.

[3] Arend Lijphart, *The Politics of Accommodation: Pluralism and Democracy in the Netherlands* (Berkeley, University of California Press, 1968). See also Eric A Nordlinger, *Conflict Regulation in Divided Societies*, Occasional Papers, No 29, Center for International Affairs (Cambridge, MA, Harvard University, 1972).

[4] Arend Lijphart, 'Consociational Democracy' (1969) 21 *World Politics* 216.

[5] ibid. See also Arend Lijphart, *Democracy in Plural Societies: A Comparative Exploration* (New Haven, Yale University Press, 1977); Arend Lijphart, *Democracies: Patterns of Majoritarian and Consensus Government in Twenty-one Countries* (New Haven, Yale University Press, 1984); Arend Lijphart, *Power-Sharing in South Africa* (Berkeley, Institute of International Studies University of California, 1985); Arend Lijphart, 'The Framework Document on Northern Ireland and the Theory of Power-Sharing' (1996) 31(3) *Government and Opposition* 267; Arend Lijphart and Carlos H Waisman (eds), *Institutional Design in New Democracies* (Boulder, Westview, 1996).

have a better record than consensus-based systems in terms of effective policy-making in settings with highly diverse ethnic or religious groups.[6] 'Power-sharing', he reasoned, would allow 'the participation of the representatives of all significant groups in political decision-making, especially at the executive level'.[7] The terms consociationalism and power-sharing are used as synonyms by Lijphart, but for practical reasons he preferred the latter in order to promote the concept 'beyond the confines of academics'.[8]

Subsequent discussions among consociationalists have concentrated on what kind of power-sharing is more likely to lay the foundations for democracy.[9] Consociationalists have claimed that they have a more inclusive model of democracy than majoritarians. In their view, a greater number of people may be able to influence or control the executive. However, there is no unanimity about the normative merits of consociations, their establishment, maintenance or breakdown. Disagreement also arises between empirical and normative approaches within consociational thinking.[10]

B. Scholarly Controversy about How to Attain a Stable Democracy

Lijphart's consociational concept has been criticised for its weak empirical support.[11] Ian Lustick, for example, commented that the unsolved situations in Cyprus, Northern Ireland and Lebanon have clearly demonstrated the 'failure of consociationalism'.[12] Richard Hrair Dekmejian suggested that the models used by Lijphart – Belgium, Canada, and Switzerland – are not fully comparable with the countries in post-conflict transitions after civil wars, such as Lebanon.[13]

[6] Arend Lijphart, 'The Wave of Power-sharing Democracy' in Reynolds, above n 1, 37.

[7] ibid, 38.

[8] As he explains: 'The term "consociational" worked well enough in scholarly writing, but I found it to be an obstacle in communicating with policy-makers who found it too esoteric, polysyllabic, and difficult to pronounce. Using "power sharing" instead has greatly facilitated the process of communication beyond the confines of academic political science': Arend Lijphart, *Thinking about Democracy: Power Sharing and Majority Rule in Theory and Practice* (London, Routledge, 2008) 6.

[9] For an overview, see Brendan O'Leary, 'Debating Consociational Politics: Normative and Explanatory Arguments' in Sid Noel (ed), *From Power Sharing to Democracy: Post-conflict Institutions in Ethnically Divided Societies* (Montreal, McGill-Queen's University Press, 2005) 3–4.

[10] Matthijs Bogaards, 'The Uneasy Relationship between Empirical and Normative Types in Consociational Theory' (2000) 12(4) *Journal of Theoretical Politics* 395. In response, see Arend Lijphart, 'Definitions, Evidence, and Policy: A Response to Matthijs Bogaards' Critique' (2000) 12(4) *Journal of Theoretical Politics* 425.

[11] Brian Barry, 'Political Accommodation and Consociational Democracy' (1975) 5 *British Journal of Political Science* 477; Rinus van Schendelen, 'The Views of Arend Lijphart and Collected Criticisms' (1984) 19(1) *Acta Politica* 19.

[12] Ian Lustick, 'Stability in Deeply Divided Societies: Consociationalism Versus Control' (1979) 31(3) *World Politics* 325.

[13] Richard Hrair Dekmejian, 'Consociational Democracy in Crisis: The Case of Lebanon' (1978) 10(2) *Comparative Politics* 254.

Similarly, Sean Byrne noted that Lijphart focused mainly on institutional, constitutional and legal characteristics of accommodation.[14] He criticised that Lijphart paid little attention to how external powers, the socio-economic process and policy outputs can obstruct social relations between communities. Byrne pinpointed as a weakness the fact that elites may resort to conflict to further their own opportunistic interests. According to his findings, the elite bargaining model does not give parties the chance to settle their dispute comprehensively.

Donald Horowitz called Lijphart's consociationalist approach a tenuous 'coalition of convenience'.[15] He argues that it fosters little or nothing beyond the necessity for ethnic parties to establish a government which only lasts for a short period. As Horowitz elaborated:

> Coalitions of convenience are easy to form but hard to sustain. They crumble readily under pressure … Such coalitions make no progress on policies of accommodation. Rather, they tend to dissolve in violent disagreement over basic ethnic issues … When coalitions of convenience break up, they reinforce pre-existing ethnic party systems. A common aftermath of their dissolution has been widespread violence and military intervention.[16]

Drawing on sociology and social psychology, Horowitz favours an integrative approach, which suggests to bring competing groups together on social issues like wealth-sharing and recognition.[17]

C. A Dilemma: Power-Sharing Tendency to Instability

Other authors have described the potential dilemmas of power-sharing, such as the tendency to repeated conflict and unstable peace. As Philip Roeder and Donald Rothchild explain, peacemakers introduced power-sharing arrangements 'in an attempt to guarantee ethnic groups a role in governmental decision-making or to ensure policy outcomes with a fair allocation of scare governmental resources'.[18] However, practice quickly revealed that the 'short term benefits' of granted power-sharing accommodations come 'with high long-term costs', as political 'hard-liners'

[14] Sean Byrne, 'Consociational and Civil Society Approaches in Peacebuilding in Northern Ireland' (2001) 38(3) *Journal of Peace Research* 327 at 333.

[15] Donald Horowitz, 'Conciliatory Institutions and Constitutional Process in Post-Conflict States' (2008) 49(4) *William and Mary Law Review* 1213. See also Donald Horowitz, *A Democratic South Africa? Constitutional Engineering in a Divided Society* (Berkeley, University of California Press, 1991).

[16] Donald Horowitz, *Ethnic Groups in Conflict. Theories, Patterns and Politics* (Berkeley, University of California Press, 1985) 369, 394–95.

[17] Donald Horowitz, 'Constitutional Design: Proposals Versus Processes' in Reynolds, above n 1, 22.

[18] Philip G Roeder and Donald S Rothchild, 'Dilemmas of State-Building in Divided Societies' in Philip G Roeder and Donald S Rothchild (eds), *Sustainable Peace: Power and Democracy after Civil Wars* (Ithaca, NY, Cornell University Press, 2005) 5.

from each group are likely to 'stir popular demands for a larger share' of power.[19] Roeder and Rothchild summarise:

> Power-sharing may get ethnic leaders to leave the battlefield, but then after a short lull transforms the bargaining room into a new battlefield.[20]

Instead, they recommend a constitutional system based on 'power-division' including separation of powers, checks and balances, and judicially safeguarded civil liberties.[21]

D. Durability of Power-Sharing Settlements

Research about peace agreements suggests that there is no general answer to whether or not power-sharing enhances the durability of peace. In 2003, an empirical study by Caroline Hartzell and Matthew Hoddie stated that the 'more extensive' power-sharing arrangements are in a negotiated civil war settlement, 'the more likely' is it that 'peace will endure in the long run'.[22] Their statistical results showed that conflicts in which parties are divided along ethnic lines have a significantly greater risk of return to war.[23] Hartzell and Hoddie examined 38 civil wars that were resolved through negotiations between 1945 and 1998, finding that civil war settlements 'have consistently higher survival rates over time' if they include 'multifaceted power-sharing arrangements' in territorial, military, political and economic areas of state power.[24] Hartzell and Hoddie concluded that power-sharing institutions 'effectively address security concerns' and ensure influence in the decision-making process 'by guaranteeing all groups a share of state power'.[25] They advised:

> Mediators at the negotiating table should support rival parties in their attempts to structure power-sharing institutions and encourage them to create a diverse array of mechanisms of this nature. These efforts to produce extensive power-sharing institutions through the process of brokered negotiations have the greatest potential for establishing self-enforcing peace in the long term.[26]

In 2009, research by Karl Derouen, Jenna Lea and Peter Wallensteen produced more nuanced results.[27] They observed that political power-sharing arrangements

[19] ibid, 7.
[20] ibid, 8–9.
[21] ibid, 17.
[22] Caroline Hartzell and Matthew Hoddie, 'Institutionalizing Peace: Power Sharing and Post-Civil War Conflict Management' (2003) 47(2) *American Journal of Political Science* 318 at 319. Similarly, in Hartzell's previous study, she advocated that settlements which provide institutional guarantees prove to be more stable. See Caroline Hartzell, 'Explaining the Stability of Negotiated Settlements to Intrastate Wars' (1999) 43(1) *Journal of Conflict Resolution* 3.
[23] Hartzell and Hoddie, ibid, 328.
[24] ibid, 327, 330.
[25] ibid, 330.
[26] ibid.
[27] Karl Derouen Jr, Jenna Lea and Peter Wallensteen, 'The Duration of Civil War Peace Agreements' (2009) 26(4) *Conflict Management and Peace Science* 367.

are costlier to government, more difficult to implement and thus likely to decrease the life span of the peace agreement. Though power-sharing governments 'might on some level provide rebels with a degree of confidence in the peace process', they are 'risky' and 'unstable' as the chances increase that the government will back out or that the opposition will strike pre-emptively.[28] As they analysed, a government might abandon the agreement because it concedes too much or opposition members could cancel the arrangement because of delays in implementation.

III. Mechanisms

The debate about the categories of power-sharing and their conceptual distinction is robust.[29] On the other hand, there is a lack of consistency in the wide array of definitions and systematics in recent research.[30] The following overview summarises some of the many possible mechanisms.[31]

A. Power-Sharing Spectrum

For the purposes of this study, power-sharing is understood in a broad way, beyond Lijphart's original consociationalism concept: power can be shared on a political, territorial, economic or military level.[32] In practice, these layers are often complementary to each other.

i. Political Power-Sharing

Political power-sharing usually comprises the distribution of shares in the government or legislature.[33] This can include systems involving proportional representation, grand coalitions or minority vetoes.[34]

[28] ibid, 383.

[29] For an overview, see Andreas Mehler, *Not Always in the People's Interest: Power-sharing Arrangements in African Peace Agreements*, GIGA Working Papers No 83, July 2006, 6.

[30] See Ben Hillman, 'Power-sharing and Political Party Engineering in Conflict-prone Societies: The Indonesian Experiment in Aceh' (2012) 12(2) *Conflict, Security and Development* 149; Matthew I Mitchell, 'Power-sharing and Peace in Côte d'Ivoire: Past Examples and Future Prospects' (2012) 12(2) *Conflict, Security and Development* 171; Leonardo Avritzer, 'The Different Designs of Public Participation in Brazil: Deliberation, Power-sharing and Public Ratification' (2012) 6(2) *Critical Policy Studies* 113; Jai Kwan Jung, 'Power-sharing and Democracy Promotion in Post-Civil War Peace-Building' (2012) 19(3) *Democratization* 486.

[31] For an overview, see Appendix, Table 1.

[32] Hartzell and Hoddie, above n 22, 320. See also Derouen et al, above n 27, 367.

[33] Hartzell and Hoddie, ibid.

[34] See details on consociationalism above, n 5.

Proportional representation can involve quotas for certain political, ethnic or religious groups in the parliament, cabinet or also in the judiciary. For example, in the peace agreement between the Government of Sierra Leone and the Revolutionary United Front of Sierra Leone (RUF/SL) in 1999, a broad-based government of national unity and with fixed cabinet appointments for the RUF/SL was created.[35]

Post-election governments can be structured as grand coalitions, unity governments or collective presidencies consisting of the key political groups, aside from majoritarian electoral considerations. For instance, in the case of Iraq in 2010, a national partnership government was formed by Iraq's leaders to stipulate a 'pluralistic and unified Iraq'.[36] Between November 2011 and May 2012, a national unity government was formed in Greece under Prime Minister Lucas Papademos in order to reach a consensus between all political parties during the debt crisis.[37] This example illustrates that power-sharing settlements are not merely a phenomena of post-conflict peace agreements, but a common element of political processes.[38]

Minority veto rights can offer ethnic and confessional groups the guarantee that *vital interests* will not be compromised by majority voting; draft laws can be blocked or suspended by a minority veto. A frequent option is that certain constitutional amendments relating to self-government and laws that directly affect culture, language and education need the approval by minority representatives. This was the solution in Macedonia in 2001, where the Ohrid Framework Agreement stipulated an end to the armed conflict between the Albanian National Liberation Army and the Macedonian security forces by guaranteeing those special parliamentary procedures as amendments to the Constitution.[39]

Another option is to introduce safeguards of parallel consent, which requires the approval of a majority of both former conflict parties. Such a mechanism was included in the Good Friday Agreement in Northern Ireland in 1989, granting Unionists and Nationalists mutual veto rights.[40]

[35] Peace Agreement between the Government of Sierra Leone and the Revolutionary United Front of Sierra Leone [hereafter Lomé Peace Agreement], Art V, signed in Lomé, 7 July 1999, UN Doc S/1999/777, 12 July 1999, Annex. For details, see SC Res 1270, 22 October 1999, para 1.

[36] UN Doc S/PRST/2010/27, 15 December 2010.

[37] 'Greece Bailout Crisis: President Seeks Unity Government' *BBC News* (12 May 2012).

[38] Wolfgang C Müller and Kaare Strom, 'Coalition Governance in Western Europe: An Introduction' in Wolfgang C Müller and Kaare Strom (eds), *Coalition Governance in Western Europe* (Oxford, Oxford University Press, 2003) 1. See also Tables 1 and 2.

[39] Framework Agreement (Ohrid Agreement), signed in Ohrid, 13 August 2001, para 5. For details, see Ermira Mehmeti, 'Implementation of the Ohrid Framework Agreement' in *Power-Sharing and the Implementation of the Ohrid Framework Agreement* (Skopje, Friedrich Ebert Stiftung, 2008) 81.

[40] Good Friday Agreement (Belfast Agreement), The Agreement, Section on Rights, Safeguards and Equality of Opportunities, signed in Belfast, 10 April 1998, para 5(i). For details, see Brendan O'Leary, *The British-Irish Agreement: Power-Sharing Plus* (London, London School of Economics, 1998) 2.

Table 1 Transitional and interim governments after the Arab uprisings (2011)

Tunisia	**Egypt**	**Libya**	**Yemen**
Overthrow of President Ben Ali	Overthrow of President Mubarak	Overthrow of Colonel Gaddafi	Departure of President Saleh
1. Mohamed Ghannouchi as self-proclaimed acting President (January 2011)	1. Supreme Council of the Armed Forces as executive caretaker (February 2011–June 2012)	1. National Transitional Council as de facto government (February 2011–August 2012)	1. Transitional Government headed by Acting President Abed Rabbo Mansour Hadi (November 2011–February 2012)
2. Formation of Unity Government under Acting President Fouad Mebazaa (January–December 2011)	2. Civilian Cabinet under Prime Minister Essam Sharaf (March–November 2011)	2. Formation of elected General National Congress (August 2012)	2. Abed Rabbo Mansour Hadi assumes office as elected President after Yemeni presidential election (February 2012)
3. Moncef Marzouki elected as Interim President by Constituent Assembly (December 2011)	3. Civilian Cabinet under Prime Minister Kamal Ganzouri (December 2011–August 2012)	3. Abdurrahim El-Keib as Interim Prime Minister (August–November 2012)	3. National Dialogue Conference, Constitutional Referendum and legislative elections envisaged for 2013–2014
4. Elections planned for mid-2013	4. Mohamed Morsi assumes office as President (August 2012)	4. Ali Zeidan assumes office as Prime Minister (November 2012)	

ii. Territorial Power-Sharing

In order to avoid secession, territorial power-sharing can encompass self-governance for 'rebellious regions' on the basis of federalism or regional autonomy.[41] It guarantees local control over limited aspects of the political and social life of a concerned group.

[41] Eiki Berg and Guy Ben-Porat, 'Introduction: Partition vs. Power-sharing?' (2008) 14(1) *Nations and Nationalism* 29, 33.

Among other possibilities, one option is to designate areas as autonomous provinces or autonomous regions. Examples are the autonomous provinces of Trentino and South Tyrol which form the autonomous region of Trentino-South Tyrol in Italy.[42] Prominent cases of autonomous regions include the Autonomous Region in Muslim Mindanao, which is part of the Mindanao island group of the Philippines; the Autonomous Region of Bougainville in Papua New Guinea; and Aceh in Indonesia.[43] Another option is to establish an autonomous republic within a unitary state. An example in this regard is the Crimea, which is an autonomous republic within the unitary state of the Ukraine.[44] It is also possible to grant a region temporary autonomy for an interim period and subsequently hold a referendum about secession. This was the case in Sudan in 2005, where the Comprehensive Peace Agreement granted Southern Sudan autonomy for six years, which was followed by a referendum about the region's independence.[45] After a referendum passed by 98.8% of all votes, South Sudan became the independent Republic of South Sudan in 2011.[46]

Federal solutions may involve symmetric federalism, where all groups enjoy equal status and autonomy.[47] Sub-categories of symmetric federalism are federations or confederations.[48] Federations emerge from an agreement between a number of separate states. Examples are the Federal Republic of Germany or the United States of America. In comparison, confederations are loose unions of sovereign states. An example in this regard is the German Confederation, which was an association of Central European states created by the Congress of Vienna in 1815 and which lasted until 1866.[49] Federalism may also be asymmetrical, where certain regions hold more power than the others. An example is India, which consists of a federal union of 28 states and 7 union territories.[50] States in India have their own elected governments, whereas union territories are ruled directly by the federal government. Another option is the recognition of federal regions.

[42] Jan Markusse, 'Power-sharing and 'Consociational Democracy' in South Tyrol' (1997) 43(1) *GeoJournal* 77.

[43] Mark Turnera, 'Autonomous Regions and the Contribution of International Relations to Peace and Development: Mindanao, Bougainville and Aceh' (2007) 6.1 *Ethnopolitics* 89.

[44] Bill Bowring, 'The Crimean Autonomy: Innovation or Anomaly?' in Marc Weller and Stefan Wolff (eds), *Autonomy, Self-Governance and Conflict Resolution: Innovative Approaches to Institutional Design in Divided Societies* (London, Routledge, 2005) 75.

[45] Comprehensive Peace Agreement between the Government of the Sudan and the Sudan People's Liberation Movement/Sudan People's Liberation Army [hereafter Naivasha CPA], Ch II (Power-Sharing), para 2.12.10, signed in Naivasha, 9 January 2005.

[46] 'UN Welcomes South Sudan as 193rd Member State' *UN News* (14 July 2011).

[47] Marc Weller, 'Introduction' in Marc Weller and Katherine Nobbs (eds), *Asymmetric Autonomy and the Settlement of Ethnic Conflicts* (Philadelphia, University of Pennsylvania Press, 2010) 7.

[48] Ronald Watts, 'Models of Federal Power Sharing' (2001) 53 *International Social Science Journal* 23.

[49] ibid.

[50] M Govinda Rao and Nirvikar Singh, *Asymmetric Federalism in India*, UC Santa Cruz International Economics Working Paper Series No 04-08, April 2004, 3.

Such a solution was included in the Iraqi Constitution in 2005, which recognises 'the region of Kurdistan, along with its existing authorities, as a federal region'.[51] Other provinces were given the option to form a region within the federal system of Iraq at a later stage.

iii. Economic Power-Sharing

Economic power-sharing means primarily *wealth-sharing*, which is most often realised by introducing shared control over natural and other economic resources.[52] Major state corporations, agencies and state-owned enterprises could be distributed between conflict parties. In the Accra Peace Agreement, for instance, several public corporations of Liberia were 'allocated to the warring parties', such as the country's public broadcasting system, electricity corporation, petroleum refining corporation, water and sewer corporation, and others.[53]

It is also possible to divide the leadership of public enterprises on a percentage base. For example, under the Pretoria Protocol settling the Burundi conflict, the major armed group was granted the leadeshp in 20 percent of all public enterprises.[54] Oil revenues are often divided on a percentage basis. For instance, the net oil revenues derived from oil-producing wells in Southern Sudan were allocated between the South and the North on a 50-50 basis.[55] An option in practice has been also to establish a commission for the management of strategic resources and development, which can be governed by a joint board of the government, civil society and representatives of armed groups. In Sierra Leone, such a commission was charged with the 'responsibility of securing and monitoring the legitimate exploitation' of the country's 'gold and diamonds, and other resources that are determined to be of strategic importance for national security and welfare as well as cater for post-war rehabilitation and reconstruction'; the chairmanship was granted to a former rebel commander.[56] Yet, this power-sharing agreement did certainly not addressed the potential for great personal profits from corruption for those participating in the deal.

[51] Iraq Constitution, Art 117, adopted on 15 October 2005. For details, see John McGarry and Brendan O'Leary, 'Iraq's Constitution of 2005: Liberal Consociation as Political Prescription' (2007) 5(4) *International Journal of Constitutional Law* 670.

[52] Hartzell and Hoddie, above n 22, 320.

[53] Comprehensive Peace Agreement Between the Government of Liberia and the Liberians United for Reconciliation and Democracy (LURD) and the Movement for Democracy in Liberia (MODEL) and Political Parties [hereafter Accra Peace Agreement], Annex 4, para 9, signed in Accra, 17 June 2003. For details, see Kwesi Aning and Samuel Atuobi, 'The Neglected Economic Dimensions of ECOWAS's Negotiated Peace Accords in West Africa' (2011) 46(3) *Africa Spectrum* 27.

[54] Pretoria Protocol on Political, Defence and Security Power Sharing in Burundi [hereafter Pretoria Protocol], signed in Pretoria, 8 October 2003, Political Power Issues.

[55] Naivasha CPA, above n 45, Ch III Wealth Sharing, para 5.6.

[56] Lomé Peace Agreement, above n 35, Art VII, paras 1, 12.

iv. Military Power-Sharing

Military power-sharing frequently leads to the integration of former non-state belligerents into the state's army.[57] A practice has been to only integrate a substantial number of officers into the national army and to demobilise the remaining combatants. In the case of Angola, for instance, general officers, senior officers, junior officers, non-commissioned officers and junior enlisted personnel were integrated into the Angolan Armed Forces 'in accordance with existing vacancies', while remaining soldiers were disarmed.[58]

Another option has been the allocation of command posts for a joint command structure along a 50-50 ethnic balance, as happened in Burundi.[59] Alternatively, there may be a proportional recruitment into the new armed forces to reflect regional interests in the country.[60] A practice has been to allow separate armies to operate in their specific geographical regions, while a joint army is maintained for disputed territories. In Sudan, for instance, the Comprehensive Peace Agreement established that the North and South would operate with separate armies while an 'Area Joint Military Committee' was created for disputed territories.[61] Senior officers from the main armed groups may form a technical committee to carry out the coordination between the former belligerents.[62]

v. Differences between Arrangements and Agreements, and between Transitional and Permanent Settlements

In this prior overview, two different facets of conflict settlements can be distinguished: distinctions between arrangements and agreements, as well as between transitional and permanent solutions.[63]

With regard to the first distinction, the terms arrangements and agreements are sometimes used interchangeably and seen as synonymous; yet legally they have nuances of meaning. 'Arrangement' is the umbrella term for modalities, whether on security issues, wealth-sharing or political issues, whereas an 'agreement' is an actual undertaking by the parties who consent to the arrangement.[64]

[57] Katherine Glassmyer and Nicholas Sambanis, 'Rebel-Military Integration and Civil War Termination' (2008) 45(3) *Journal of Peace Research* 365.

[58] Memorandum of Understanding between the Government of the Republic of Angola and UNITA on the Peace Process Ch II 2 C), signed in Luanda, 4 April 2002, UN Doc S/2002/483, 26 April 2002, Annex.

[59] Pretoria Protocol, above n 54, paras I. 1.3.4, 1.4.1.

[60] Lomé Peace Agreement, above n 35, Art XVII, para 3.

[61] Naivasha CPA, above n 45, Annexure I Permanent Ceasefire and Security Arrangements Implementation Modalities and Appendices, para 14.7.

[62] ibid, paras 17.1.3, 17.1.4.

[63] See Figure 1 below.

[64] See, eg, Naivasha CPA, above n 45, Chapeau of the Comprehensive Peace Agreement, para 5 (for example, 'Agreement on Security Arrangements', 'in accordance with the arrangements agreed to by the Parties').

Arrangements can result from traditions and informal custom, whereas an agreement is the promise to comply with and implement the proposed solution.[65] In this respect, the distinction between arrangements and agreements reflects a degree of formality ranging between informal and formal settlements.[66]

On the other hand, whereas transitional power-sharing is intended to end after a certain time, for instance after elections or constitutional reforms, permanent power-sharing structures can become a part of the constitution and the state's societal system.[67] This aspect illustrates that the spectrum of power-sharing has, besides a mechanism-specific side, a decisive temporal component. Temporal considerations are especially relevant in matters of proportionality concerning justified differential treatment in power-sharing settlements: as the in-depth case studies on Bosnia and Herzegovina in Chapter 3 and on Lebanon in Chapter 4 will show in detail. While temporary discriminatory power-sharing settlements might be justified, permanent discriminatory power-sharing structures tend to be unproportionate, and are thus unjustified.[68]

Figure 1 Difference between arrangements and agreements, and transitional or permanent settlements

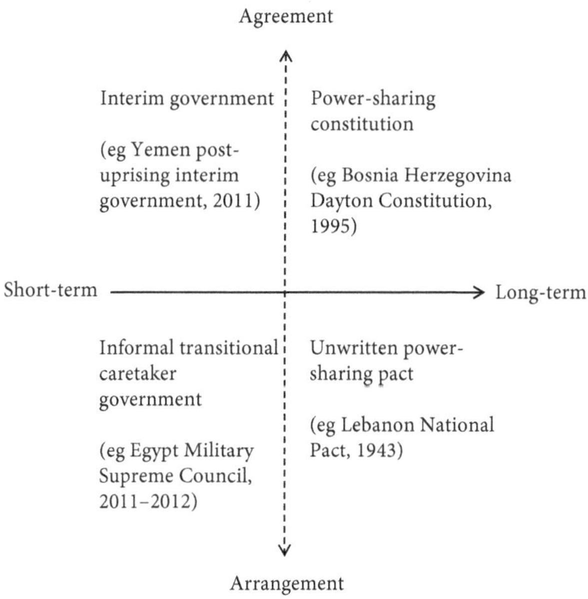

[65] See, eg, The General Framework Agreement for Peace in Bosnia and Herzegovina [hereinafter Dayton Accords], Art 2-8, signed in Paris, 14 December 1995.

[66] Anthony Aust, *Modern Treaty Law and Practice* (Cambridge, Cambridge University Press, 2007) 32.

[67] Caroline Hartzell, 'Structuring the Peace: Negotiated Settlements and the Construction of Conflict Management Institutions' in T David Mason et al (eds), *Conflict Prevention and Peacebuilding in Post-War Societies: Sustaining the Peace* (London, Routledge, 2006) 31.

[68] For details, see the case studies on Bosnia and Herzegovina in Ch 3 and on Lebanon in Ch 4.

B. Ethnic Power-Sharing in Bosnia and Herzegovina

Bosnia and Herzegovina is one of the most multifaceted cases of constitutional ethnic power-sharing and has often been called the 'most extensive democratization' initiative of the international community in contemporary history.[69] Indeed, the Dayton Peace Agreement was a trial run for modern post-conflict ethnic state building in Europe and used shortly thereafter as a blueprint for Kosovo.[70] In textbook fashion, the Constitution of Bosnia and Herzegovina resembles a combination of power-sharing provisions, including vetoes, quota and territorial autonomy.[71] The Dayton Peace Accords split state powers among the former conflict parties, who are also the largest ethnic groups: Bosniaks, Croats, and Serbs. Under the Constitution, they are privileged as the 'constituent people', apart from 'other' ethnic minorities.[72]

Table 2 Features of power-sharing in Bosnia and Herzegovina

Type of power-sharing	Elements	Provisions
Political power-sharing	Three-headed Presidency	Equally distributed between Bosniaks, Croats and Serbs ('constituent people')
	Proportional representation	Equal representation of Bosniaks, Croats and Serbs in the House of Peoples
	Vital interest veto	Veto by one of the 'constituent people' against any Parliamentary Assembly decision
Territorial power-sharing	Autonomy	Internal autonomy of the Federation of Bosnia and Herzegovina and the Republika Srpska within the State of Bosnia and Herzegovina
	Condominium	Brčko District as a Special Administrative Zone: condominium of the Republika Srpska and the Federation of Bosnia and Herzegovina

[69] Sumantra Bose, *Bosnia after Dayton: Nationalist Partition and International Intervention* (Oxford, Oxford University Press, 2002) 202.

[70] Joseph Marko, 'The New Kosovo Constitution in a Regional Comparative Perspective' (2008) 33(4) *Review of Central and East European Law* 437.

[71] For an overview, see Table 2. For a synopsis of power-sharing provisions in the Constitution of Bosnia and Herzegovina, see Appendix, Table 2.

[72] Bosnia and Herzegovina Constitution, Preamble, para 9, adopted on 1 December 1995 [hereinafter BiH Constitution].

i. The Federation of Bosnia and Herzegovina, the Republika Srpska and the Brčko as Elements of Territorial Power-Sharing

As a component of territorial power-sharing, Bosnia and Herzegovina is partitioned into two entities: the Serb-dominated (mainly Orthodox Christian) Republika Srpska, and the Bosniak-dominated (mainly Muslim) Federation of Bosnia and Herzegovina.[73] Both entities have the right to establish special parallel relationships with neighbouring states, as long as they are consistent with the sovereignty and territorial integrity of Bosnia and Herzegovina.[74] The Federation and the Republika Srpska also maintain their own civilian law enforcement agencies.[75] The police, the entities' Supreme Courts and lower courts, customs services and postal services are separated.[76]

In 2009, pursuant to an arbitral award, the independent Brčko District was created.[77] The Brčko area in north-eastern Bosnia was left out in the demarcation, as there was no consensus on the location of the boundaries.[78] The final arbitration award declared the territory a 'condominium' governed by both the Republika Srpska and the Federation of Bosnia and Herzegovina.[79] Among other responsibilities, the district organises its own finances, public property, cultural affairs, education, health care, social welfare, judiciary and legal services and law enforcement.[80]

ii. The Multi-Ethnic Presidential Troika, Bicameral System and Veto Rights as Components of Political Power-Sharing

As a part of political power-sharing, a presidential troika was created consisting of one Bosniak and one Croat elected from the Federation, as well as one Serb elected

[73] BiH Constitution, Art 1, para 3.

[74] BiH Constitution, Art 3, para 2 a).

[75] BiH Constitution, Art 3, para 2 c).

[76] For details, see Jan Christoph Nemitz, 'The Legal Status of the Republika Srpska' (1997) 43 *Osteuropa Recht* 89.

[77] Final Award, Arbitral Tribunal for Dispute over Inter-Entity Boundary in Brčko Area, 5 March 1999. See Amendment I to the Constitution of Bosnia and Herzegovina, adopted by the House of Representatives on 25 March 2009, and by the House of Peoples on 26 March 2009.

[78] Instead, all parties signed up to a binding arbitration process which would define the shape of the disputed area. See Dayton Accords, above n 65, Annex 2, Agreement on Inter-Entity Boundary Line and Related Issues, Art 5, para 1.

[79] Final Award, para 11, above n 77. Technically, the Brčko District became a special 'administrative unit of local self-government'. See Statute of the Brčko District of Bosnia and Herzegovina, adopted on 6 May 2008, Art 1, para 1.

[80] ibid, Art 8, para 1.

from the Republika Srpska, who together serve as a collective head of the state.[81] Each member of the Presidency has a veto right against decisions of the Presidency if they consider the decisions to be 'destructive of a vital interest' of the entity from which he or she was elected.[82]

A bicameral Parliamentary Assembly tries to balance the entities' interests in the legislative. The House of Peoples, as the upper house of the Parliament, draws its members from among the three constituent ethnicities: five Croats and five Bosniaks have to be from the Federation, and five Serbs have to come from the Republika Srpska.[83] In the House of Representatives, as the lower house of the Parliament, two-thirds of the members are elected from the territory of the Federation and one-third from the territory of the Republika Srpska.[84] The Constitution guarantees Bosniaks, Croats, or Serbs as the 'constituent people' a veto right, when vital interests are concerned.[85]

Alongside power-sharing in the executive and legislative, the highest judiciary similarly ensures proportional representation: four members of the Constitutional Court are selected by the House of Representatives of the Federation, and two members by the Assembly of the Republika Srpska.[86] Additionally, three international judges serve in the Court.

iii. Joint Economic Power-Sharing of Public Entities

Guaranteeing economic power-sharing, the first Governing Board of the Central Bank comprised two members from the Federation with one Bosniak and one Croat who share one vote, as well as one member from the Republika Srpska.[87] In order to share the financial burden, the Federation is constitutionally obliged to provide two-thirds, and the Republika Srpska one-third, of the revenues required by the budget.[88] The Dayton Accords also contained an agreement on establishing a Commission on Public Corporations to 'operate joint public facilities, such as for the operation of utility, energy, postal and communication facilities, for the benefit of both Entities'.[89]

[81] BiH Constitution, Art 5.
[82] BiH Constitution, Art 4, para 2 d).
[83] BiH Constitution, Art 4, para 1.
[84] BiH Constitution, Art 4, para 2.
[85] BiH Constitution, Art 4, para 2 e).
[86] BiH Constitution, Art 4, para 1 a).
[87] BiH Constitution, Art 7, para 2.
[88] BiH Constitution, Art 7, para 3.
[89] Two members of the Commission are appointed by the Federation of Bosnia and Herzegovina and one by the Republika Srpska. Two further members are appointed by the President of the European Bank for Reconstruction and Development, which also designates one international member as the chairperson. See Dayton Accords, above n 65, Annex 9, Agreement on Establishment of Bosnia and Herzegovina Public Corporations, Art 1.

C. Confessional Power-Sharing in Lebanon

In comparison to ethnic power-sharing in Bosnia and Herzegovina, Lebanon's political system is based on confessional proportions.[90] Instead of a rule by majority, decision-making relies on consensus, which aims to accommodate religious pluralism. Lebanon has 18 state-recognised communities with distinctive religious, political or philosophical beliefs, among them Shi'a, Sunni, Druze, Isma'ili, Alawite Muslims, and Maronite Christians, Roman Catholic, Chaldean Catholic, Copts, Protestants, Greek Catholic, Greek Orthodox, Armenian Catholic, Armenian Orthodox, Syriac Catholic, Syriac Orthodox, Assyrian Christians, and Jews.[91]

Lebanon's confessional system comprises two components: first, matters related to status law can be regulated by each confession independently.[92] Religious courts are granted exclusive jurisdiction over marriage, divorce and inheritance. Marriages across sects need either a religious conversion or marriage under civil law in another country.[93] Second, political confessionalism establishes that posts within the state are distributed among the various sects and religious communities. In the Lebanese Parliament, seats are equally divided between Christians and Muslims.[94]

Table 3 Lebanon's eighteen state-recognised communities

1 Shi'a	7 Roman Catholic	13 Armenian Catholic
2 Sunni	8 Chaldean Catholic	14 Armenian Orthodox
3 Druze	9 Copts	15 Syriac Catholic
4 Isma'ili	10 Protestants	16 Syriac Orthodox
5 Alawite	11 Greek Catholic	17 Assyrian Christians
6 Maronite Christian	12 Greek Orthodox	18 Jews

[90] In the context of Lebanon's political system, the terms 'confessionalism' and 'sectarianism' are often used interchangeably. The terminological difference between confessions and sects is not always coherent, which can be seen in the fact that both terms are used synonymously. Confessionalism often relates to the different sub-divisions in a religion, particularly concerning different churches (eg Orthodox, Anglican, Lutheran, Catholic Christian; but also regarding the Sunni-Shi'a schism), whereas sects are described as religious sub-movements which broke away from one religious denomination under a certain leader (eg Bazighiyya, Dhammiyya, Hafizi as extinct Shia sects; but also Sunni and Shia are often considered as different sects of Islam). In practice in Lebanon, clashes between Christians and Muslims are described as 'confessional' violence, and clashes when there is a focus on Shi'a-Sunni differences are described as 'sectarian'. For terminological guidance, see 'Sects' in John Bowker (ed), *The Oxford Dictionary of World Religions* (Oxford, Oxford University Press, 1999) 871.

[91] Law No 553 (Lebanon), issued on 24 July 1996. See Table 3.

[92] For details, see UN Doc CEDAW/C/LBN/3, 7 July 2006, para 22.

[93] Michael Humphrey, *Islam, Multiculturalism and Transnationalism* (London, IB Tauris, 1998) 76.

[94] For an overview, see Table 4. For a synopsis of power-sharing provisions in the Lebanese Constitution, see Appendix, Table 3.

Table 4 Features of power-sharing in Lebanon

Type of confessionalism	Elements	Provisions
Political power-sharing	Three Presidencies	Lebanese President: Maronite Christian; Prime Minister: Sunni Muslim; Speaker of the Parliament: Shi'a Muslim
	Unity Government	Tendency and aim to form coalition governments of all political parties
	Proportional representation	50:50 quota for Christians and Muslims in the Lebanese Parliament; Confessional quota for high-level posts ('Grand One')
	Consensus	Each confessional group regulates matters of personal status independently
Status laws	Religious independence	Each confessional group regulates matters of personal status independently

i. Lebanon's Secular Constitution and the Unwritten 'National Pact'

Crafted during the French mandate in 1926, Lebanon's Constitution initially founded democracy in the country on a strong secular base, following the French concept of laïcité, separating governmental and religious affairs.[95] However, continuing the tradition of the Ottoman *millet* system, governmental posts were split among the different religious groups in order to strike a political balance between them in the country.[96]

In 1943, after the country's independence from France, the 'National Pact' formally divided public positions between Christians and Muslims.[97] Arranged as a 'gentleman's agreement' between Lebanon's first President, Bishara al-Khuri (Maronite Christian) and its first Prime Minister, Riyad al-Sulh (Sunni Muslim), the National Pact arrangement comprised three principles: first, sectarian proportionality; second, sectarian autonomy, and third, foreign policy neutrality.[98]

Accommodating Sunni and Shi'a interests, the Christian leadership of Lebanon committed themselves to refrain from military pacts with Western powers. In return, Lebanon's Islamic religious authorities agreed to accept the territorial

[95] Kamal S Salibi, *The Modern History of Lebanon* (Delmar New York, Caravan Books, 1965) 167.
[96] ibid.
[97] Eyal Zisser, *Lebanon: The Challenge of Independence* (London, IB Tauris Publishers, 2000) 57.
[98] Although the pact was never signed or ratified by Parliament, it was considered to be binding and considered to be an 'unwritten' part of the constitution: ibid, 59.

borders of Lebanon and stop pushing for incorporating the country into a single Arab or Syrian state. It was established that future Lebanese presidents should always be Maronite Christian, the Prime Minister should be Sunni Muslim and the Speaker of the Parliament Shi'a Muslim.[99] Influential positions within the public administrations, so-called 'Grade One' posts, were shared out according to religion.[100] This confessional partnership in jointly running the affairs of the state remained in place for three decades until its collapse in 1975 with the outbreak of the Lebanese Civil War.[101]

ii. The Taif Agreement and the Post-War Hope for a Phase-Out of the Confessional Divide

After 16 years of Civil War in Lebanon, the Taif Agreement called for a gradual abolishment of political sectarianism as a 'fundamental national objective'.[102] Agreed to by the remaining members of the Lebanese Parliament in the Mecca Province city Taif in Saudi Arabia in 1989, the peace settlement stipulated that 'people may not be categorized on the basis of any affiliation whatsoever and there shall be no fragmentation, no partition'.[103] Among others, the Taif Agreement demanded the removal of sectarian labels from identity cards and promoted administrative decentralisation by expanding the power of provinces.[104] Notably, the Taif Agreement suggested that appointments to the civil service should be merit-based, except for high level Grade One posts, which remain distributed between the different confessions through informal custom.[105]

Under the umbrella of political reforms, the Taif Agreement envisaged that the Chamber of Deputies would pass an 'election law free of sectarian restriction'.[106] In the meantime, parliamentary seats were divided 'equally between Christians and Muslims' and 'proportionately between the denominations of each sect', as well as 'proportionately between the districts'.[107] The agreement increased the

[99] From Lebanon's independence up until today, this custom of maintaining three authorities as a troika has only been broken a few times. For details, see 'Myth #16: The Post of the Parliament Speaker is historically and constitutionally reserved to the Shi'a' (2008) 75 *The Monthly* 25.

[100] For example, the Minister of Defence was usually a Druze, while the Chief-of-Staff of the Lebanese Army was a Maronite, and the five provincial governors were from the main five sects: Maronite, Sunni, Shi'a, Greek Orthodox and Druze. See Zisser, above n 97, 59.

[101] Fawwaz Traboulsi, *A History of Modern Lebanon* (London, Pluto Press, 2007) 111.

[102] Taif Agreement, signed in Taif, 22 October 1989, I, para G. The terms 'Taif Agreement', 'Taif Accord', 'National Reconciliation Accord' and 'Document of National Accord' are often used interchangeably in this context. The original Arabic title is 'الطائف اتفاقية', which can be translated as 'sectarian agreement' or 'confessional agreement'.

[103] ibid, First Part, I.H.

[104] ibid, First Part, I.G.b; III.A.2.

[105] ibid, First Part, II.G.a. For a comprehensive overview about confessional posts in Lebanese public entities, see Appendix, Table 4. See also 'Sharing the Lebanese Government Apparatus' (2010) 100 *The Monthly* 5; 'Embassies Reserved for Confessions' (2010) 92 *The Monthly* 5.

[106] ibid, First Part, II.A.5.

[107] ibid, First Part, II.A.5.a–c.

number of parliamentary seats from 99 deputies (54 Christians, 45 Muslims) to 108 deputies (54 Christians, 54 Muslims), shifting slightly the previous 6:5 ratio to an equal 1:1 split of seats between Christians and Muslims.[108]

The Taif Agreement also partly transferred executive authority from the President (Christian Maronite) to the cabinet, and thereby increased the power of the Prime Minister (Muslim Sunni).[109] The term of the Speaker of Parliament (Muslim Shia) was extended from one year to four years.[110] The Chamber of Deputies, the Parliament, was also strengthened at the expense of Presidential powers by the inclusion of binding parliamentary consultations for the nomination of the Prime Minister.[111] The President was intended to embody 'the country's unity'.[112]

Technically, the Taif Agreement was adopted by a constitutional law by the Lebanese Parliament, which amended the Constitution.[113] The Preamble of the Constitution now calls for the 'abolition of political confessionalism [to] be a basic national goal'.[114] However, a specific deadline or timeline for the gradual removal of political confessionalism was not set.

iii. Post-Taif Electoral Reform Attempts (1992–2006)

Several efforts to change the sectarian electoral framework have been attempted since the signing of Taif. In 1992, the number of seats in the Lebanese Parliament was extended to 128 seats, equally attributed between Christians and Muslims.[115] Within the non-Muslim grouping, one seat got reserved for minorities such as Latin Catholics, Syriacs (Catholic or Orthodox), Chaldean Catholics, Assyrians, Copts and Jews.[116]

Table 5 50:50 Muslim-Christian rule for the distribution of seats in the Lebanese Parliament

	Christians		**Muslims**	
Confessions	Maronites	(34)	Sunnis	(27)
	Greek Orthodox	(14)	Shi'as	(27)
	Catholics	(8)	Druze	(8)

(continued)

[108] ibid, First Part, II.A.6.
[109] ibid, First Part, II.C.
[110] ibid, First Part, II.A.1.
[111] ibid, First Part, II.C.2.
[112] ibid, First Part, II.B.
[113] Constitution of the Lebanese Republic [hereafter Lebanese Constitution], adopted on 23 May 1926, amended by Amendment to the Constitution of Lebanon, Constitutional Law, adopted on 21 September 1990.
[114] ibid.
[115] For details, see Vanessa E Shields, 'Political Reform in Lebanon: Has the Cedar Revolution Failed?' (2008) 14(4) *Journal of Legislative Studies* 474.
[116] Farid El-Khazen, *Prospects for Lebanon: Lebanon's First Postwar Parliamentary Election, 1992* (London, IB Tauris, 2007) 15. See Table 5 above.

Table 5 ***(Continued)***

	Christians		**Muslims**	
	Armenian Orthodox	(5)	Alawites	(2)
	Armenian Catholic	(1)		
	Protestant	(1)		
	Minority group member	(1)		
Proportion		(64)		(64)
Total	(128)			

In 1996, a change in the election law extended the boundaries of electoral districts in order to overcome confessional fragmentation.[117] In 2000, the district boundaries shifted once more to ensure outcomes in favour of the Syrian presence in certain areas.[118] In 2006, the National Commission for Electoral Law under Fouad Boutros proposed a mixed majority and proportionate system.[119] Yet, the proposal was never adopted by the Lebanese Parliament.

iv. The Doha Agreement (2008)

In 2008, the Doha Agreement re-emphasised Lebanon's consensus principle to keep the country stable.[120] It ended an 18-month-long political struggle which brought Lebanon to the brink of another civil war. The Doha Agreement entailed four main points: first, the Chief of Staff of the Lebanese Army, General Michel Sleiman, was elected as the 'consensus' President of the country; second, a 'National Unity Government' was to be formed; third, new rules for the Parliamentary elections in the subsequent year were to be agreed upon; and fourth, all sides undertook to abstain from armed force and continue the dialogue.[121] Within the National Unity Government, the opposition was given a third of cabinet posts, the so called 'blocking third', which created veto power.[122] The Doha Agreement also led to recourse to the 1960 election law, which nearly doubled the number of electoral districts to arrange a power equilibrium through fragmentation.[123]

[117] Paul Salem, *Electoral Law Reform in Lebanon: The Experience and Recommendations of the National Commission*, Arab Reform Brief No 10, Arab Reform Initiative, 2006, 2.

[118] *Assessment of the Election Framework: Election Law of 2008*, Democracy Reporting International (DRI) and the Lebanese Association for Free Elections (LADE), Berlin/Beirut, December 2008, 18–20.

[119] *A Guide to the Proposed Draft Law*, Civil Campaign for Electoral Reform, 2007, 2.

[120] In November 2006, Shi'a minister of the Amal party and Hezbollah resigned from Prime Minister's Fouad Siniora unity government following disagreements over the establishment of the Special Tribunal for Lebanon. For details, see Jim Muir, 'Lebanon Deal Holds Prospect of Peace' *BBC News* (21 May 2008).

[121] Doha Agreement, signed in Doha, 21 May 2008.

[122] 'Doha Agreement Achieved its Aims' *The Daily Star (Lebanon)* (26 June 2009).

[123] 'Lebanon Dialogue Committee Agreed to Adopt 1960 Electoral Law' *Yalibnan* (18 May 2008).

v. Post-Doha Elections (2009) and Forthcoming Ballots (2014)

In 2009, although the Western-allied bloc, referred to as the 'March 14' alliance, won a majority of seats in the Parliamentary elections, a National Unity Government was formed for the sake of internal peace in the spirit of the Doha Agreement.[124] After months of brokering a deal with the opposition, a 30-member cabinet was formed along a 15:10:5 formula whereby 15 ministers were selected by the March 14 alliance, ten from the opposition March 8 Alliance, and five posts allocated to politicians close to the President.[125] The set-up ensured that the March 14 coalition did not have an absolute majority, and the March 8 opposition did not have a vetoing third, as it did after Doha. The arrangement gave the President's ministers, who were supposedly impartial, a swing vote on cabinet decisions. Since 2009, the government has changed several times, most lately in March 2013 over disputes about the electoral law reform.[126] New elections to the Lebanese Parliament were initially scheduled for summer 2013 and finally took place in 2018.

The cases of Lebanon and Bosnia and Herzegovina illustrate how difficult it is for states in transition to actually overcome old power structures. Lebanon still operates under a political system initiated nearly a century ago, which is hard to overcome despite the formal committement in the Taif Agreement to phase out the custom of poltical confessionalism. In the case of Bosnia and Herzegovina, the Dayton Accords struck a constitutional balance between the major ethnicities, which brought an end to hostilities but also resulted in a stalemate on reforms. As will be detailed in Chapters 3 and 4, international law can play a crucial role in those post-conflict situations by catalysing change and motivating state transitions.

IV. The Legal Debate

Legal scholars have been assessing state transitions and power-sharing arrangements in peace settlements from various angles. Parallel to Lijphart's writings, legal thinking revolved around the requirements for successful federalism.[127] Addressed topics have ranged from self-determination, human rights, minority rights, the structural analysis of peace accords, to the influence of international

[124] Under the electoral system in place at the time, the March 14 coalition had gained about 45% of the total electoral votes, but won 71 of the 128 available seats. The March 8 coalition won 54.7% of the votes, but only gained 57 seats. For details, see Lebanon: Final Report, Parliamentary Election, European Union Election Observation Mission, 7 June 2009, 28.

[125] Nadim Ladki, 'Lebanon's Hariri Forms Unity Government with Hezbollah' *Reuters* (9 November 2009).

[126] Donna Abu-Nasr and Nadeem Hamid, 'Lebanon's Premier Resigns After Dispute on Electoral Law' *Bloomberg* (23 March 2013).

[127] Thomas Franck, 'Why Federations Fail' in Thomas Franck, *Why Federations Fail: An Inquiry into the Requisites for Successful Federalism* (New York, New York University Press, 1968) 213.

law on constitutional designs. Whether and what kind of power-sharing can constitute discrimination or violate participation rights has been a particular focus of critical legal reflection.

A. Power-Sharing as a Term in Public International Law?

Terminologically, power-sharing is an atypical category used in international law, which explains the asynchrony between research on the topic in political science and international law.[128] For instance, neither the UN Charter nor human rights conventions explicitly classify power-sharing or elaborate on its purpose or limitations.[129] A reason is that power-sharing primarily concerns the internal structure of a state, which remains as a *domaine réservé* for them.[130] It is rather constitutional law that employs concepts such as 'state powers', the 'division of powers', and the 'balance of powers' between courts and legislatures.

Nonetheless, the concept of shared power is not absent in international law. For example, Philip Allott used the term 'power-sharing' to explain the political, economic and legal modifications in international maritime law which the newly signed UN Convention on the Law of the Sea entailed.[131] Another angle has been the lawfulness of international treaty-making in the light of constitutional law vis-à-vis the different authorities of a state.[132]

Terms in international law which are close to power-sharing, but focus on inter-state relations, are the concepts of *servitudes* and *condominiums*. Servitudes are shared territorial rights and obligations established by treaty; for instance, for the joint exploitation of natural resources or the joint access to a territory.[133]

[128] For instructive thoughts on the overall academic challenge of bridging political science and the legal scholarship, see Anne-Marie Slaughter, Andrew S Tulumello and Stepan Wood, 'International Law and International Relations Theory: A New Generation of Interdisciplinary Scholarship' (1998) 92(3) *American Journal of International Law* 367.

[129] Hardly any contemporary textbook in international law mentions power-sharing as a key term for legal assessment. See Anthony Aust, *Handbook of International Law* (Cambridge: Cambridge University Press, 2010); Donald R Rothwell et al (eds), *International Law: Cases and Materials With Australian Perspectives* (Cambridge, Cambridge University Press, 2010); Wolfgang Vitzthum (ed), *Völkerrecht* (Berlin, Walter de Gruyter, 2007); Joe Verhoeven, *Droit International Public* (Bruxelles, Larcier, 2001).

[130] Concerning the intersection of responsibility, accountability and human rights, see Ch 1, Part III.A.

[131] Philip Allott, 'Power Sharing in the Law of the Sea' (1983) 77 *American Journal of International Law* 1. The observation that international treaties regulate powers between states has also been scrutinised by other authors. See also Richard H Steinberg and Jonathan M Zasloff, 'Power and International Law' (2006) 100(1) *American Journal of International Law* 64.

[132] Joseph R Biden, Jr and John B Ritch, III, 'The Treaty Power: Upholding a Constitutional Partnership' (1989) 137(5) *University of Pennsylvania Law Review* 1529. See also Uwe Leonardya, 'Federation and Länder in German Foreign Relations: Power-sharing in Treaty-making and European Affairs' (1992) 1(3) *German Politics* 119.

[133] Pitman B Potter, 'The Doctrine of Servitudes in International Law' (1915) 9(3) *American Journal of International Law* 627, 638. See also Lassa FL Oppenheim, *International Law: A Treatise* vol 1 (ed) Ronald F Roxburgh (Clark, New Jersey, The Lawbook Exchange, 2005) 364, para 203.

Condominiums, on the other hand, entail joint territorial sovereignty of two or more states over the same external territory.[134] An example is Pheasant Island in the Bidasoa River, which has been formally administered by Spain and France since the Peace Treaty of the Pyrenees in 1659.[135]

B. The Self-Determination Trap

The roots of the legal debate about inter-state power-sharing can be found in one of the cardinal principles of modern international law: the right to self-determination. While self-determination aims to strengthen peace, it is also one of the major causes of armed conflict.[136] Self-determination allows all peoples to 'freely determine their political status and freely pursue their economic, social and cultural development'.[137] However, when, by whom and to what extent the right to self-determination can be exercised is disputed in practice.[138]

Although territorial breakaways have occurred in practice, a right to secession is not enshrined in current international law.[139] At the same time, secessions are not explicitly outlawed. Legal scholars argue that a remedial right of unilateral secession should be granted when a minority is oppressed by a tyrannical government.[140] Some scholars suggest that, as a last resort, a people could be entitled to remedy extreme persecution through secession.[141] In any case, unilateral secession may only be considered under extreme circumstances in which the coexistence of different groups within a state would obviously be impossible and a peaceful solution unimaginable.[142]

As a way out of this 'self-determination trap', states are unrestricted in their choice of means for balancing the interests of opposing ethnic or confessional fractions.[143] Power-sharing can be used to avoid a forced secession by allocating

[134] Kay Hailbronner, 'Der Staat und der Einzelne als Völkerrechtssubjekte', *Völkerrecht*, paras 123–24.

[135] For more examples, see Christopher C Joyner, *International Law in the 21st Century: Rules for Global Governance* (Oxford, Rowman & Littlefield Publishers, 2005) 33.

[136] For details, see Marc Weller, 'Settling Self-determination Conflicts: An Introduction' in Marc Weller, Barbara Metzger and Niall Johnson, *Settling Self-Determination Disputes: Complex Power-sharing in Theory and Practice* (Leiden, Brill, 2008) xi. For the connection between self-determination and peace, see UN Charter, Art 1, para 2.

[137] See ICCPR and ICESCR, Art 1, para 1.

[138] See Milena Sterio, *The Right to Self-determination under International Law: 'Selfistans', Secession, and the Rule of the Great Powers* (London, Routledge, 2012) 4.

[139] James Crawford, 'State Practice and International Law in Relation to Unilateral Secession' in Anne Bayefsky (ed), *Self-Determination in International Law: Quebec and Lessons Learned* (Cambridge, Kluwer Law International, 2000) 60.

[140] Christian Tomuschat, 'Secession and Self-determination' in Marcelo G Kohen (ed), *Secession: International Law Perspectives* (Cambridge, Cambridge University Press, 2006) 42.

[141] Thomas Franck, 'Postmodern Tribalism and the Right to Secession' in Catherine Brölmann, René Lefeber and Marjoleine Zieck (eds), *Peoples and Minorities in International Law* (Boston, Brill, 1993) 13.

[142] Georg Nolte, 'Session and External Intervention' in Kohen, above n 140, 65, 85–86.

[143] Marc Weller, *Escaping the Self-Determination Trap* (Leiden, Brill, 2008) 13.

autonomy, veto rights and proportional representation to rival groups, as described above. States are thus maintained as cornerstones to stabilise international order.[144]

C. Increased Minority Rights and Human Rights Protections as Frameworks for Peace

The second layer to the legal perspective on power-sharing results from the process of enhanced human rights and minority rights protections. Since the last century, human rights protections at regional and international levels have increased.[145] In the wake of World War I with the collapse of the old Habsburg, Romanov and Ottoman Empires and the creation of new 'nation-states' with mixed ethnic and diverse religious populations, the protection of minority rights became crucial.[146] At the Paris Peace Conference in 1919, provisions for the protection of specific minorities were included in a series of adopted bilateral and multilateral peace treaties and declarations.[147] The treaties gave certain minorities some autonomy, but guarantees lacked implementation and the scope of minority rights remained disputed.[148] Following World War II, international law became even more sensitive to matters of discrimination and equality. Minority rights began to be perceived as part of the solution to international disputes rather than the problem.[149] As a counter-strategy to secession and ethno-nationalism, guarantees for minority rights were developed as a 'constructive alternative' in order to maintain the stability of states facing ethnically fragmented societies.[150] Subsequently, comprehensive minority rights provisions gradually found their way into peace agreements.[151]

[144] Three months after the outbreak of armed conflict in Bosnia and Herzegovina, Boutros Boutros-Ghali pronounced in the Agenda for Peace in 1992: 'If every ethnic, religious or linguistic group claimed statehood, there would be no limit to fragmentation, and peace, security and economic well-being for all would become ever more difficult to achieve'. See Report of the UN Secretary-General, 'Agenda for Peace', UN Doc A/47/277-S/24111, 17 June 1992, para 17.

[145] For a synopsis of relevant universal rights affected by power-sharing, see Appendix, Table 6.

[146] For an instructive historical summary, see Thomas Buergenthal, 'The Normative and Institutional Evolution of International Human Rights' (1997) 19(4) *Human Rights Quarterly* 703.

[147] For details on the League of Nations' Minority Treaties, see Athanasia Spiliopoulou Åkermark, *Justifications of Minority Protection in International Law* (The Hague, Athanasia Spiliopoulou Åkermark, 1997) 104.

[148] For the series of minority disputes before the Permanent Court of International Justice, see ibid, 108–11.

[149] Patrick Thornberry, *International Law and Rights of Minorities* (Oxford, Oxford University Press, 1993) 398.

[150] Asbjørn Eide, 'In Search of Constructive Alternatives to Secession' in Christian Tomuschat (ed), *Modern Law of Self-Determination* (Martinus Nijhoff, Dordrecht, 1993) 139.

[151] David Wippman, 'The Evolution and Implementation of Minority Rights' (1997) 66(2) *Fordham Law Review* 597, 611. For empirical analysis, see also Fernand de Varennes, 'Political Participation and Power-sharing in Ethnic Peace Settlements' in Marc Weller and Katherine Nobbs (eds), *Political Participation of Minorities: A Commentary on International Standards and Practice* (Oxford, Oxford University Press, 2010) 453, 468.

D. Legal Counter-Ideals of Minority Rights in the Struggle Over Autonomy

Parallel to the growing appraisal of minority rights, legal scholars have been debating the tension between individual and group rights.[152] Questions have been raised as to whether special minorities' measures lead to an opt-out from individual rights and whether minority protection thus inevitably entails inequality.[153] This discourse correlates with the earlier reflection about the tension between liberalism versus communitarianism, vis-à-vis justice, equality and liberty, at the beginning of the 1980s.[154]

The debate centres on the question of whether liberal states 'behave better' and whether or not liberal democracy could actually stabilise international relations, based on the proposition that liberal states cause less internal and external conflict.[155] Unlike liberalism, the core idea of communitarianism is the belief that there has been too much emphasis on individual liberty. Both theories struggle with the problem of how to encourage group life without sacrificing individual identity. A fundamental critique of communitarism has been that group autonomy could undermine rather than advance communities, as the rhetoric used for group affiliations can reinforce exclusion and domination under the guise of community.[156] Balancing the notions of individualism and communitarianism, critical pluralists have argued that a more sensible route is one 'where group differences are acknowledged to be an important aspect of social and political life, but where these very differences are adjusted and reconstituted in a process of constant and genuine dialogue'.[157]

At the beginning of the 1990s, the legal debate about individual versus group rights, intensified parallel to the preparation of the UN Declaration on the Rights of Persons Belonging to National or Ethnic, Religious and Linguistic Minorities.[158] Henry Steiner assessed how autonomy can both strengthen and undermine

[152] For a detailed overview, see Nicola Wenzel, *Das Spannungsverhältnis zwischen Gruppenschutz und Individualschutz im Völkerrecht* (Berlin, Springer, 2008) 17.

[153] Gillian Triggs, 'The Rights of "Peoples" and Individual Rights: Conflict or Harmony?' in James Crawford (ed), *The Rights of Peoples* (Oxford, Oxford University Press, 1988) 148.

[154] See John Rawls, *A Theory of Justice* (Cambridge, MA, Harvard University Press, 1971) 3, and Michael Walzer, *Spheres of Justice: A Defense of Pluralism and Equality* (New York, Basic Books, 1983) 4.

[155] For a thorough introduction, see Tobias Bunde, 'Das Völkerrecht der Demokratien: Ambivalenzen einer liberalen Weltordnung' in Christian Tomuschat (ed), *Weltordnungsmodelle für das 21. Jahrhundert* (Baden-Baden, Nomos, 2009) 99. See also José E Alvarez, 'Do Liberal States Behave Better?: A Critique of Slaughter's Liberal Theory' (2001) 12(2) *European Journal of International Law* 183.

[156] Gregory S Alexander, 'Dilemmas of Group Autonomy: Residential Associations and Community' (1989) 75 *Cornell Law Review* 1.

[157] Adeno Addis, 'Individualism, Communitarianism, and the Rights of Ethnic Minorities' (1991) 67 *Notre Dame Law Review* 615, 674.

[158] Declaration on the Rights of Persons Belonging to National or Ethnic, Religious and Linguistic Minorities, GA Res 47/135, 18 December 1992.

human rights.[159] Analysing the Flemish issue in Belgium, the Basques in Spain, the Tamils in Sri Lanka or the Francophone population in Canada, Steiner argued that autonomy 'may improve chances for pacific co-existence and provide the only realistic alternative not only to continuing oppression, but to a split of the contending ethnic groups into two states'.[160] Steiner observed that, although autonomy regimes may reinforce underlying human rights, they may in fact weaken them. Steiner concluded that the individual's link to the relevant group in itself constitutes the occasion for discrimination. He warned that the 'manifestations of ethnic bonds will become the cardinal obstacle to a human rights consciousness, at least with respect to attitudes of members of the ethnic group towards "the other"'.[161]

E. Ethnic Conflict, the Dayton Peace Accords and International Law

The sealing of the Dayton Peace Accords gave rise to in-depth thinking about conflict settlements and international law.[162] Paul Szasz noted that the 'nature and bitterness of the conflict and the expressed unwillingness of a substantial fraction of the Bosnian population to live peacefully with other Bosnians have led to a plethora of unprecedented and necessarily experimental constitutional proposals'.[163] Legal practitioners initially applauded the achievement of the Dayton Peace Accords, but soon critical voices were raised, pointing to the risk of ethnic discrimination.

Among others, Anne-Marie Slaughter underscored the impact of ethnic conflict on human rights law, elaborating on the tension between individual versus group rights.[164] Fernando Tesón assessed the relation between ethnicity, human rights and self-determination, concluding that:

> The recognition of special group rights and self-determination is linked to, and dependent on, the imperatives to respect human rights and promote social justice. Only to

[159] Henry J Steiner, 'Ideals and Counter-Ideals in the Struggle over Autonomy Regimes for Minorities' (1991) 66 *Notre Dame Law Review* 1539.

[160] ibid, 1557.

[161] ibid, 1554.

[162] For example, see Niccoló Figa-Talamanca, 'The Role of NATO in the Peace Agreements for Bosnia and Herzegovina' (1996) 7 *European Journal of International Law* 164, and James Sloan, 'The Dayton Peace Agreement: Human Rights Guarantees and their Implementation' (1996) 7 *European Journal of International Law* 245; Zoran Pajic, 'A Critical Appraisal of Human Rights Provisions of the Dayton Constitution of Bosnia and Herzegovina' (1998) 20 *Human Rights Quarterly* 125.

[163] Paul C Szasz, 'The Quest for a Bosnian Constitution: Legal Aspects of Constitutional Proposals Relating to Bosnia' (1995) 19(2) *Fordham International Law Journal* 363, 407.

[164] Anne-Marie Slaughter, 'Pushing the Limits of the Liberal Peace: Ethnic Conflict and the "Ideal Polity"' in David Wippman (ed), *International Law and Ethnic Conflict* (Ithaca, NY, Cornell University Press, 1998) 128.

the extent that ethnicity is linked to political or territorial injustice may ethnic groups legitimately claim special rights.[165]

Following the work of Steiner, David Wippman investigated the practical and legal constraints on internal ethnic power-sharing.[166] He argued that it sounds absurd that federalism was proposed as a device to manage ethnic conflict in the former Yugoslavia as it failed to prevent violent disintegration. In reference to the Nagorno-Karabakh and Cyprus conflict, Wippman pointed out that the UN and the EU tend to propose ethnic power-sharing systems despite the constraints those political settlements impose on human rights.[167]

An alternative would be partition, yet this would require the resettlement of some parts of the population and result in an equally grave violation of human rights. Rule by one ethnic group, with the risk of the expulsion of undesired ethnic groups, would be an even worse choice. Thus, he deduced, even if consociational practices cannot avoid interethnic political violence, 'they may be still the only means by which members of ethnic groups can maintain their identities and still participate meaningfully in the life of the larger society'.[168]

Normatively, Wippman pointed to a violation of three human rights guarantees: the prohibition of discrimination, the right of political participation, and the freedom of movement and residence. His assessment was that 'positive discrimination' in favour of minorities has become accepted in state practice, seeing that various power-sharing settlements have been endorsed by the UN.[169] The proportionate distribution of governmental positions or posts in public services to minority groups is acceptable in order to correct prior discrimination, as 'long as the intent is to protect rather than to discriminate against such groups'.[170] On the subject of freedom of movement and residence, he concluded that territorial based autonomy regimes for a particular ethnic group 'may require some ability to exclude members of other ethnic groups from taking up residence in the area designated as the autonomous region'.[171] Yet, this should not be 'confused with apartheid schemes designed to suppress subordinate populations', as the 'voluntary separation produced by some autonomy regimes may be a necessary price to pay for the protection of ethnic minorities in deeply divided societies'.[172]

Other scholars, such as Ronald Slye, raised the point that ethnic limitations on governmental officeholders and institutional representation create 'incentives for further ethnic segregation' by embedding ethnic-citizenship criteria in the

[165] Fernando R Tesón, 'Ethnicity, Human Rights, and Self-Determination' in Wippman, above n 164, 111.

[166] David Wippman, 'Practical and Legal Constraints on Internal Power Sharing' in Wippman, above n 164, 211.

[167] David Wippman, 'International Law and Ethnic Conflict on Cyprus' (1996) 31 *Texas International Law Journal* 141.

[168] Wippman, above n 166, 240.

[169] ibid, 232.

[170] ibid, 237.

[171] ibid, 238.

[172] ibid, 239.

constitutional structure.[173] Fionnuala Ni Aolain warned with regard to the Dayton Peace Accords that 'an agreement born out of the policies of ethnic cleansing and massive human rights violations must ensure that it is not a vehicle to facilitate the continuation of the war by other means'.[174]

F. Undemocratic and Unconstitutional Change through Peace Agreements?

Another strand in the debate about transitions to peace and international law has been a focus on the process leading to constitutional change. Although peace settlements address substantial elements of state powers and human rights, they are often negotiated behind closed doors by a small elite group without public participation.[175]

In the case of the Dayton Accords and the revision of the Constitution of Bosnia and Herzegovina, Sienho Yee highlighted that the method by which constitutional provisions were prepared and put into force was undemocratic.[176] Technically, the new constitution came into effect upon the signature of the General Framework Agreement by the Republic of Bosnia and Herzegovina, the Republic of Croatia and the Federal Republic of Yugoslavia, despite the fact that the rules for constitutional amendments under the old constitution required a two-thirds majority of the deputies of every Assembly chamber.[177] In Yee's opinion, these declarations were 'decisions of the various governments, and not necessarily those of the people'.[178] He stressed that the 'New Constitution was primarily hammered out at the international level in Dayton, rather than drafted by the Assembly'.[179] As other scholars noted, the Constitution therefore appears to be the outcome of an external and not an internal constitution-making process.[180]

[173] Ronald C Slye, 'The Dayton Peace Agreement: Constitutionalism and Ethnicity' (1996) 21 *Yale Journal of International Law* 459, 471.

[174] Fionnuala Ni Aolain, 'The Fractured Soul of the Dayton Peace Agreement: A Legal Analysis' (1998) 19 *Michigan Journal of International Law* 957, 960–61.

[175] About the practical challenges of peacemaking, see Ch 1, Part II.A.

[176] Sienho Yee, 'The New Constitution of Bosnia and Herzegovina' (1996) 7 *European Journal of International Law* 176, 180.

[177] As Yee spelled out: 'After the Serb members abandoned the Assembly, 161 members remained. The Assembly at a joint session approved the Dayton Peace Agreement on 30 November 1995, with 85 members present and voting in favour. On 12 December 1995, the Assembly at a joint session passed a Constitutional Law on Amendments and Additions to the Constitution … with 92 members voting in favour. Accordingly, less than a two-thirds majority of the remaining members voted in favour at either session. If the total members of the 1990 Assembly were counted, no simple majority existed at these sessions', ibid, 178.

[178] ibid, 180.

[179] ibid, 178.

[180] As Paola Gaeta argued, it is 'no coincidence that the Constitution was drafted in English and not in the three languages of the peoples concerned': Paola Gaeta, 'The Dayton Agreements and International Law' (1996) 7 *European Journal of International Law* 147, 160. See also Urs Saxer, *Die internationale Steuerung der Selbstbestimmung und der Staatsentstehung* (Heidelberg, Springer, 2000) 993.

As mentioned in the introduction to this study, Jeremy Levitt argued that power-sharing 'forces war victims to live under the rule of alleged war criminals and other abusers'.[181] Levitt commented that power-sharing 'sets a negative precedent, as it sends a dangerous message to would-be insurrectionists that violence is a legitimate means to effectuate change and obtain political power'.[182] Levitt posits that the Accra and Lomé Peace Agreements 'derived from a lawless black hole of unsubstantiated authority in which illegally sharing power for the perceived good of peace is acceptable despite the existence of well-established governing rules to the contrary'.[183]

G. Human Rights in Post-Conflict State Transitions

Temporal aspects play another crucial role in *post-conflict* transitions. The current discourse about *jus post bellum* is only one of many ways in which law, peace and time can be linked conceptually.[184] A temporal dimension in this context was initially added to international law by the debate about 'Transitional Justice' aiming at accountability for human rights violations.[185] Subsequently, Christine Bell attached a focus on time by arguing that 'peace agreements are best understood as a form of transitional constitution'.[186] Building on Ruti Teitel's concept of 'transitional constitutionalism', Bell stressed that peace agreements are 'distinctively partial and temporary'.[187]

The derogation of human rights at times of public emergency is another temporal factor. Gro Nystuen presented maybe the most comprehensive legal analysis to date of peace agreements, power-sharing and human rights law, focusing on the Dayton Accords and state transitions.[188] She tested whether prohibition of discrimination could be violated, and upheld the justification of ethnic differentiation and the temporary derogation of human rights as an option.

[181] Jeremy I Levitt, 'An Inquiry into the Legality of Power-Sharing with Warlords and Rebels in Africa' (2006) 27(2) *Michigan Journal of International Law* 499. See also Jeremy I Levitt, *Illegal Peace in Africa: An Inquiry into the Legality of Power Sharing with Warlords, Rebels, and Junta* (Cambridge, Cambridge University Press, 2012).

[182] Levitt (2006), above n 181, 499.

[183] ibid, 571–72.

[184] See Ch 1.

[185] Paige Arthur, 'How 'Transitions' Reshaped Human Rights: A Conceptual History of Transitional Justice' (2009) 31(2) *Human Rights Quarterly* 321.

[186] Christine Bell, *Peace Agreements and Human Rights* (Oxford, Oxford University Press, 2000) 9.

[187] ibid. Teitel had previously explored the phenomenology of transition and had suggested 'that there is a close tie between the normative shift in understandings of justice and law's role in the construction of transition'. Touching on temporal limitations, Teitel argued that the conception of justice during periods of political change is inherently 'extraordinary and constructivist'. See Ruti Teitel, 'Transitional Jurisprudence: The Role of Law in Political Transformation' (1997) 106 *Yale Law Journal* 2014.

[188] Gro Nystuen, *Achieving Peace or Protecting Human Rights: Conflicts between Norms Regarding Ethnic Discrimination in the Dayton Peace Agreement* (Leiden, Martinus Nijhoff Publishers, 2005) 183.

Continuing the discourse about temporality, Antoine Buyse and Michael Hamilton drew attention to the legal challenge as to whether regional mechanisms 'can remain true to the rule of law whilst also meaningfully recognising the acute social, economic and political exigencies which characterise periods of transition'.[189] Focusing on 'transitional jurisprudence', they criticised the fact that regional courts such as the European Court of Human Rights lack 'temporal and cultural-spatial proximity' to events on the ground in countries of transition.[190] However, transition must also not be a 'trump card' which overrules existing human rights norms.[191] They propose that whereas 'in the immediate aftermath of a change of regime, broad and sweeping measures may be allowed, the more time elapses, the more individualised the assessment of interferences with people's rights should be'.[192]

Table 6 Summary of relevant universal rights affected by power-sharing

<table>
<tr><th>Explanation</th><th>Rights</th><th>Relevant for type of power-sharing</th></tr>
<tr><td>Overall principle in international law:</td><td>• Self-determination</td><td rowspan="4">Political, territorial, military and economic power-sharing</td></tr>
<tr><td rowspan="3">Vulnerable groups:</td><td>• Minority rights</td></tr>
<tr><td>• Women's rights</td></tr>
<tr><td>• Indigenous Peoples' rights</td></tr>
<tr><td rowspan="3">Risk of infringed human rights through power-sharing (depending on the particular case):</td><td>• Prohibition of discrimination</td><td>Political, economic and military power-sharing</td></tr>
<tr><td>• Right to political participation and equal access to public service</td><td>Political power-sharing</td></tr>
<tr><td>• Freedom of movement and residence</td><td>Territorial power-sharing</td></tr>
</table>

V. Conclusion: The Necessity and Challenges of Bridging Interdisciplinary Perspectives

It is striking in the outlined scholarly discourse that the trajectories of debate in socio-political science, conflict resolution theory and the legal field about state

[189] Michael Hamilton and Antoine Buyse, 'Introduction' in Michael Hamilton and Antoine Buyse (eds), *Transitional Jurisprudence and the ECHR: Justice, Politics and Rights* (Cambridge, Cambridge University Press, 2011) 2–3.
[190] Michael Hamilton and Antoine Buyse, 'Conclusion' in ibid, 288.
[191] ibid, 293.
[192] ibid, 292.

transitions, power-sharing peace agreements and constitutional change processes hardly ever intersect. As Jennifer Jackson-Preece commented, legal provisions are 'often ignored, or at least downplayed, within the existing literature on ethnic regulation'.[193] She speculates that it could be due to the 'methodological predisposition toward social science positivism, which tends to avoid normative claims and categories to the detriment of empirical analysis in this area'.[194] Maybe the challenge of interdisciplinary exchange is another piece of the puzzle that could help explain why conflict settlements are imperfect.

A. Strengthening the Human Rights Focus Instead of Blurring the Perception of International Law

The conflict settlement and state transition theme eventually highlights a tension which is symptomatic of the relation between international law and politics. On one side, issues of contextual justice cannot be solved by the application of ready-made rules or principles, as Koskenniemi noted; their solution 'requires venturing into fields such as politics, [and] social and economic casuistry' beyond the point at which a legal argument is supposed to remain 'legal'.[195] Koskenniemi rightly commented that legal interpretation reflects 'arenas of political struggle'.[196] On the other side, conflict parties and peacemakers cannot pretend that there are no rules at all. As Hart put it, there is no 'formalist heaven', but a great range of legal concepts which should not encourage normative scepticism.[197] As he detailed:

> The rule-sceptic is sometimes a disappointed absolutist; he has found that rules are not all they would be in a formalist's heaven, or in a world where men were like gods and could anticipate all possible combinations of fact, so that open-texture was not a necessary feature of rules. The sceptic's conception of what it is for a rule to exist, may thus be an unattainable ideal, and when he discovers that it is not attained by what are called rules, he expresses his disappointment by the denial that there are, or can be, any rules.[198]

At the intersection of law and politics is the discussion about liberalism, which is found too in the discourse about state transitions, power-sharing and constitutional change.[199] The spread of liberal democracy impacted the contours

[193] Jennifer Jackson-Preece, 'The Role of Human and Minority Rights in Complex Power-sharing' in Weller, Metzger and Johnson, above n 136, 627–28.
[194] ibid.
[195] Martti Koskenniemi, 'The Politics of International Law' (1990) 1(4) *European Journal of International Law* 4, 32.
[196] ibid, 31.
[197] HLA Hart, *The Concept of Law* (Oxford, Clarendon Press, 1961) 135.
[198] ibid.
[199] See Slaughter, above n 164; Wippman, above n 166.

of international law.[200] The twentieth century witnessed 'waves of democracy' that led to the liberalisation of political systems in several countries.[201] Views among states and within societies about liberty, community and justice ideals remain heterogeneous.[202] Although there are universal elements, the perceptions about what human rights should encompass as common values still differ.[203] Legal opinions are diverse regarding the understanding of equality, the accommodation of religious and ethnic minorities, as well the limits of tolerance.[204] The 2005 World Summit Outcome Document, for instance, highlights democracy as a 'universal value' but also stressed that there is 'no single model of democracy'.[205] As the document notes, states have different 'national and regional particularities and various historical, cultural and religious backgrounds'.[206]

The question about how to reconcile universal human rights with the demands of particular forms of community cultures will need to be answered by state practice, judicial decisions and developing rules expressly recognised by states.[207] The historical overview in this chapter about the evolution of human rights and minority rights regimes illustrated that the process of agreeing on standards for constitutional designs by enhancing rights and protection guarantees is progressing slowly but steadily.

Although some scholars write that minority rights declarations and conventions 'do not provide clear guidance as to how the balance with individual rights should be struck', international law is not blurry, yet it leaves some room for manoeuvre.[208] Claiming that there is a 'law of peacemakers' could risk obscuring what can be systematically analysed as a distinct component of international law: that is, international human rights law.[209] So far, only a few scholars have examined peace settlements and consociationalism precisely through the lens of international law while providing a deep and systematic assessment of human rights.[210]

[200] Gregory H Fox and Brad R Roth, 'Introduction: The Spread of Liberal Democracy and its Implications for International Law' in Gregory H Fox and Brad R Roth (eds), *Democratic Governance and International Law* (Cambridge, Cambridge University Press, 2000) 1.

[201] Samuel P Huntington, *The Third Wave: Democratization in the Late 20th Century* (Norman, University of Oklahoma Press, 1991) 15.

[202] About the concept of *jus cogens* as a reflection of common values, see Ch 5, Part II.

[203] Nehal Bhuta, 'Rethinking the Universality of Human Rights' in Anver Emon, Mark Ellis and Benjamin Glahn (eds), *Islamic Law and International Human Rights Law: Searching for Common Ground?* (Oxford, Oxford University Press, 2012) 123.

[204] Ratna Kapur, 'Unveiling Equality: Disciplining the "Other" Woman through Human Rights Discourse', in Emon, Ellis and Glahn, above n 203, 265. See also Anver M Emon, 'Religious Minorities and Islamic Law: Accommodation and the Limits of Tolerance': ibid, 323.

[205] GA Res 60/1, 24 October 2005, para 135.

[206] ibid, para 121.

[207] On this matter, see also Ruti Teitel, *Humanity's Law* (Oxford, Oxford University Press, 2011) 20.

[208] For the quote, see Bell, above n 186, 4.

[209] On the idea of a '*lex pacificatoria*', the law of peacemakers, see Christine Bell, *On the Law of Peace: Peace Agreements and the Lex Pacificatoria* (Oxford, Oxford University Press, 2008).

[210] See Nystuen, above n 188.

As outlined in this chapter, the principles and rights established in international law remain coherent: first, there is no right but also no outlawing of secession; second, international law enshrines minorities' rights, which generate state obligations depending on whether a state is a signatory to them; and third, of particular concern for peacemakers has to be the prohibition of discrimination, which could be violated by certain power-sharing arrangements. The interpretation of these principles and rights varies depending on the cases at hand. The ambiguity of individual and community rights, as well as the paradox that peace agreements may enhance yet also infringe human rights, is needed in order to leave leeway for specific circumstances.

B. Complex Legal Answers for Complex Conflict Settlements

Mainstream legal advocates in the field of peace settlements and international law have reasoned that the unconditional 'compatibility of consociationalism with the individual rights of international human rights law cannot be assumed'.[211] Yet, it would equally be a mistake to jump to the conclusion that all consociational arrangements violate international law. In reality, many constitutions in the world contain elements of power-sharing.[212]

Regarding the tension between liberalism and communitarianism, Wippman commented that the international community has 'unfortunately' yet 'to develop a principled or fully coherent political or legal response to ethno-nationalist claims'.[213] He admits that the validity of power-sharing practice depends on the extent of human rights infringement, the breadth and importance of the infringed right, its duration and the political circumstances.[214] For example, to conclude that every power-sharing deal with warlords and rebels in Africa creates an 'illegal peace' would be ill-judged. Given the complexity of available conflict settlement mechanisms, only a case-by-case evaluation seems truly capable of accommodating the intricacy of legal conditions and consequences. Wippman's call for a fully coherent legal response to ethno-nationalist claims is difficult to achieve. A static, inflexible legal approach towards peacemaking would contradict the right to self-determination. The strength of international law is, in fact, its ability to accommodate a multitude of colliding legal norms and values.

[211] Bell, above n 209, 4. See also Jackson-Preece, above n 193; Levitt (2006), above n 181; Nystuen, above n 188; Wippman, above n 166.
[212] For a synopsis of power-sharing mechanisms, see Appendix, Table 1.
[213] David Wippman, 'Introduction: Ethnic Claims and International Law' in Wippman, above n 164, 7.
[214] Wippman, above n 166, 238.

Much of the previous research on state transitions, power-sharing and international law has focused on Africa and Europe.[215] The law and peace research agenda is clearly shaped by historical and contemporary events.[216] Since 2011, several of the uprisings in the Middle East and Northern Africa have resulted in multifaceted power-sharing arrangements.[217] Yemen, Libya, Egypt, Tunisia and other countries in the region have begun transforming their constitutions. Whether and, if so, which forms of 'liberal democracy' the region will ultimately adopt is as yet unclear. The outcome of the constitutional change processes in the Arab world will probably impact upon the debate about state stability across academic disciplines, which will also shape the future interpretation of international law.

C. International Law as Both a Blessing and a Burden

Gary Friedman and Jack Himmelstein, who both have been working on turning mediation into a profession since the 1970s, observed that mediators often try to keep the law out, even if it is inevitably the 'elephant in the room' and may creep onto the agenda nonetheless.[218] They noticed that the 'power and authority of the law will inevitably dominate, making it impossible for the parties to focus on their business and personal interests'.[219] Friedman and Himmelstein recommended to reduce the 'destructive potential' of law by working with the opposing parties to identify in a 'straight forward manner' which statutes and rules underlie the conflict.[220] Their experience in conflict resolution suggests that it is better to address legal issues openly and transparently despite, or even because of, the difficulties which will surface. The result 'can be a revelation to the parties' that facilitates the deal-making.[221] The metaphor illustrates how sensitive the treatment of international law is in conflict settlements.

[215] The reason for the relevance of these cases may be the high international engagement in those regions, given the colonial past in Africa and essential security interests in Europe after the end of the Cold War. See Bell, above n 209, 4; Wippman, above n 166, 241; Levitt (2006), above n 181, 495. See also Scott P Sheeran, 'International Law, Peace Agreements and Self-Determination: The Case of the Sudan' (2011) 60(2) *International and Comparative Law Quarterly* 423; Geoff Gilbert, Colin Warbrick and Dominic McGoldrick, 'The Northern Ireland Peace Agreement, Minority Rights and Self-Determination' (1998) 47(4) *International and Comparative Law Quarterly* 943.

[216] David J Dunn, *The First Fifty Years of Peace Research: A Survey and Interpretation* (Aldershot, Ashgate, 2005) 2.

[217] See Table 1 above.

[218] 'When Law is the Elephant in the Room' (2003) 18.2 *Tikkun Magazine* 40. See also Gary J Friedman and Jack Himmelstein, *Challenging Conflict: Mediation Through Understanding* (Cambridge, MA, American Bar Association, Harvard Law School Program of Negotiation, 2008) 139.

[219] ibid.

[220] ibid.

[221] ibid.

This chapter has exhibited that there has been no shortage of critical legal voices reflecting on consociational arrangements, although the quantity of work is miminal in comparison with the vast scholarly literature within political science. As a way out of the 'self-determination trap', power-sharing is frequently intended to enhance the compliance of states with human rights. Sometimes, it is the only way to achieve an end to hostilities by satisfying the demands of those who would continue an armed confrontation if they were not included in political decision-making. The negotiation of legally imperfect peace settlements reflects the fact that compromises have to be made. In this endeavour, international law embodies a legal paradox: it can be a blessing and a burden at the same time.

3

Power-Sharing on Trial

Sejdić and Finci v Bosnia and Herzegovina

'We expected the decision for 15 years. Indeed this is good news, because it took someone from outside to rule on the Constitution of Bosnia and Herzegovina, which is discriminatory and does not provide equal rights for all citizens'.

Srdjan Dizdarevic, President of the Helsinki Committee for Human Rights in Bosnia and Herzegovina[1]

'The Bosnian peace plan was hard-won and its particulars contained bitter pills for both sides, but it would bring an end to four bloody years that claimed more than 250,000 lives and caused more than two million people to flee their homes'.

US President Bill Clinton[2]

'I trust that one day we'll look back and say Dayton was the place where fundamental choices were made; this is where, this is the place where the parties chose peace over war, dialogue over destruction, reason over revenge'.

US Secretary of State Warren Christopher[3]

I. Bosnia and Herzegovina between Transition and Transformation

The Balkans continue to struggle with the compromises for peace which were necessary requisites to end hostilities, mass atrocities and a genocide. As one of the most prominent cases of external state building and intervention in Europe after World War II, Bosnia and Herzegovina exemplifies the crux of the *peace, human rights* and *justice* dilemma in all its complexity.[4] Nearly two decades after

[1] Gordana Sandić-Hadžihasanović, 'Strazbur Osudio BiH Zbog Diskriminacije Roma i Jevreja' *Radio Free Europe/Radio Liberty* (22 December 2009) [translation provided by the author].

[2] Bill Clinton, *My Life* (New York, Alfred A Knopf, 2004) 644.

[3] 'A New Constitution for Bosnia' *PBS NewsHour* (22 November 2005).

[4] For a legal assessment of foreign intervention in Bosnia and Herzegovina in 1995, see Georg Nolte, *Eingreifen auf Einladung* (Berlin, Springer, 1999) 538. On the false dichotomy of *peace versus justice*, or *peace versus human rights* in detail, see Ch 5, Part I.C.

the signing of the Dayton Peace Accords, the country remains ethnically divided.[5] In 2013, the Report of the High Representative of the European Union highlighted that the situation in Bosnia and Herzegovina is still characterised by 'political instability and a lack of substantial progress'.[6] Political parties 'so far failed to reach a compromise' on necessary constitutional reforms.[7] Bosnia and Herzegovina is about to apply for EU membership, but the 'non-compliance with the European Convention on Human Rights' and 'discrimination against citizens on the grounds of ethnicity' remain issues of 'serious concern', as the EU Commission commented in its progress report in 2012.[8] In addition, the distribution of political powers between Bosniaks, Croats and Serbs, as well as the territorial integrity of the country, continues as a matter of dispute.[9] As one of the 'bitter pills', as former US President Clinton put it, Dayton created a paradox by securing equality between the three major ethnic groups and decreasing the participation rights of other minorities, all while attempting to uphold international human rights standards.[10] Although the fundamental choice was to foster 'peace over war', new forms of inequality and persistent instability resulted.[11]

This chapter focuses on how human rights courts tackle state transitions, power-sharing and international law. A significant reference point in international human rights law is the landmark decision of the European Court of Human Rights (ECtHR) in *Sejdić and Finci v Bosnia and Herzegovina*.[12] In this case, the ECtHR assessed whether exclusive constitutional rights for particular ethnic groups that discriminate against minorities can be justified for the sake of peace.

The first part of this chapter summarises the controversy surrounding the case. Prior to the ECtHR decision, several appeals to Bosnia and Herzegovina's Constitutional Court had tried to remove ethnic provisions in the constitution and electoral law. These developments reveal how judicial proceedings can be used by conflict parties as an extension to their previous peace negotiations. The second part of this chapter analyses the main legal arguments raised in *Sejdić and Finci v Bosnia and Herzegovina* and examines whether the decision is consistent with comparative ECtHR case law. This part focuses on the practice of the Convention concerning the prohibition of discrimination. The third part of this chapter

[5] As the Report of the High Representative of the European Union underlined in February 2013: 'Inflammatory nationalistic rhetoric continued' and 'contributed to increased political tension': Report of the High Representative of the European Union for Foreign Affairs and Security Policy on the Activities of the European Union Military Mission in Bosnia and Herzegovina, UN Doc S/2013/90, 12 February 2013, Annex, para 12.

[6] ibid, para 12.

[7] ibid, para 4.

[8] Enlargement Strategy and Main Challenges 2012–2013, Communication from the Commission to the European Parliament and the Council, COM(2012) 600 Final, European Commission, 10 October 2012, paras 1.3, 2.1.

[9] ibid, para 1.2.

[10] Clinton, above n 2, 644. For details, see Ch 2, Part IV.E.

[11] Quote by US Secretary of State Warren Christopher, see above n 3.

[12] *Sejdić and Finci v Bosnia and Herzegovina*, ECtHR Judgment, App Nos 27996/06 and 34836/06, 22 December 2009.

reflects on the limits and consequences of judicial review for states in transition that are trying to appease internal conflict while pleasing the court.

II. Relevant Decisions of Bosnia and Herzegovina's Constitutional Court (1997–2009)

Between 1997 and 2009, a series of cases were brought before the Constitutional Court of Bosnia and Herzegovina in attempts by political parties to topple the country's constitutional order.[13] Just a few years after the signing of the Dayton Peace Accords, these cases were a serious legal test for the rule of law.

Table 1 Cases at the Constitutional Court of Bosnia and Herzegovina addressing ethnic power-sharing

Year	Decision
1997	Croatian 1861 Law Party (Hrvatska Stranka prava 1861) and the Bosnia-Herzegovina 1861 Law Party (Bosansko-hercegovačka Stranka prava 1861) Decision, Constitutional Court of Bosnia and Herzegovina, No U-7/97, 22 December 1997
2000	Alija Izetbegović, Chair of Presidency of Bosnia and Herzegovina, Partial Decision, Constitutional Court of Bosnia and Herzegovina, No U-5/98 I, 29 January 2000
	Alija Izetbegović, Chair of Presidency of Bosnia and Herzegovina, Partial Decision, Constitutional Court of Bosnia and Herzegovina, No U-5/98 II, 18 February 2000
	Alija Izetbegović, Chair of Presidency of Bosnia and Herzegovina, Partial Decision, Constitutional Court of Bosnia and Herzegovina, No U-5/98 III, 1 July 2000
	Alija Izetbegović, Chair of Presidency of Bosnia and Herzegovina, Partial Decision, Constitutional Court of Bosnia and Herzegovina, No U-5/98 IV, 18 August 2000
2006	Sulejman Tihić, Chair of the Presidency of Bosnia and Herzegovina, Decision on Admissibility, Constitutional Court of Bosnia and Herzegovina, No U-5/04, 31 March 2006
	Sulejman Tihić, Chair of the Presidency of Bosnia and Herzegovina, Decision on Admissibility, Constitutional Court of Bosnia and Herzegovina, No U-13/05, 26 May 2006
2009	Stranka za Bosnu i Hercegovinu (Party for Bosnia and Herzegovina) and Mr Ilijaz Pilav, Decision on Admissibility and Merits, Constitutional Court of Bosnia and Herzegovina, No AP-2678/06, 29 September 2009

[13] See Table 1. All decisions are available in English at http://www.ccbh.ba (accessed 30 January 2019).

A. The Cases and Legal Arguments

In 1997, two Croat parties petitioned the Constitutional Court for a review of the Dayton Peace Accords. They alleged that the peace agreement undermined the 'integrity of the state' and that it could 'cause the dissolution of Bosnia and Herzegovina'.[14] The Constitutional Court dismissed the admissibility of the cases, seeing itself 'not competent to evaluate the constitutionality' of the Dayton Accords, as it was deliberately established to maintain the ethnic power-sharing structures.[15]

In 1998, Bosnia and Herzegovina's first elected Bosniak to the Presidency, Alija Izetbegović, himself turned to the Constitutional Court, objecting to parts of the Constitutions of the Republika Srpska and the Federation of Bosnia and Herzegovina. He argued that the entities' constitutions exaggerated their constitutionally granted right of internal self-determination.[16] These circumstances, Izetbegović suggested, could 'prevent the return of displaced persons and the restoration of property as well as the restoration of a multi-ethnic society'.[17] Agreeing with him, the Constitutional Court declared parts of the entities' constitutions unconstitutional.

In 2004, Sulejman Tihić lodged an abstract review procedure of the Dayton Constitution. Tihić, who had succeeded Izetbegović as the Bosniak member of the tripartite Presidency of Bosnia and Herzegovina, claimed that exclusive division of power in the House of Peoples and Presidency among the *constituent people* violates the prohibition of racial discrimination in the European Convention on Human Rights (ECHR) and the International Convention on the Elimination of All Forms of Racial Discrimination (ICERD).[18] In 2005, Tihić turned again to the Constitutional Court, this time concerning the Election Law. Both cases were rejected by the Constitutional Court as inadmissible. The Court concluded that a decision on the conformity of constitutional provisions with the ECHR and the ICERD simply 'falls out of the scope of its competence'.[19]

In 2006, the Party for Bosnia and Herzegovina and its candidate Ilijaz Pilav filed an appeal with the Constitutional Court against the Central Election Commission's rejection of Pilav's candidacy to become a member of the Presidency of

[14] Croatian 1861 Law Party (Hrvatska Stranka prava 1861) and the Bosnia-Herzegovina 1861 Law Party (Bosansko-hercegovačka Stranka prava 1861) Decision No U-7/97, 22 December 1997, para 4.

[15] ibid, para 7.

[16] For example, Art 1 of the Republika Srpska Constitution provided that 'the Republika Srpska is a State of the Serb people and of all its citizens'. Article 28 of the Republika Srpska Constitution postulated 'material State support of the Orthodox Church and cooperation between the State and the Orthodox Church in all fields'. Other articles in both entities' constitutions narrowed the scope of official languages. See Alija Izetbegović, Partial Decision No U-5/98 I, 29 January 2000, para I.1.a) g).

[17] Alija Izetbegović, Partial Decision No U-5/98 III, 1 July 2000, para III.A.a) 47.

[18] For details about ethnic power-sharing in Bosnia and Herzegovina, see Ch 2, Part III.B.

[19] Sulejman Tihić, Decision on Admissibility No U-5/04, 30 March 2006, paras 14–15; Sulejman Tihić, Decision on Admissibility, No U-13/05, 26 May 2005, para 10.

Bosnia and Herzegovina.[20] The Commission had barred him from running for elections on the ground that he was a Bosniak residing in the Republika Srpska, whereas the electoral law stipulates that only Bosniaks living in the Federation can run for the Bosniak seat in the Presidency. Pilav argued that the territorial ethnic distinction was discriminatory and violated his right to stand for election. In this case, the Constitutional Court admitted the complaint, but decided that ethnic discrimination was justified.[21]

B. The Reasoning of the Constitutional Court: Defending Human Rights Compromises of the Dayton Peace Accords

Throughout its judgments from 1997 to 2009, the Constitutional Court developed the line of argument that it needs to protect the power-sharing equilibrium of the Dayton Peace Accords. The Court consistently defended the human rights compromises of the imperfect Dayton Accords and argued that it does not have the authority to change the Constitution.

On one hand, the Constitutional Court acknowledged that, in principle, ethnic distinctions contradict international human rights law and minority guarantees, as the 'accommodation of cultures and ethnic groups prohibits not only their assimilation but also their segregation'.[22] The Constitutional Court recognised that the designation as constituent people and others 'may be discriminatory'.[23] In the *Izetbegović* judgment, the Court stressed that the territorial delimitation of Bosnia and Herzegovina into two entities 'cannot serve as a constitutional legitimacy for ethnic domination, national homogenisation, or a right to uphold the effects of ethnic cleansing'.[24]

On the other hand, the Constitutional Court upheld that the special rights granted by the Dayton Accords are 'necessary in order to maintain the possibility of a pluralist society'.[25] In the *Pilav* case, the Constitutional Court summarised:

> The said restrictions are justified by the specific nature of internal order of Bosnia and Herzegovina that was agreed upon by the Dayton Agreement and whose ultimate goal was the establishment of peace and dialogue between the opposing parties ...[26]

[20] As a part of political power-sharing in Bosnia and Herzegovina, the Presidency of the country consists of one Bosniak and one Croat elected from the Federation, as well as one Serb elected from the Republika Srpska. For details, see Ch 2, Part III.B.ii.

[21] Stranka za Bosnu i Hercegovinu (Party for Bosnia and Herzegovina) and Mr Ilijaz Pilav, Decision No AP-2678/06, 29 September 2009.

[22] Partial Decision No U-5/98 III, above n 17, para III.A.a) 57.

[23] ibid, para 107.

[24] ibid, para 96.

[25] ibid, paras 114–16.

[26] Decision No AP-2678/06, above n 21, para VII, 21.

The Court emphasised that ethnic power-sharing is based on the legitimate aim of politically stabilizing and gradually democratising the country.[27] Concluding that democracy 'requires a compromise', the Constitutional Court argued that collective rights outweigh individual rights for the sake of peace in the case of Bosnia and Herzegovina.[28]

C. Controversy and Political Reactions

The judgments of the Constitutional Court caused wide public controversy. The independence of the Court was challenged not only by media and civil society groups, but also by members of the Government.[29] Judge Zovko noted in his dissenting opinion that public pressure on the judges included 'serious insults' and 'most grave threats'.[30] As he complained, the national judges at the Constitutional Court were told by their ethnic communities and political parties to decide according to their ethnic association.[31]

Judge Popović alleged that the decision-making in the Constitutional Court was actually politicised. He and Judge Miljko observed in the *Izetbegović* decision that the ruling 'was adopted in a manner that the judges from amongst Bosniaks and foreign judges voted for the Decision and that the Judges from amongst Serbs and Croats voted against it'.[32]

The international judges were also criticised. There was an attempt to dismiss the Austrian judge, Judge Marko, as biased, as he had shown himself to be in favour of a harmonisation of the Constitution with the ECHR while serving as a member of the Venice Commission prior to his duty as an international judge at the Constitutional Court.[33] Similarly, the President of the Court, Judge Begić, who had participated as an expert during the adoption of the Dayton Peace Accords, was accused of bias. In the end, all claims against both were dismissed.

D. The European Court of Human Rights as the Last Resort

As the International Crisis Group pointed out, the cases at the Constitutional Court were worrisome evidence of how 'pervasive ethnic cleansing' persisted in

[27] Partial Decision No U-5/98 III, above n 17, para III.A.a).

[28] ibid, para 56.

[29] See ibid, Dissenting Opinion of Judge Mirko Zovko, 86.

[30] ibid.

[31] As Judge Zovko noted: 'I feel sad and resigned since an entire propaganda mechanism tried to influence my consciousness in a most ruthless way by using all means, including threats against my freedom and the integrity of a judge …': ibid, 86–89.

[32] ibid, Dissenting Opinion of Judge Vitomir Popović, 84. See also ibid, Separate Opinion of Judge Zvonko Miljko, 90.

[33] The request for Marko's exclusion on the grounds of bias was dismissed. See ibid, Dissenting Opinion of Judge Mirko Zovko, 84.

Bosnia and Herzegovina's post-conflict present.[34] The Constitutional Court itself noted that 'following the entering into force of the Dayton Agreement, there was and still is a systematic, long-lasting, purposeful discriminatory practice of the public authorities' in both entities.[35] Direct participation in violent incidents, harassment, intimidation and violent attacks on grounds of ethnic origin are just some of the examples of discrimination the Court mentioned.

Just a few years after the end of hostilities and ethnic massacres in the region, the decisions marked a crucial phase of post-conflict transition, exemplifying how heavily the war-time past can weigh on judicial processes.[36] The cases symbolise a strategy shift of the antagonists, transferring their struggle about an 'imperfect' peace settlement from the negotiation table to the court room.

Eventually, the rulings of the Constitutional Court to justify human rights restrictions with the aim of political stabilisation and the Court's mandate to honour the Constitution reflect a strength rather than a weakness of the Court: the judges fulfilled their duty to protect the established constitutional framework of ethnic power-sharing and not change it. Quite reasonably, the Constitutional Court refused to rewrite the consensus of Dayton, as this would have disrupted the state's separation of powers and might also have reduced the Court's own credibility at such an early stage of post-conflict institution building.

All these circumstances explain why the ECtHR was finally approached as the judicial last resort, in order to re-evaluate an ethnic power-sharing system which resisted being altered from the inside.

III. ECtHR Definition of Ethnic-Racial Discrimination in *Sejdić and Finci*

In August 2006, Dervo Sejdić and Jakob Finci turned to the ECtHR in Strasbourg, shortly after it became evident that the so-called 'April Package' of amendments to the Constitution of Bosnia and Herzegovina would fail.[37] Sejdić, a prominent Bosnian Roma Union activist who served as the Roma Rights Coordinator for the OSCE, and Finci, who headed the Jewish Community of Bosnia Herzegovina, had been excluded by the Central Election Commission from running for seats in the

[34] *Bosnia's Nationalist Governments: Paddy Ashdown and the Paradoxes of State Building*, International Crisis Group, Report No 146, 22 July 2003, 3.

[35] Partial Decision No U-5/98 III, above n 17, para III.A.a) 95.

[36] Tapping as they did into the most sensitive issues of ethnic constitutionality in Bosnia and Herzegovina, the decisions were far from unanimous. In Decision No U-5/98, four judges voted against the application and five judges voted in favour, maintaining that the challenged provisions are unconstitutional. In case U-13/05, three judges submitted a separate opinion. In decision AP-2678/06, a 7-2 majority of the Court decided against the applicants.

[37] In April 2006, the Parliament of Bosnia and Herzegovina missed by just two votes the required two-thirds majority in the House of Representatives which would have allowed reform of the power-sharing system of Dayton. For details, see Sofia Sebastián, *Leaving Dayton Behind: Constitutional Reform in Bosnia and Herzegovina*, FRIDE, Working Paper No 46, November 2007, 4.

Presidency and the House of the Peoples, which was solely reserved for Bosniaks, Croats and Serbs as the major ethnic groups and former belligerents.

Sejdić stated:

> The main reason why I decided to take the case and submit the lawsuit before the European Court of Human Rights was due to lack of representation of national minorities in the government, especially Roma, who have always suffered historical discrimination, to the extent that such discrimination is now part of the constitution of this country'.[38]

'The not-so-immediate impact that was sought with this demand was to change the mindset of citizens and open their minds so that when choosing a politician, this election is not be based on ethnicity, but on their capacities and capabilities to carry out their work', he added.[39] 'All citizens should be equal before the law,' commented Finci.[40] The ECtHR Grand Chamber released its judgment in December 2009, just in time to stipulate reforms before the 2010 elections.

In the following, before elaborating on the Court's decision, the normative framework of the *Sejdić and Finci* judgment will be outlined, and prior ECtHR jurisprudence will be explored.

A. Normative Framework

With regard to regional human rights law, Sejdić and Finci argued that the Government of Bosnia and Herzegovina has breached its obligations under the ECHR and its Protocols. Among others, they pointed to Article 14 of the Convention which prohibits discrimination on:

> [A]ny ground such as sex, race, colour, language, religion, political or other opinion, national or social origin, association with a national minority, property, birth or other status.[41]

In conjunction with Article 14 ECHR, the applicants referred to Article 3 of Protocol No 1 of the Convention, which guarantees the right to free elections:

> The High Contracting Parties undertake to hold free elections at reasonable intervals by secret ballot, under conditions which will ensure the free expression of the opinion of the people in the choice of the legislature …[42]

[38] 'Interview with Dervan Sejdić' *Movimiento Por la Paz Balkans E-Newsletter* (12 April 2010).

[39] ibid.

[40] Finci stressed: 'In our country there are several hundred thousand people who come from "mixed" marriages. They need to declare that they belong to one of the constitutive nations, whether they like it or not. Even among the religiously defined Muslims, Catholics and Orthodox …, there are many who reject this assignment, because they feel secular'. Erich Rathfelder, 'Fünf Minute mit Jakob Finci: Über Menschenrechte, Gleichheit und einen gewonnenen Prozess' *Jüdische Allgemeine* (14 January 2010) [translation provided by the author].

[41] ECHR, 3 September 1953, Art 14, 213 UNTS 222.

[42] Protocol to the Convention for the Protection of Human Rights and Fundamental Freedoms [hereafter Protocol No 1], 18 May 1954, Art 3.

Moreover, the complaints were based on Article 1 of Protocol No 12 to the Convention, which widened and solidified the general prohibition against discrimination:

1. The enjoyment of any right set forth by law shall be secured without discrimination on any ground such as sex, race, colour, language, religion, political or other opinion, national or social origin, association with a national minority, property, birth or other status.
2. No one shall be discriminated against by any public authority on any ground such as those mentioned in paragraph 1.[43]

Protocol No 12 became applicable as the applicants contested provisions in the electoral law rendering them ineligible to stand for election to the Presidency of Bosnia and Herzegovina, which was seen by them as a discrimination in the enjoyment of rights 'set forth by law'.[44] Protocol No 12 was drawn up within the Council of Europe by the Steering Committee for Human Rights to extend the framework of anti-discrimination law.[45] *Sejdić and Finci v Bosnia and Herzegovina* was one of the first cases which activated those strengthened protection mechanisms in the Council of Europe human rights system.[46]

B. Prior Jurisprudence

Although Article 14 of the Convention does not specifically enumerate 'ethnicity' as a category for discrimination, ECtHR jurisprudence has established a wide interpretation to encompass the term.

[43] Protocol No 12 to the Convention for the Protection of Human Rights and Fundamental Freedoms [hereafter Protocol No 12], 1 April 2005, Art 1.

[44] See Protocol No 12, Art 1, para 1.

[45] It was opened to signature by the Member States of the Council of Europe in November 2000, and finally entered into force after the ratification by 10 Member States in April 2005. Bosnia and Herzegovina signed Protocol No 12 in April 2002, and ratified it in July 2003. The additional scope of protection under Art 1 Protocol No 12 especially concerns cases where a person is discriminated against: (i) in the enjoyment of any right specifically granted to an individual under national law; (ii) in the enjoyment of a right which may be inferred from a clear obligation of a public authority under national law, that is, where a public authority is under an obligation under national law to behave in a particular manner; (iii) by a public authority in the exercise of discretionary power (for example, granting certain subsidies); (iv) by any other act or omission by a public authority (for example, the behavior of law enforcement officers when controlling a riot). See Explanatory Report to the Convention on the Protection of Human Rights and Fundamental Freedoms, ETS No 177, 4 June 2000, para 22. On the impact of Protocol No 12 in the case of *Sejdić and Finci v Bosnia and Herzegovina*, see Part III.D below.

[46] Sejdić also claimed a violation of ECHR, Art 3 arguing that his ineligibility to stand for elections was an 'affront to his human dignity' and reduced him as well as other members of national minorities to 'second-class citizens'. Art 3 of the Convention provides that 'no one shall be subjected to torture or to inhuman or degrading treatment or punishment'. However, the Court held that the difference of treatment did 'not denote any contempt or lack of respect for the personality of the applicant and that it was not designed to, and did not, humiliate or debase', but was intended solely to achieve peace. See *Sejdić and Finci v Bosnia and Herzegovina*, above n 12, paras 47–48.

In 2005, the ECtHR determined in *Timishev v Russia* that ethnic discrimination can be a form of racial discrimination.[47] In this case, Ilyas Yakubovich Timishev, an ethnic Chechen and Russian national, was refused registration of his permanent residence outside the Chechen Republic. Due to his Chechen ethnic origin he was refused access into neighbouring regions, and his children were denied entry to state schools outside of Chechnya and Ingushetia. Timishev successfully established to be discriminated and infringed upon his right to liberty of movement. The ECtHR reasoned that 'ethnicity and race are related and overlapping concepts':

> Whereas the notion of race is rooted in the idea of biological classification of human beings into subspecies according to morphological features such as skin colour or facial characteristics, ethnicity has its origin in the idea of societal groups marked by common nationality, tribal affiliation, religious faith, shared language, or cultural and traditional origins and backgrounds …[48]

Previously in the same year, the Court had established in *Nachova and Others v Bulgaria*:

> Racial violence is a particular affront to human dignity and, in view of its perilous consequences, requires from the authorities special vigilance and a vigorous reaction. It is for this reason that the authorities must use all available means to combat racism and racist violence, thereby reinforcing democracy's vision of a society in which diversity is not perceived as a threat but as a source of its enrichment.[49]

In this case, criminal investigations were carried out ineffectively because of the Roma origin of the victims. The Court found that the authorities had failed in their duty under Article 2 and Article 14 of the Convention to take all possible steps to investigate and unmask whether or not discrimination may have played a role in the events.[50] The ECtHR's ruling made clear that European states have an obligation to investigate possible racist motives behind acts of violence.[51]

In 2007, the ECtHR reaffirmed its practice in *DH and Others v Czech Republic*.[52] In this case, Czech nationals of Roma origin showed that Roma children in the Czech Republic were systematically assigned to special segregated schools for children with learning difficulties, according to their racial or ethnic identity

[47] *Timishev v Russia*, ECtHR Judgment, App Nos 55762/00 and 55974/00, 13 December 2005, para 58.

[48] The ECtHR referred to the General Policy Recommendation No 7 authored by the European Commission against Racism and Intolerance in 2002, which states that: '"Direct racial discrimination" shall mean any differential treatment based on a ground such as race, colour, language, religion, nationality or national or ethnic origin …' ibid, para 55. See also General Policy Recommendation No 7, ECRI CRI(2003)8, 13 December 2002, para I.1.b).

[49] *Nachova and Others v Bulgaria*, ECtHR Judgment, App Nos 43577/98 and 43579/98, 6 July 2005, para 145.

[50] ibid, para 168.

[51] ibid, para 151.

[52] *DH and Others v the Czech Republic*, ECtHR Judgment, App No 57325/00, 13 November 2007, para 44.

rather than their intellectual capacities. The Court highlighted that discrimination can take place even if it has not been the intention:

> If a policy or general measure has disproportionately prejudicial effects on a group of people, the possibility of its being considered discriminatory cannot be ruled out even if it is not specifically aimed or directed at that group ...[53]

The ECtHR confirmed in *DH and Others v Czech Republic* that the Czech Government engaged in indirect discrimination against Roma children.[54] Statistical data submitted by the applicants had revealed a dominant trend that Roma pupils were disproportionately assigned to special schools.[55] The Court concluded that there has been a violation in the instant case of Article 14 of the Convention taken in conjunction with Article 2 of Protocol No 1, as relevant school legislation as applied in practice at the time had a disproportionately prejudicial effect on the Roma community.[56]

C. Decision of the ECtHR: Confirming Unequal Treatment

In *Sejdić and Finci v Bosnia and Herzegovina*, the fact that the exclusive distribution of power in the House of Peoples and Presidency among the major ethnic groups constitutes a direct infringement of rights of other minorities was actually not doubted by any side and was admitted by the Government.[57]

Following its practice on minority protection, the ECtHR restated in *Sejdić and Finci* that the definition of discrimination goes beyond the Convention's wording:

> Discrimination means treating differently, without an objective and reasonable justification, persons in similar situations.[58]

The Court agreed with the applicants, and clarified:

> Discrimination on account of a person's ethnic origin is a form of racial discrimination.[59]

Technically, discrimination was caused by the circumstance that the applicants, 'who describe themselves to be of Roma and Jewish origin respectively and who do not wish to declare affiliation with a 'constituent people', are, as a result, excluded'.[60]

[53] ibid, para 46.
[54] ibid, para 195.
[55] ibid, paras 190–92.
[56] ibid, para 209.
[57] *Sejdić and Finci v Bosnia and Herzegovina*, above n 12, paras 34–35.
[58] ibid, para 42. See also *Willis v the United Kingdom*, ECtHR Judgment, App No 36042/97, 11 September 2002, para 8; *Okpisz v Germany*, ECtHR Judgment, App No 59140/00, 25 October 2005, para 33.
[59] *Sejdić and Finci v Bosnia and Herzegovina*, above n 12, para 43.
[60] ibid, para 45.

D. Impact of Protocol No 12

Sejdić and Finci v Bosnia and Herzegovina was the first judgment ever in which the ECtHR found a violation of Protocol No 12, making it a landmark in the Court's jurisprudence. As mentioned, Protocol No 12 was introduced to enhance equality before the law and equal legal protection.[61] As Article 3 of Protocol No 1 to the Convention only guarantees the right to vote and to stand for parliamentary elections, the exclusion of certain ethnic groups from the government was previously outside the scope of human rights protection under the Convention.[62]

In *Sejdić and Finci v Bosnia and Herzegovina*, the ECtHR did not elaborate on the possible extent of the general prohibition of discrimination under Protocol No 12, which did not satisfy some of the participating judges. Judge Mijović and Judge Hajiyev noted critically that the application of Protocol No 12 'was set out in only two paragraphs'.[63] They argued that the tripartite structure of the Presidency in Bosnia and Herzegovina 'is, like many other State institutions in that country, a result of the political compromise achieved by the peace accord'.[64] In their view, the key question that required an answer was whether that tripartite structure was ever justified.

Indeed, a more detailed analysis of the normative framework of Protocol No 12 could have helped to define the general limits of constitutional designs for states in post-conflict transitions more precisely. Yet, the reluctance of the Court in *Sejdić and Finci v Bosnia and Herzegovina* to generally comment on the scope of Protocol No 12 will allow flexibility in other cases, which could ultimately strengthen the protection of human rights by refraining from overregulating them in advance.[65]

E. Importance of Ethnic Diversity and Religious Equality in Europe

In times of growing xenophobia and Romaphobia, the ECtHR decision in support of citizens of Jewish and Roma background is particularly crucial.[66]

[61] For details on the normative framework, see Part III.A above. See also Protocol No 12, Preamble.

[62] Marko Milanovic, 'Peacemaking or Discrimination: Bosnia's Dayton Constitution before the European Court of Human Rights', *EJIL Reports*, 1 June 2009.

[63] *Sejdić and Finci v Bosnia and Herzegovina*, above n 12, Partly Concurring and Partly Dissenting Opinion of Judge Mijović, joined by Judge Hajiyev, para IV. 1.

[64] ibid.

[65] On the debate about 'certainty' versus 'flexibility' in the protection of human rights, see also Stefan Sottiaux and Gerhard Van der Schyff, 'Methods of International Human Rights Adjudication: Towards a More Structured Decision-Making Process for the European Court of Human Rights' (2008) 31(1) *Hastings International and Comparative Law Review* 115. See also Eva Brems, *Human Rights: Universality and Diversity* (The Hague: Martinus Nijhoff, 2001) 343.

[66] For details, see Anti-Semitism: Summary Overview of the Situation in the European Union 2001–2010, European Union Agency for Fundamental Rights, April 2011, 31.

As the Explanatory Report to Protocol No 12 states, the Convention was extended in order to counter 'discriminatory attitudes and racist violence' currently 'spreading in many European countries' facing 'the resurgence of racist ideologies and religious intolerance' within Europe.[67] As the OSCE Annual Report on Hate Crimes regularly documents, Jewish citizens and Sinti and Romas continue to be harassed, threatened and attacked by right-wing groups.[68] As ethnic minorities, they have suffered heavily from discrimination under the Communist regime in the former Yugoslavia and are still experiencing socially accepted stigmatisation.[69] From this perspective, the recognition of discrimination of Jews and Romas in *Sejdić and Finci v Bosnia and Herzegovina* set a precedent and sent a strong signal for the importance of ethnic diversity and religious equality in Europe.[70]

IV. Justifying Human Rights Restrictions

The justification of human rights infringements was one of the key aspects in *Sejdić and Finci v Bosnia and Herzegovina.* The Government of Bosnia and Herzegovina argued that states enjoyed 'considerable latitude in establishing rules within their constitutional order to govern parliamentary elections and the composition of the Parliament'.[71] Sejdić and Finci claimed that discrimination on race or ethnicity cannot be justified under any circumstances.[72]

A. Normative Framework

In comparison with other rights in the Convention, the prohibition of discrimination in Article 14 ECHR includes no option for limitation.[73] A concession could have been only given through derogation, which allows human rights restrictions 'in time of war or other public emergency threatening the life of the nation'.[74] However, this scenario was not addressed in *Sejdić and Finci v Bosnia*

[67] Explanatory Report to the Convention on the Protection of Human Rights and Fundamental Freedoms, above n 46, para 7.

[68] Hate Crimes in the OSCE Region: Incidents and Responses, OSCE Annual Report for 2010, 44, 52. See also Hate Crimes in the OSCE Region: Incidents and Responses, OSCE Annual Report for 2012, 44, 55.

[69] Jan Briza, *Minority Rights in Yugoslavia* (Minority Rights Group, 2000) 7. See also Judith Latham, 'Roma of the former Yugoslavia' (1999) 27(2) *Nationalities Papers* 205.

[70] See also Lindsey E Wakely, 'From Constituent Peoples to Constituents: Europe Solidifies Fundamental Political Rights for Minority Groups in Sejdić v Bosnia' (2010) 36(1) *North Carolina Journal of International Law* 253.

[71] *Sejdić and Finci v Bosnia and Herzegovina*, above n 12, para 34.

[72] ibid, para 32.

[73] For an overview, see Table 2.

[74] ECHR Art 15, para 1.

and Herzegovina, as the state of public emergency was lifted after the signing of the Dayton Peace Accords.[75]

Table 2 ECHR provisions for human rights limitations

Concerned right	ECHR provision	Limitation
Liberty of movement	Article 2, para 3	(+)
Fair and public hearing	Article 6, para 1	(+)
Respect for private and family life	Article 8, para 2	(+)
Freedom of thought, conscience and religion	Article 9, para 2	(+)
Freedom of expression	Article 10, para 2	(+)
Freedom of peaceful assembly and freedom of association	Article 11, para 2	(+)
Prohibition of discrimination	Article 14	(−)

B. General Jurisprudence

Apart from the wording of Article 14 of the Convention, the ECtHR developed the practice that differential treatment can be justified under certain conditions. In 1968, the ECtHR established in the *Belgium language cases* that:

> [T]he principle of equality of treatment is violated if the distinction has no objective and reasonable justification. The existence of such a justification must be assessed in relation to the aim and effects of the measure under consideration, regard being had to the principles which normally prevail in democratic societies.[76]

In the cases, French-speaking Belgian citizens complained that the state did not provide any French-language education in their municipality, while Dutch-speaking children were supported. The ECtHR decided in favour of the applicants, arguing that the differential treatment of French-speaking Belgian citizens by the state was unjustified. As a general rule, the ECtHR established that an 'objective and reasonable justification' of human rights restrictions requires three conditions: first, a legitimate aim; second, proportionate means; and third, objective grounds.[77] As it will be shown in the following part of this chapter, the requirement of a 'legitimate aim' means the existence of plausible reasons, while 'proportionality' demands the probing of necessity and alternatives to the human rights restriction,

[75] On the consideration of derogation for states in transition, see Ch 4.

[76] Case 'Relating to Certain Aspects of the Laws on the Use of Languages in education in Belgium' v Belgium, ECtHR Judgment, App Nos 1474/62; 1677/62; 1691/62; 1769/63; 1994/63; 2126/64, 23 July 1968, para 10.

[77] ibid, para 10.

which need to be based on convincing evidence that are establishing the 'objective grounds' for the justification.[78]

C. 'Legitimate Aim': Identifying Reasons

The practice of the ECtHR in applying this formula has varied over the years.[79] Nonetheless, justifications for human rights constraints have been common for the purpose of protecting democratic order and national security, especially in the context of post-conflict state transitions.[80] Meanwhile, Sejdić and Finci claimed that ethnic domination 'cannot promote peace and reconciliation', but instead harms state stability.[81]

i. Prior Jurisprudence

In the mentioned decision *Timishev v Russia*, the ECtHR unanimously ruled that discrimination based on race or ethnicity cannot be justified on any grounds:

> In any event … no difference in treatment which is based exclusively or to a decisive extent on a person's ethnic origin is capable of being objectively justified in a contemporary democratic society built on the principles of pluralism and respect for different cultures.[82]

In 2006, the ECtHR decided in *Ždanoka v Latvia* that limitations on the exercise of electoral rights can be justified based on the 'principle of the rule of law and the general objectives of the Convention, namely the protection of the State's independence, democratic order and national security'.[83] The ECtHR established that restrictions are compatible with the Convention, and stated:

> Convention provisions do not prevent, in principle, Contracting States from introducing general policy schemes by way of legislative measures whereby a certain category or group of individuals is treated differently from others, provided that the interference with the rights of the statutory category or group as a whole can be justified under the Convention.[84]

In this case, Tatjana Ždanoka, a Latvian national, was disqualified from standing for election to the Latvian Parliament and to municipal elections. The reason was

[78] See Part III.C–E above. For a summary of the ECtHR methodology, see Appendix, Table 7. For an overview, see Appendix, Table 3.

[79] For details, see Frédéric Edel, *The Prohibition of Discrimination Under the European Convention on Human Rights* (Strasbourg, Council of Europe, 2010) 58.

[80] ibid.

[81] Applicants' Written Submission to the Grand Chamber, ECtHR App Nos 27996/06 and 34836/06, 28 April 2009, para 91.

[82] *Timishev v Russia*, above n 47, para 58.

[83] *Ždanoka v Latvia*, ECtHR Judgment, App No 58278/00, 16 March 2006, para 118.

[84] ibid, para 112.

her prior affiliation with the Communist Party of Latvia in the 1970s. The party was declared unconstitutional due to attempted coups following Latvia's declaration of independence. Ždanoka alleged that her exclusion from the parliamentary elections infringed her rights under the Convention.

The ECtHR emphasised that electoral legislation can take into consideration the 'political evolution' of a country.[85] Although the state has no 'carte blanche', special measures may be 'considered acceptable' given the 'historic-political context' and 'threat to the new democratic order'.[86]

ii. Decision of the ECtHR: Post-Conflict Transitions Can Justify Restricted Human Rights

In *Sejdić and Finci v Bosnia and Herzegovina*, the ECtHR upheld that the principles of justification established in the *Belgium language cases* are 'well entrenched in the Court's case law'.[87] It decided that the Convention does not prohibit states from treating groups differently in order to correct 'factual inequalities' between them.[88] The ECtHR referred to the major reason for the Dayton Peace Accords as the legitimate aim: namely 'the restoration of peace'.[89] As the Court elaborated:

> When the impugned constitutional provisions were put in place a very fragile cease-fire was in effect on the ground. The provisions were designed to end a brutal conflict marked by genocide and 'ethnic cleansing'. The nature of the conflict was such that the approval of the 'constituent peoples' (namely, the Bosniaks, Croats and Serbs) was necessary to ensure peace.[90]

This aim for peace is 'broadly compatible with the general objectives of the Convention'.[91] The Convention explicitly enumerates 'the foundation of justice and peace in the world' in its Preamble.[92]

iii. The Restoration of Peace as a Challenge for Human Rights

The formulation of a legitimate aim for justifying human rights restrictions does not usually pose difficulties. Some scholars even argue that it has become 'a rhetorical and artificial assertion that has nothing to do with the issues truly deciding the case'.[93] In the context of state transitions and regime changes, the

[85] ibid, paras 105, 106, 122.
[86] ibid, para 113.
[87] *Sejdić and Finci v Bosnia and Herzegovina*, above n 12, para 39.
[88] ibid, para 44.
[89] ibid, para 45.
[90] ibid.
[91] ibid.
[92] ECHR, Preamble, para 4.
[93] Oddný Mjöll Arnardóttir, *Equality and Non-Discrimination under the European Convention on Human Rights* (The Hague, Martinus Nijhoff Publishers, 2003) 45.

ECtHR has referred to the 'protection of State independence', 'democratic order' or 'national security'.[94] *Sejdić and Finci v Bosnia and Herzegovina* was the first time that the ECtHR acknowledged the 'restoration of peace' as a cause.[95]

It is noteworthy that the ECtHR did not dismiss the arguments of the Government on the ground that ethnic discrimination can never be justified, as decided in *Timishev v Russia*.[96] In the *Izetbegović* case, the Constitutional Court of Bosnia and Herzegovina had also stated that ethnic segregation can never aid the aim of peace.[97] By pursuing a further assessment, the ECtHR followed its practice established in *Ždanoka v Latvia*, where it held that there are 'numerous ways of organising and running electoral systems and a wealth of differences', in which states can decide about their 'own democratic vision'.[98]

D. 'Proportionality': Probing Necessity and Alternatives

Whether ethnic power-sharing as an employed means is proportional to the aim of restoring peace was one of the central points of debate in the decision in *Sejdić and Finci v Bosnia and Herzegovina*. Sejdić and Finci argued that viable alternative political structures have been proposed, which suggest that ethnic power-sharing in its current form 'is not necessary' any more.[99] The Government maintained that the contested constitutional provisions are still required, since 'the time was still not ripe for a political system which would be a simple reflection of majority rule'.[100]

i. Prior Jurisprudence

Previously, the ECtHR had held in *Glor v Switzerland* that if there are less drastic but equally efficient alternatives, the chosen measures are not proportionate:

> The Court considers that in order for a measure to be considered to be proportional and necessary in democratic society, another measure must not exist which achieves the same aim but infringes upon the fundamental right in issue to a lesser extent.[101]

In this case, a Swiss national was discharged from military and civil service because of diabetes. He alleged that he had been subjected to discriminatory

[94] For an overview, see Athanasia Spiliopoulou Akermark, *Justifications of Minority Protection in International Law* (The Hague: Springer, 1997) 208.

[95] The Venice Commission had previously argued in a similar direction. See Opinion on the Constitutional Situation in Bosnia and Herzegovina and the Powers of the High Representative, Venice Commission, Doc CDL-AD(2005)004, 11 March 2005, para 80.

[96] *Timishev v Russia*, above n 47, para 58.

[97] Partial Decision No U-5/98 III, above n 17, para III.A.a) 96.

[98] *Ždanoka v Latvia*, above n 83, para 103.

[99] Applicants' Written Submission to the Grand Chamber, above n 81, para 100.

[100] *Sejdić and Finci v Bosnia and Herzegovina*, above n 12, para 34.

[101] *Glor v Switzerland*, ECtHR Judgment, App No 13444/04, 6 November 2009, para 94.

treatment by being requested to pay an exemption tax although he had wanted to join the military. The ECtHR concluded that states need 'to secure a fair balance between safeguarding the interests of the community and respecting the rights and liberties' of an individual.[102] It emphasised that as long as there are alternative means available which can achieving the same end, unequal treatment cannot be justified.

In *DH and Others v the Czech Republic*, the ECtHR demonstrated that it usually considers various Council of Europe sources in its assessment of necessity, such as: recommendations of the Council of Ministers, the Parliamentary Assembly, reports of the European Commission against Racism and Intolerance (ECRI) and the European Commission for Democracy through Law (Venice Commission), governmental reports with regard to the Framework Convention for the Protection of National Minorities, and statements by the European Commissioner for Human Rights.[103]

ii. Decision of the ECtHR: Possibility of Phasing Out of Human Rights Constraints

In *Sejdić and Finci v Bosnia and Herzegovina*, the ECtHR underlined that the drafters and international mediators of the Dayton Peace Accords were 'fully aware' that the arrangements 'were most probably conflicting with human rights', which makes it 'especially important' to consider the Constitution 'a dynamic instrument' and provide for a 'possible phasing out' of restrictions.[104] The ECtHR emphasised that Bosnia and Herzegovina has 'voluntarily agreed' to meet the relevant standards of the European Convention on Human Rights, which require adherence.[105] Finally, the Court concluded that in the case of Bosnia and Herzegovina, the constitutional ethnic system does 'not satisfy the requirement of proportionality', as less drastic but equally efficient alternatives exist.[106] The ECtHR summarised:

> While the Court agrees with the Government that there is no requirement under the Convention to abandon totally the power-sharing mechanisms peculiar to Bosnia and Herzegovina and that the time may still not be ripe for a political system which would be a simple reflection of majority rule, the Opinions of the Venice Commission … clearly demonstrate that there exist mechanisms of power-sharing which do not automatically lead to the total exclusion of representatives of the other communities.[107]

[102] ibid, para 96.

[103] *DH and Others v the Czech Republic*, above n 52, paras 54–80.

[104] *Sejdić and Finci v Bosnia and Herzegovina*, above n 12, para 14.

[105] ibid, para 49. Technically, the ECHR has been directly applicable since the adoption of the Constitution in 1995 (BiH Constitution, Art 2, para 2). After becoming a member of the Council of Europe in 2002, the Convention was formally ratified as an international treaty. In this way Bosnia and Herzegovina made the commitment to harmonise its legislation with the international obligations deriving from the treaty. See Compatibility of Laws in BiH with the Requirements of the ECHR, Council of Europe, Directorate General of Human Rights and Legal Affairs, Dec. 2006.

[106] *Sejdić and Finci v Bosnia and Herzegovina*, above n 12, para 46.

[107] ibid, para 48.

As the Court stressed, the Venice Commission had urged Bosnia and Herzegovina to pursue constitutional change while acknowledging that the country is 'in transition'.[108]

iii. *The Internal Logic of the ECHR System*

As in *DH and Others v the Czech Republic*, a key focus in *Sejdić and Finci v Bosnia and Herzegovina* has been on other conclusions from within the Council of Europe system. These references of the ECtHR for substantiating its decisions about proportionality follow an internal logic, maintaining the coherency of the European human rights system.

a. Role of the Venice Commission

Recommendations from the Venice Commission and the Council of Europe Parliamentary Assembly often play a decisive role.[109] The challenge for the ECtHR, the Venice Commission, the Parliamentary Assembly and other Council of Europe institutions is to try to give states in transition enough leeway in deciding their own affairs, while gently assisting them towards democracy and adherence to human rights standards.[110] Though the ECtHR judges are not obliged to follow the legal opinion of the Venice Commission, the Commission was deliberately set up as an 'independent consultative body' which functions like an informal expert witness.[111] Hence, the decision in *Sejdić and Finci v Bosnia and Herzegovina* appears consistent as it is based on the sum of analogous conclusions by various human rights monitoring bodies of the Council of Europe.

b. Proposed Reform Options

The constitutional reform process of Bosnia and Herzegovina has not been short of proposed alternatives.

Among others, the Venice Commission recommended 'an electoral system ensuring representation of both Entities', under the condition that 'not more than

[108] ibid, para 22. See also Venice Commission, Doc CDL-AD(2005)004, above n 95, para 29.

[109] In comparison, see also *Republican Party of Russia v Russia*, ECtHR Judgment, App No 12976/07, 12 April 2011, para 88; *Bulanov and Kupchik v Ukraine*, ECtHR Judgment, App Nos 7714/06 and 23654/08, 9 December 2010, para 25; *Tanase v Moldova*, ECtHR Judgment, App No 7/08, 27 April 2010, para 135; *Yumak and Sadak v Turkey*, ECtHR Judgment, App No 10226/03, 8 July 2008, para 129; *The Georgian Labour Party v Georgia*, ECtHR Judgment, App No 9103/04, 8 July 2008, para 88; *Oya Ataman v Turkey*, ECtHR Judgment, App No 74552/01, 5 December 2006, para 16.

[110] For details, see Julia Raue, *Der Europarat als Verfassungsgestalter seiner Neuen Mitgliedsstaaten: Vom Beobachter zum Reformer in Osteuropa* (Zürich et al, Schulthess, 2005) 47.

[111] See Revised Statute of the European Commission for Democracy through Law, Art 1, para 1, Council of Europe, Committee of Ministers, Res(2002)3, 21 February 2002. See also On a Partial Agreement Establishing the European Commission for Democracy through Law, Art 1, para 1, Council of Europe, Committee of Ministers, Res(90)6, 10 May 1990.

one member of the Presidency' may belong to the same constituent people or the group of 'others'.[112] Another option put forward was to abolish the collective Presidency and replace it with 'an indirectly elected President with very limited powers'.[113] The executive power could also be concentrated in the Council of Ministers.[114]

Another discussed option was to incorporate an additional rotating member for the Presidency to represent minorities, and to add three seats for representatives from national minorities in the Parliament.[115] An alternative idea was to have a single President, with Vice-Presidents belonging to different ethnic groups with a rotation of the Presidency between all ethnic groups.

A further debated option was to ensure that the President, Prime Minister and the Presidents of the two parliamentary houses do not belong to the same ethnic group, to allow ethnic diversity.[116] Another option was to establish a five-seat Presidency, combined with the establishment of a single national electoral district.[117] This model would guarantee a seat for each of the three constituent people, leaving the fourth and the fifth seats for inter-ethnic electoral competition, in order to allow the representation of political minorities by at least safeguarding their chances to participate in elections.[118]

None of the proposals found sufficient consensus. As the Report of the High Representative of the European Union in February 2013 summarised, Bosnia and Herzegovina's political parties 'have submitted for parliamentary consideration various proposals on how to implement the ruling of the Court but have so far failed to reach a compromise that would meet the requirements of the European Union and other relevant European institutions'.[119]

c. Difference between Legislative and Executive Power-Sharing?

A distinction which could serve as guidance for assessing the proportionality of power-sharing has been hinted at by Judge Feldman in the second *Tihić* decision

[112] Venice Commission, Doc CDL-AD(2005)004, above n 95, para 77. See also Opinion on the Electoral law of Bosnia and Herzegovina, Venice Commission, Doc CDL-INF(2001)21, 24 October 2001, para 26.

[113] Venice Commission CDL-AD(2005)004, above n 95, para 77.

[114] Joint Opinion on Amendments to the Election Law of Bosnia And Herzegovina, Venice Commission, Doc CDL-AD(2006)004, 20 March 2006, para 17.

[115] For details, see Daniel Bochsler, 'Non-Discriminatory Rules and Ethnic Representation: The Election of the Bosnian State Presidency' (2011) 10(3) *Ethnopolitics* 5.

[116] ibid, 6.

[117] As Bochsler proposed, a single nationwide electoral district could 'help moderate candidates to win more votes across ethnic boundaries', and allow 'politicians to get a national mandate … to be accountable to the electorate in the whole country' and in the long run encourages the promotion of 'programs that are popular with voters of all parts of the country': ibid, 9.

[118] Given that each voter has only one vote for one candidate, the political majority would not have sufficient votes to occupy all seats, allowing the political minority to concentrate on fielding one candidate or a small number of candidates: see ibid, 10. Further proposals had been brought forward.

[119] UN Doc S/2013/90, above n 5, para 4.

of the Constitutional Court of Bosnia and Herzegovina. He argued convincingly that ethnic privileges could be legitimised for the Presidency, but not for the legislature.[120] At least for law-making bodies, 'the normal principles of electoral democracy' must apply, Judge Feldman concluded.[121]

Reading between the lines of his thoughts, this differentiation makes sense: at least in parliamentary systems, parliaments represent the core of democratic representation. As the President of the Inter-Parliamentary Union, Pier Ferdinando Casini, has put it, parliaments are 'the central institution of democracy'.[122] Their purpose is to represent all citizens in some way, much more than the executive. As Grégoire Webber concluded:

> In a democratic constitutional State, only the legislature is an institution … which, albeit with many imperfections, can purport to represent all citizens. And only through the legislature can all citizens be said to be represented in the process that determines what shall be limitation of constitutional rights left open by the constitution.[123]

Along the same lines, the Venice Commission suggested with regard to Bosnia and Herzegovina that proposals for a three-, four- or five-headed Presidency are too 'complicated', 'with too many steps' and with 'possibilities for stalemate' after elections.[124] The Commission's recommendation was therefore for 'a simpler procedure with more focus on the House of Representatives as the body having direct democratic legitimacy derived from the people as a whole'.[125]

Similarly, some scholars have argued that any model that does not continue to guarantee giving the three constituent people in the Presidency a say is most likely to be 'politically unfeasible'.[126] A concern is that the abolition of the Presidency quota could lead to domination by one ethnicity, leading to an even more intense political stalemate.

d. The Proportionality Hypothesis

As Jeremy Gunn pointed out critically, 'the problems of a proportionality analysis can perhaps most easily be illustrated by a hypothetical example, where different

[120] Decision on Admissibility No U-13/05, above n 19, Separate Concurring Opinion of Judge David Feldman, 15.

[121] ibid.

[122] David Beetham, *Parliament and Democracy in the Twenty-First Century* (Geneva, Inter-Parliamentary Union, 2006) vii.

[123] Grégoire CN Webber, *The Negotiable Constitution: On the Limitation of Rights* (Cambridge, Cambridge University Press, 2009) 215.

[124] Joint Opinion on Amendments to the Election Law of Bosnia And Herzegovina, Venice Commission, above n 114, para 21.

[125] The Venice Commission elaborated: 'The possibility to nominate candidates should be reserved to members of the House of Representatives, selection among these candidates could take place in the three separate ethnic caucuses of the House of Peoples to ensure that the interests of all three constituent peoples are respected and the slate of candidates would have to be confirmed by the majority of the composition of the House of Representatives, ensuring that all three members have legitimacy as representatives of the people of Bosnia and Herzegovina as a whole': ibid, para 22.

[126] Bochsler, above n 115, 7, 17.

courts can reach different judgments based upon the weight they provide to different factors'.[127] Likewise, Stavros Tsakyrakis argued that 'proportionality constitutes a misguided quest for precision and objectivity in the resolution of human rights disputes and suggests that courts should instead focus on the real moral issues underlying such disputes'.[128] Yutaka Arai-Takahashi called the use of the proportionality doctrine 'rhetorical'.[129] Ultimately, one could compromise along with Jeremy McBride, who stated that 'it is perhaps inevitable' that the specific application of the principle of proportionality will continue 'to be controversial'.[130]

In the ECtHR's practice, the question is not *which* alternative power-sharing model is better suited.[131] The Court can only assess *whether there are* viable constitutional alternatives.[132] The actual way to choose a solution is via legislative processes, and only subsequent developments can prove whether the preferred power-sharing model is less discriminatory but still able to preserve peace.

Courts are deliberately established as checks and balances, to enhance the protection of rights by generating a dynamic for a discourse about them. In negating the proportionality of the existing power-sharing structures in Bosnia and Herzegovina, the ECtHR followed its practice of encouraging states to improve when change is possible.

E. 'Objective Grounds': Questions of Time and Proof

Whether human rights restrictions for the restoration of peace are still justifiable on objective grounds, years after the end of armed conflict, was another major issue of dispute in *Sejdić and Finci v Bosnia and Herzegovina*.

The Government of Bosnia and Herzegovina pointed to the fact that citizens voted mainly for national parties, which in its view reflects ongoing ethnic tension justifying the need for power-sharing among the major ethnic groups in order to prevent a relapse into hostilities.[133] The Government maintained

[127] T Jeremy Gunn, 'Deconstructing Proportionality in Limitations Analysis' (2005) 19 *Emory International Law Review* 471.

[128] Tsakyrakis Stavros, *Proportionality: An Assault on Human Rights?*, Jean Monnet Working Paper No 9 (2008) 1.

[129] Yutaka Arai-Takahashi, *The Margin of Appreciation Doctrine and the Principle of Proportionality in the Jurisprudence of the ECHR* (Antwerp, Intersentia, 2001) 15.

[130] Jeremy McBride, 'Proportionality and the European Convention on Human Rights' in Evelyn Ellis (ed), *The Principle of Proportionality in the Laws* (Oxford, Hart, 1999) 23.

[131] On the so-called 'less restrictive alternative doctrine' of the ECtHR, see Arai-Takahashi, above n 129, 14.

[132] Gunn, above n 127, 466. See also Marc-André Eissen, 'The Principle of Proportionality in the Case-Law of the European Court of Human Rights' in Ronald St J Macdonald, Franz Matscher and Herbert Petzold (eds), *The European System for the Protection of Human Rights* (Dordrecht, Martinus Nijhoff Publishers, 1993) 125.

[133] Additional Written Observations and Comments of Bosnia and Herzegovina on the Claims for Just Satisfaction, ECtHR, App Nos 27996/06 and 34836/06, 26 December 2008, para 43.

that the unfinished work of the International Criminal Tribunal for the Former Yugoslavia and the continuing 'Transitional Justice' process was an indication that peace was not completely restored in the country. The presence of NATO troops and enduring interventions of the High Representative on behalf of the international community were seen as further evidence that Bosnia and Herzegovina was not considered to be stable.

Sejdić and Finci submitted that 'the length of time during which the exclusion had continued increased even more the burden' on the Government to objectively justify ethnic distinction.[134] They portrayed Bosnia and Herzegovina's steps towards EU accession as an indication for the country's stability.[135]

i. *Normative Framework*

In general, the furnishing of evidence is governed in the Annex to the Rule of the Court.[136] Like other human rights courts, the ECtHR has increased investigative powers. The judges can, for instance, at the request of one of the parties, a third party or ex officio, collect evidence.[137] However, concrete obligations or a checklist about which facts the Court has to consider are not codified.

ii. *Prior Jurisprudence*

In its practice, the ECtHR established that it judges 'in the light of the case as a whole':

> ... on the basis of the different data available to it, whether the reasons given by the national authorities to justify the actual measures of 'interference' they take are relevant and sufficient.[138]

As a principle, the ECtHR follows the rule *affirmanti incumbit probation*, which postulates that whoever alleges something must prove that allegation.[139]

[134] *Sejdić and Finci v Bosnia and Herzegovina*, above n 12, para 33.

[135] Sejdić's counsel, Francisco Javier Leon Diaz stated that Bosnia and Herzegovina 'has clearly expressed its conviction that the country is moving from a peace implementation process to a process of European integration'. In June 2008, Bosnia and Herzegovina signed a Stabilization and Association Agreement (SAA) with the EU, which also includes legislative reform of electoral rights. See Reply of Mr Dervo Sejdić to the Government's Observation on Admissibility and Merits of 4 July 2008, ECtHR, App Nos 27996/06 and 34836/06, 2009, para 24.

[136] ECtHR Rules of Court, 1 April 2011, Annex to the Rules (Concerning Investigations) Rule A1-A8.

[137] ibid, Rule A1.

[138] *Handyside v The United Kingdom*, ECtHR Judgement, App No 5493/72, 7 December 1976, paras 50, 59.

[139] *DH and Others v the Czech Republic*, above n 52, paras 177, 179. See also *Timishev v Russia*, above n 47, para 56; *Moldovan v Romania*, ECtHR Judgment, App Nos 41138/98 and 64320/01, 12 July 2005, para 140; *Nachova and Others v Bulgaria*, above n 49, para 157; *Chassagnou and Others v France*, ECtHR Judgment, App Nos 25088/94, 28331/95 and 28443/95, 29 April 1999, paras 91–92.

ECtHR case law provides that the onus of justification is with the respondent government, once an applicant has established a difference in treatment. The ECtHR has continually repeated that 'where the events in issue lie wholly, or in large part, within the exclusive knowledge of the authorities', the burden of proof rests on the authorities to provide a 'satisfactory and convincing explanation'.[140] In *DH and others v Czech Republic*, the ECtHR explained:

> Where an applicant alleging indirect discrimination thus establishes a rebuttable presumption that the effect of a measure or practice is discriminatory, the burden then shifts to the respondent State, which must show that the difference in treatment is not discriminatory.[141]

Though a respondent government may disprove an arguable allegation of discrimination, it is generally considered that the proof of justification is 'difficult', especially in cases of discrimination motivated by racial prejudice.[142] The ECtHR stressed:

> Where the difference in treatment is based on race, colour or ethnic origin, the notion of objective and reasonable justification must be interpreted as strictly as possible.[143]

In 2004, the ECtHR decided *Aziz v Cyprus* on power-sharing concerning the Cypriot conflict. Without elaboration, the ECtHR rejected the attempt to justify human rights constraints, and stated:

> Although the Court takes note of the Government's arguments, it considers that they cannot justify this difference on reasonable and objective grounds, particularly in the light of the fact that Turkish Cypriots in the applicant's situation are prevented from voting at any parliamentary election.[144]

Similarly to the circumstances in *Sejdić and Finci v Bosnia and Herzegovina*, Ibrahim Aziz, a Cypriot national of Turkish origin living in the Cypriot part of Nicosia, tried unsuccessfully to be registered on the Greek-Cypriot electoral roll for the parliamentary elections of 2001. In order to maintain peace, this had been forbidden by the Constitution of Cyprus. The ECtHR upheld that an exclusion of citizens, due to the fact that they are Turkish Cypriots, is not justified on reasonable and objective grounds.

iii. Decision of the ECtHR: Assessing Indicators of Post-Conflict Transitions

In *Sejdić and Finci v Bosnia and Herzegovina*, the ECtHR admitted that the progress made in the post-conflict transition of the country 'might not always

[140] *DH and Others v the Czech Republic*, above n 52, para 179. See also *Anguelova v Bulgaria*, ECtHR Judgment, App No 38361/97, 12 September 2002, para 111; *Salman v Turkey*, ECtHR Judgment, App No 21986/93, 27 June 2000, para 100.
[141] *DH and Others v the Czech Republic*, above n 52, para 177.
[142] ibid, para 179.
[143] ibid, para 196.
[144] *Aziz v Cyprus*, ECtHR Judgment, App No 69949/01, 22 June 2004, para 37.

have been consistent and challenges remain'.[145] However, six reasons convinced the Court that the restoration of peace was completed:

(1) In 2005 the former parties to the conflict surrendered their control over the armed forces and transformed them into a small, professional force;
(2) in 2006 Bosnia and Herzegovina joined NATO's Partnership for Peace;
(3) in 2008 it signed and ratified a Stabilisation and Association Agreement with the European Union;
(4) in March 2009 it successfully amended the State Constitution for the first time;
(5) and it has recently been elected a member of the United Nations Security Council for a two-year term beginning on 1 January 2010.
(6) Furthermore, whereas the maintenance of an international administration as an enforcement measure under Chapter VII of the United Nations Charter implies that the situation in the region still constitutes a 'threat to international peace and security', it appears that preparations for the closure of that administration are under way.[146]

Referring to the 2008 European Commission progress reports on Bosnia and Herzegovina as a potential candidate for EU membership and the 2009 documentation of the International Crisis Group, the ECtHR endorsed Bosnia and Herzegovina as having made 'significant positive developments' since the 1995 Dayton Peace Agreement.[147] The ECtHR also mentioned the CERD concluding observations on Bosnia and Herzegovina, which documented as positive aspects the fact that the country is engaged in a constructive dialogue about equality between all ethnic groups.[148]

iv. Unanswered Questions by the Court

The decision has been criticised, in that the ECtHR left unanswered the question why Bosnia and Herzegovina could be seen as stable enough to modify key parts of the war-ending power-sharing deal itself, while still needing to be under international supervision.[149] And indeed, the facts assessed by the Court can be seen as ambiguous. In the following paragraphs, a few thoughts on an alternative reasoning of the Court are discussed.

a. Ambiguity of Facts: An Alternative Reasoning

Ambiguity of facts reveals itself in several points: on one side, the ECtHR noted in *Sejdić and Finci* that the authors of the Dayton Peace Accords foresaw a

[145] *Sejdić and Finci v Bosnia and Herzegovina*, above n 12, para 47.
[146] ibid.
[147] ibid.
[148] ibid. See also UN Doc CERD/C/BIH/CO/6, 11 April 2006, para 5.
[149] *Sejdić and Finci v Bosnia and Herzegovina*, above n 12, Partly Concurring and Partly Dissenting Opinion of Judge Mijović, joined by Judge Hajiyev, para V.

phasing-out of the power-sharing agreement.[150] On the other side, the Dayton Peace Accords do not declare when the right moment is for this to happen. Time limits and deadlines were deliberately excluded from the peace agreement in order to allow flexibility.[151] The Court's argument that Bosnia and Herzegovina has voluntarily committed itself to adhere to the Convention and review electoral legislation within one year after the admission to the Council of Europe in 2002 is only partially persuasive.[152] Certainly, this reminder of the Court upholds the principle of international law that states have to obey their obligations (*pacta sunt servanda*). However, despite the Court's observation that 'significant positive developments' have been achieved, 'progress' does not necessarily mean that full stability has been attained, which is also recognised in the judgment.[153] It would be an oversimplification to argue that states in transition have to fulfil self-imposed human rights standards immediately, as constitutional and legislative change in the aftermath of conflict needs time. The Court itself admits that 'progress might not always have been consistent and challenges remain' in the country.[154]

In this light, a more convincing line of argument could have been to acknowledge the ambiguity of the facts. For instance, the international military presence and the High Representative provide a security mechanism, but do not necessarily prove that peace has been restored. Even the potential EU candidacy of Bosnia and Herzegovina would not automatically imply re-established peace; in fact, EU membership in itself is seen an incentive for peacebuilding and a factor of stability, which indicates that the restoration of peace remains an ongoing process. There is a nuanced difference between the end of an armed conflict, the maintenance of law and order by foreign actors, and the restoration of peace, which the ECtHR refrained from commenting on.

b. Judicial Discretion in the Assessment of Evidence

From the perspective of international practice, international courts and tribunals have a wide discretion in the assessment of evidence.[155] Although they must satisfy themselves that claims are 'well founded in fact and in law', it is within their authority to judge on the facts of a case.[156] As the ICJ upheld in *Nicaragua v United*

[150] *Sejdić and Finci v Bosnia and Herzegovina*, above n 12, para 14.

[151] An option could have been to include a 'sunset' clause indicating the expiry or the need for review of the Dayton Accords. See Timothy D Sisk, 'Peacebuilding as Democratization: Findings and Recommendations' in Anna K Jarstad and Timothy D Sisk (eds), *From War to Democracy: Dilemmas of Peacebuilding* (Cambridge, Cambridge University Press, 2008) 254, 239.

[152] *Sejdić and Finci v Bosnia and Herzegovina*, above n 12, para 49.

[153] ibid, para 47.

[154] ibid.

[155] Rüdiger Wolfrum, 'International Courts and Tribunals, Evidence', *Max Planck Encyclopaedia of Public International Law* paras 2, 8.

[156] For details, see Markus Benzing, *Das Beweisrecht vor internationalen Gerichten und Schiedsgerichten in zwischenstaatlichen Streitigkeiten* (Berlin, Springer Verlag, 2010) 493.

States of America in 1986, 'within the limits of its statute and rules', international courts have 'freedom in estimating the value of the various elements of evidence'.[157] Legally, procedural law of international courts and tribunals traditionally does not include strict rules on admissibility of evidence.[158] And, as has been criticised, international courts and tribunals are 'reluctant to deal in depth with questions of evidence'.[159] It is particularly regrettable that judges 'do not explain which standard of proof they have used and how they have reached conclusions on disputed facts'.[160] This was unfortunately also the case in the decision in *Sejdić and Finci v Bosnia and Herzegovina*, where the ECtHR only evaluated some aspects of the presented facts.

c. A Non-Liquet Situation?: Protecting Human Rights while Showing Sensitivity Towards State Transitions

An alternative reasoning with more sensitivity to the difficult post-conflict political environment of Bosnia and Herzegovina could have concluded that the presented facts were actually inconclusive (*non-liquet*). This approach could have valued the benefit of the doubt in judicial decisions.[161] The rationale behind the principle is that a judge shall not be forced to take a decision while being uncertain about the facts, as such a judgment would be random and against the rule of law.[162] Situations which are *non liquet* are decided on the basis of applying the burden of proof.[163] Potentially, the *non liquet* approach could make for sounder judicial reasoning in ambiguous cases about whether or not state transitions are completed and peace is restored.

However, in contrast to domestic judiciaries, international human rights courts are reluctant to apply the concept of *non liquet* explicitly.[164] The ECtHR's practice is that decisions on evidence cannot be left *non liquet*.[165] According to

[157] *Military and Paramilitary Activities in and against Nicaragua (Nicaragua v US)*, Merits, 27 June 1996, ICJ Reports 14, 27 June 1986, para 60.

[158] Wolfrum, above n 155, para 23.

[159] ibid, para 2.

[160] ibid.

[161] Thomas Riehm, *Abwägungsentscheidungen in der Praktischen Rechtsanwendung: Argumentation, Beweis, Wertung* (München, Verlag CH Beck, 2006) 122.

[162] Juliane Kokott, *The Burden of Proof in Comparative and International Human Rights Law: Civil and Common Law Approaches with Special Reference to the American and German Legal Systems* (The Hague, Kluwer Law International, 1998) 171.

[163] Hanns Prütting, *Gegenwartsprobleme der Beweislast* (Munich, CH Beck Verlag, 1983) 120.

[164] In international law, the term *non liquet* is mainly used for legal gaps, or lacunae, concerning the substance of positive or customary law. For details, see Lucien Siorat, *Le Problème des Lacunes en Droit International* (Paris, LGDJ, 1958) 191. See also Durward V Sandifer, *Evidence Before International Tribunals* (Charlottesville, University Press of Virginia, 1975) 31.

[165] Jonas Christoffersen, *Fair Balance: Proportionality, Subsidiarity and Primarity in the European Convention on Human Rights* (The Hague, Brill, 2009) 173. See also Rebecca Schorm-Bernschütz, *Die Tatsachenfeststellung im Verfahren vor dem Europäischen Gerichtshof für Menschenrechte* (Münster, LIT Verlag, 2004) 138.

Jonas Christoffersen, the understanding of the Court is that it 'must decide whether a fact or a set of facts is proven or unproven, established or not established'.[166] Christoffersen pointed out that the general standard of proof at the ECtHR is the 'preponderance of evidence' to which 'a fact is established if its existence is 'more probable' than its non-existence'.[167] Although the ECtHR has never explicitly set general standards as to what evidence constitutes a 'satisfactory and convincing explanation', international human rights law tends to be a priori resistant to restrictions, especially in cases of ethnic-racial discrimination.[168] This practice explains why the ECtHR was reluctant to accept a justification of ethnic differential treatment in *Sejdić and Finci v Bosnia and Herzegovina*.

d. Decision by the Burden of Proof

A decision by the burden of proof would also have turned against the Government. In the moment of ambiguity about facts for or against a justification of discrimination, the responsible state carries the responsibility to answer any concerns about the necessity of restricting human rights.[169] Objective reasons for human rights restrictions have to be proven 'beyond reasonable doubt', in order to protect victims from human rights violations.[170]

Frederick Schauer made the opposite comment that the distinction between fact and value, description and prescription is often a mystery in judicial reasoning.[171] One systemic deficiency is that international law is not conclusive on directions about how to decide on which bases of evidence, and why. The practice of the ECtHR often leaves explanations on evidence in the grey zone.[172] In *Sejdić and Finci v Bosnia and Herzegovina*, more transparency by the ECtHR could have eventually made the decision more acceptable for all sides and taken heat out of the political debate about the judgment.

[166] ibid, 173.

[167] ibid, 176.

[168] Benzing, above n 156, 703. See also *DH and Others v the Czech Republic*, above n 52, para 179.

[169] *Velikova v Bulgaria*, ECtHR Judgment, App No 41488/98, 18 May 2000, para 70. In *The Sunday Times v The United Kingdom*, the dissenting judges added that an assessment has 'to be made with due care and in a reasonable manner, and which of necessity will be based on facts and circumstances prevailing in the country concerned and on the future development of those facts and circumstances': *The Sunday Times v The United Kingdom*, ECtHR Judgement, App No 6538/74, 26 April 1979, Joint Dissenting Opinion of Judges Wiarda, Cremona, Thór Vilhjálmsson, Ryssdal, Ganshof van der Meersch, Sir Gerald Fitzmaurice, Bindschedler-Robert, Liesch and Matscher, para 7.

[170] Wolfrum, above n 155, para 77.

[171] Frederick F Schauer, *Thinking Like a Lawyer: A New Introduction to Legal Reasoning* (Cambridge, MA, Harvard University Press, 2009) 205.

[172] As McBride commented, there 'might be grounds for wondering whether sometimes more attention could still be given to the capacity of the Convention institutions to make an informed judgment about the acceptability of some of the interferences to which they are prepared to allow rights and freedoms to be subjected': McBride, above n 130, 23–24.

F. Margin of Appreciation

Did the ECtHR overstep its authority by judging in a sphere which might have been purely eligible for a domestic decision? Was the ECtHR in Strasbourg the right place to demand constitutional changes, given the unfinished political debate in Bosnia and Herzegovina? The cases at the Constitutional Court of Bosnia and Herzegovina had already posed the question of whether courts are allowed to interfere and modify a state's post-conflict configuration.

i. Prior Jurisprudence

In the *Belgium language cases*, the ECtHR admitted that 'national authorities remain free to choose the measures which they consider appropriate'.[173] The ECtHR established that it cannot assume the role of a Parliament, as it would otherwise 'lose sight of its subsidiary nature'.[174]

The Court defined later in detail that a 'margin of appreciation' is left to the domestic legislator as well as to the local judiciary.[175] However, the responsibility for ensuring the Member States' compliance with the Convention remains with the ECtHR, as it was empowered by them to give a final ruling:

> The domestic margin of appreciation thus goes hand in hand with a European supervision. Such supervision concerns both the aim of the measure challenged and its 'necessity' … The Court's supervisory functions oblige it to pay the utmost attention to the principles characterising a 'democratic society'.[176]

In 1984, the ECtHR stated in *Rasmussen v Denmark* on the subject of the margin of appreciation doctrine that the existence or non-existence of common ground between the laws of the Contracting States may be a relevant factor:

> The scope of the margin of appreciation will vary according to the circumstances, the subject-matter and its background; in this respect, one of the relevant factors may be the existence or non-existence of common ground between the laws of the Contracting States.[177]

In that case, the applicant had grounds for assuming that he was not the biological father of his two sons. Under Danish law there was a time-limit on how long a husband could contest paternity, whereas the wife was entitled to institute paternity proceedings at any time. In its assessment, the ECtHR analysed whether there was common legislation among the Convention's states parties. In fact, the

[173] Case 'Relating to Certain Aspects of the Laws on the Use of Languages in education in Belgium' v Belgium, above n 76, para 10.

[174] ibid.

[175] *Handyside v The United Kingdom*, above n 138, para 49.

[176] ibid.

[177] *Rasmussen v Denmark*, ECtHR Judgment, App No 8777/79, 28 November 1984, para 40.

legislation of Denmark differed from that of most other ECHR member states. Consequently, Denmark was 'entitled to think that the introduction of time-limits for the institution of paternity proceedings was justified'.[178]

The ECtHR clarified in *Buckley v the United Kingdom* that whether the Court steps into the domestic margin of appreciation depends on the specific context:

> The scope of this margin of appreciation is not identical in each case but will vary according to the context … Relevant factors include the nature of the Convention right in issue, its importance for the individual and the nature of the activities concerned.[179]

In *Aziz v Cyprus*, the Court noted that it is an institution of last resort, and is thus allowed to undertake judicial review of electoral power-sharing provisions in the constitution and subsequent laws.[180]

In *Ždanoka v Latvia*, the ECtHR held that national authorities 'are better placed to assess the difficulties faced in establishing and safeguarding the democratic order', particularly in cases in which the state needs to gain people's trust in new constitutional institutions due to a specific historical and political context of transition:

> Those authorities should therefore be left sufficient latitude to assess the needs of their society in building confidence in the new democratic institutions, including the national parliament, and to answer the question whether the impugned measure is still needed for these purposes, provided that the Court has found nothing arbitrary or disproportionate in such an assessment.[181]

The ECtHR scrutinised in *Ždanoka v Latvia* whether the Latvian Parliament had been periodically reviewing the relevant paragraphs in the Constitution which excluded certain citizens from running for office. The ECtHR stressed that 'new democratic institutions, including the national Parliament' should 'be left sufficient latitude to assess the needs of their society' in deciding whether a restriction was still needed.[182]

ii. Decision of the ECtHR: Granted Authority to Judge

In *Sejdić and Finci v Bosnia and Herzegovina*, the ECtHR merely concluded that:

> The scope of a Contracting Party's margin of appreciation in this sphere will vary according to the circumstances, the subject matter and the background.[183]

[178] ibid, para 41.
[179] *Buckley v The United Kingdom*, ECtHR Judgment, No 20348/92, 25 September 1996, para 74.
[180] *Aziz v Cyprus*, above n 144, para 25.
[181] *Ždanoka v Latvia*, above n 83, paras 133–34.
[182] ibid, para 134.
[183] *Sejdić and Finci v Bosnia and Herzegovina*, above n 12, para 42.

This relatively short explanation was criticised by Judge Mijović and Judge Hajiyev in their partly concurring and partly dissenting opinion, where they noted that for 'the sake of the Court's case-law, it would have been very interesting to see how far the Court would have interpreted the margin of appreciation left to the State in this case'.[184] Judge Bonello added in his dissenting opinion:

> A judicial institution so remote from the focus of dissention can hardly be the best judge of this. In traumatic revolutionary events, it is not for the Court to establish, by a process of divination, when the transitional period is over, or when a state of national emergency is past and everything is now business as usual.[185]

Bonello doubted 'that the Court is better placed than the national authorities to assess the point in time when previous fractures consolidate, when historical resentments quell and when generational discords harmonise', and found that:

> Claims such as these, arguably based on self-delusory wishful thinking, show little or no respect for the inexhaustible resources of rancour. The Court does ill to shut its mind to histories in which hate validates culture.[186]

iii. About the Critical and Crucial Role of the ECtHR

From early on, the scope of judicial review by the ECtHR has been disputed.[187] In 1979, the dissenting judges argued in the ECtHR decision *The Sunday Times v The United Kingdom* that 'the national authorities are, in principle, better qualified than an international court' for the purpose of an evaluation of facts and the 'administration of justice'.[188] They proposed that the ECtHR could only determine 'whether the national authorities have acted in good faith, with due care and in a reasonable manner when evaluating those facts and circumstances, as well as the danger that might thereby be occasioned'.[189]

[184] ibid, Partly Concurring and Partly Dissenting Opinion of Judge Mijović, joined by Judge Hajiyev, para V.

[185] ibid, Dissenting Opinion of Judge Bonello.

[186] ibid.

[187] The legal literature about limited margin of appreciation is immense. For an introduction, see James A Sweeney, 'Margins of Appreciation: Cultural Relativity and the European Court of Human Rights in the Post-Cold War Era' (2005) 54 *International and Comparative Law Quarterly* 459. See also Steven C Greer, *The Margin of Appreciation: Interpretation and Discretion under the European Convention on Human Rights* (Strasbourg, Council of Europe, 2000); Nicolas Lavender, 'The Problem of the Margin of Appreciation' (1997) 4 *European Human Rights Law Review* 382; Georg Nolte, 'General Principles of German and European Administrative Law: A Comparison in Historical Perspective' (1994) 57(2) *Modern Law Review* 191.

[188] *The Sunday Times v The United Kingdom*, above n 169, Joint Dissenting Opinion of Judges Wiarda, Cremona, Thór Vilhjálmsson, Ryssdal, Ganshof van der Meersch, Sir Gerald Fitzmaurice, Bindschedler-Robert, Liesch and Matscher, para 7.

[189] ibid, para 8.

a. Debate about Judicial Activism versus Judicial Restraint

Ever since, Strasbourg has frequently been criticised for acting like 'Europe's Constitutional Court', instead of serving purely as the European Court of Human Rights.[190] Critics point to the fact that the ECtHR has been using the margin of appreciation concept in accordance with its needs for a results-oriented jurisprudence.[191] A concern has been that the doctrine is applied in an 'elusive' way.[192] Other authors have observed that the ECtHR often uses the label of the margin of appreciation 'without stating explicitly the substantive principle upon which that conclusion is based'.[193] As Eyal Benvenisti pointed out, the inconsistent application of the doctrine in seemingly similar cases has 'raised concerns about judicial double standards'.[194]

Ignacio de la Rasilla del Moral argued that the doctrine 'mirrors an intrinsic tension' within the Convention, which is 'alternatively conceived as a fundamental instrument for the protection of human rights in Europe and as a mechanism within the political framework of the underlying European integration process'.[195] In its practice, the ECtHR treats cases with the notion that it is generally competent to decide questions about common European human rights standards.[196] As Jan Helgesen, former President of the Venice Commission, recalled, the ECtHR has been a reliable safeguard mechanism for the enforcement of human rights:

> If one wishes to defend the Court, one must remember that if the Court would refrain from being active and creating new norms, there would be no normative development at all. The Court cannot, like a domestic Supreme Court or Constitutional Court, leave the challenge to develop norms to the legislator. The ECtHR cannot leave the legislative action to the States. They will certainly not act. This is a very important difference from the parallel discussion within a domestic political system.[197]

Indeed, states concerned often respond with reluctance to decisions which do not favour their positions. However, it is the very *raison d'être* of the ECtHR

[190] For the debate about judicial activism, judicial self-restraint and subsidiarity in human rights adjunction, see Paul Mahoney, 'Judicial Activism and Judicial Self-Restraint in the European Court of Human Rights: Two Sides of the Same Coin' (1990) 11 *Human Rights Law Journal* 57. See also Dragoljub Popovic, 'Prevailing of Judicial Activism over Self-Restraint in the Jurisprudence of the European Court of Human Rights' (2008–2009) 42(3) *Creighton Law Review* 361.

[191] 'The Universality of Human Rights', Speech by Lord Hoffmann at the Judicial Studies Board Annual Lecture 2009, 19 March 2009, para 27.

[192] Lester Lord of Herne Hill, 'Universality Versus Subsidiarity: A Reply' (1998) 1 *European Human Rights Law Review* 75.

[193] George Letsas, 'Two Concepts of the Margin of Appreciation' (2006) 26 *Oxford Journal of Legal Studies* 705.

[194] Eyal Benvenisti, 'Margin of Appreciation, Consensus, and Universal Standards' (1999) 31 *International Law and Politics* 844.

[195] Ignacio de la Rasilla del Moral, 'The Increasingly Marginal Appreciation of the Margin of Appreciation Doctrine' (2006) 7(6) *German Law Journal* 621.

[196] Speech by Lord Hoffmann, above n 191, para 43.

[197] 'What are the Limits to the Evolutive Interpretation of the Convention?', Speech by Jan E Helgesen at the European Court of Human Rights in Strasbourg, 28 January 2011, 5.

to defend human rights. Following this way of thinking, judicial activism is reframed as a duty to protect the values of the Convention on the basis of a majority consensus among its member states.

b. Following State Consensus

As in *Rasmussen v Denmark*, the ECtHR could have probed whether similar patterns of practice or regulation exist among the member states to the Convention.[198] This 'common ground test' or 'European consensus criterion' assesses whether there is common legislation and a joint understanding of ethnic power-sharing among states parties to the Convention.[199] The absence of a European consensus normally indicates that a wider margin of appreciation will be accorded to the state.[200]

In *Sejdić and Finci v Bosnia and Herzegovina*, the ECtHR did not address the European consensus criterion explicitly. Nonetheless, the Amicus Curiae Briefs of the Advice on Individual Rights in Europe (AIRE) Centre and the Open Society Justice Initiative provided an opinion on the matter: AIRE drew attention to the experience of post-World War II practice in Western Europe and post-communist countries in Central and Eastern Europe, where those who were associated with previous regimes were excluded from applying for certain public posts.[201] Other causes for exclusion from public posts have been criminal sanctions, restrictions based on age, mental capacity and citizenship, none of which were for ethnic reasons.[202] Thus, AIRE concluded, 'the European consensus on the practice of withdrawing an individual's right to stand for office is that such a decision must be based on the individual's conduct, as opposed to innate or inalienable characteristics'.[203] The Open Society Justice Initiative highlighted that 'no other European country, not even the other post-conflict countries of former Yugoslavia, totally excludes citizens of specific national minorities from active political participation', only Bosnia and Herzegovina.[204] The Amicus Curiae Brief of the Open Society Justice Initiative therefore reasoned that the margin of appreciation granted 'cannot extend so far as to permit the present exclusionary and discriminatory measures'.[205]

Indeed, although power-sharing systems in Europe, such as those in Northern Ireland, Belgium and Macedonia, include minority vetoes and quotas, no other constitution among the Council of Europe Member States entails a de jure

[198] *Rasmussen v Denmark*, above n 177, para 40.
[199] For details, see Rasilla del Moral, above n 195, 621.
[200] ibid, 617.
[201] Amicus Curiae Brief in the Cases Sejdić and Finci v Bosnia and Herzegovina, App Nos 27996/06 and 34836/06, The AIRE Centre, 15 August 2008, para 20.
[202] ibid, paras 2, 18.
[203] ibid, ¶ 3.
[204] Amicus Curiae Brief in the Cases Sejdić and Finci v Bosnia and Herzegovina, App No 27996/06 and 34836/06, Open Society Justice Initiative, 15 August 2008, paras 43–44.
[205] ibid.

exclusion of certain ethnic groups from running for Presidency or taking a seat in the Parliament.[206] Kosovo's constitutional framework imitated and extended the ethnic power-sharing solution for the Balkans, but Kosovo is not yet a member of the Council of Europe.[207] In Macedonia, the Ohrid Framework Agreement amended the constitution with affirmative ethnic power-sharing quotas to reflect the role of Albanians as a constituent ethnicity and introduced elements of decentralisation, but did not install an exclusive power-sharing system as the Dayton Accords did for Bosnia and Herzegovina.[208] In the Russian Federation, elements of ethnic federalism exist, such as decisions on economic, cultural and environmental issues in Tatarstan; however, territorial power-sharing in Russia does not restrict legislative or executive bodies like the Dayton Peace Agreement does.[209]

At this point, one can reasonably argue in two directions. On the one hand, the absence of ethnic power-sharing in most states suggests a European consensus that discrimination has to be avoided. On the other hand, the ECtHR could have upheld that Bosnia and Herzegovina has the only exclusive, ethnic power-sharing constitution, which can indicate a wider margin of appreciation accorded to the state. Speaking out about those nuances could have substantiated the judgment and made it more solid.

c. Constitutional Review in Post-Conflict Transitions

Systemically, *Sejdić and Finci v Bosnia and Herzegovina* falls into the pattern of ECtHR decisions concerning states in post-conflict transition. As the experience of other Central and East European states shows, the ECtHR has developed its jurisprudence towards a quasi-constitutional role, fixing systemic legal defects.[210] Instead of being a 'fine-tuner' of human rights, the Court has become a 'scrutiniser of failing legal and political systems' intervening in fundamental policy domains, as Wojciech Sadurski phrased it.[211]

[206] Matthijs Bogaard, 'Democracy and Power-Sharing in Multinational States: Thematic Introduction' (2006) 8(2) *International Journal on Multicultural Societies* 123.

[207] For a comparative overview, see Florian Bieber, 'Power Sharing as Ethnic Representation in Post-Conflict Societies: The Cases of Bosnia, Macedonia and Kosovo' in Alina Mungiu-Pippidi and Ivan Krastev (eds), *Nationalism after Communism: Lessons Learned* (Budapest, CEU Press, 2004) 229.

[208] Karl Cordell and Stefan Wolf (eds), *Ethnic Conflict* (Cambridge, Polity Press, 2010) 206.

[209] Bill Bowring, 'The Russian Constitutional System: Complexity and Asymmetry' in Marc Weller and Katherine Nobbs (eds), *Asymmetric Autonomy and the Settlement of Ethnic Conflicts* (Philadelphia, University of Pennsylvania Press, 2010) 48.

[210] Oreste Pollicino, 'The New Relationship between National and the European Courts after the Enlargement of Europe: Towards a Unitary Theory of Jurisprudential Supranational Law?' (2010) 29(1) *Yearbook of European Law* 65.

[211] Wojciech Sadurski, 'Partnering with Strasbourg: Constitutionalisation of the European Court of Human Rights, the Accession of Central and East European States to the Council of Europe, and the Idea of Pilot Judgments' (2009) 9(3) *Human Rights Law Review* 397.

The overall challenge in this context is that there are no universal rules in international law for the margin of appreciation.[212] As in *Ždanoka v Latvia*, the ECtHR could have acknowledged in *Sejdić and Finci v Bosnia and Herzegovina* that the legislature was still reviewing the relevant discriminatory provisions of the Constitution.[213] Indeed, the constitutional reform process in Bosnia and Herzegovina has been deadlocked; nonetheless, the ongoing debate in the country reflects domestic political engagement and not necessarily indifference towards human rights.

Loukis Loucaides stated that, in practice, the Court was reluctant 'to find violations in sensitive matters affecting the interests of the respondent states'.[214] Other scholars also noted that the margin doctrine is 'particularly generous with regard to actions which domestic authorities regard as critical to the prevention of disorder'.[215] In previous cases, the ECtHR has usually given member states a wide margin of appreciation in highly contentious issues.[216] Conceptually, the margin of appreciation doctrine aims to prevent a loss of the Court's legitimacy and credibility.[217] All this should have alerted the judges in *Sejdić and Finci v Bosnia and Herzegovina* to the need for hesitation, caution or at least more elaboration.

V. Post-trial Developments and Constitutional Reform Process

Legally, the ECtHR decision *Sejdić and Finci v Bosnia and Herzegovina* obliges Bosnia and Herzegovina to abide by the judgment, which ultimately requires a reform of the Constitution.[218]

In autumn 2009, just before the release of the judgment, an EU-US initiative put forward a draft for constitutional changes, but no agreement emerged.[219] Shortly after the ruling in December 2009, the Council of Ministers adopted an action plan for the implementation of the ECtHR decision and formed an inter-institutional working group in March 2010. In July 2011, Sulcjman Tihic

[212] Yuval Shany, 'Toward a General Margin of Appreciation Doctrine in International Law?' (2005) 16(5) *European Journal of International Law* 907.

[213] *Ždanoka v Latvia*, above n 83, paras 133–34.

[214] Loukis G Loucaides, 'Reflections of a Former European Court of Human Rights Judge on his Experiences as a Judge' (2010) 1 *Roma Rights* 64.

[215] Gregory H Fox and Georg Nolte, 'Intolerant Democracies' (1995) 36(1) *Harvard International Law Journal* 48.

[216] Letsas, above n 193, 705. See also Karen Reid, *A Practitioner's Guide to the European Convention on Human Rights* (London, Thomson/Sweet & Maxwell, 2008) 33.

[217] Benvenisti, above n 194, 843.

[218] ECHR, Art 46, para 1.

[219] Bosnia and Herzegovina 2010 Progress Report, European Commission, Doc 2010SEC(2010) 1331, 9 November 2010, 8. For an overview of previous efforts to change the Dayton Constitution, see Joseph Marko, 'Constitutional Reform in Bosnia and Herzegovina' (2005/06) 5 *European Yearbook of Minority Issues Online* 207.

made the ECtHR decision *Sejdić and Finci v Bosnia and Herzegovina* part of a package deal for a coalition of his Party of Democratic Action with the Social Democratic Party and the Croatian Democratic Union.[220] In 2011, the Parliamentary Assembly of Bosnia and Herzegovina established an Interim Joint Committee to agree on amendments to implement the ECtHR decision.[221]

In 2013, Report of the High Representative of the European Union highlighted in February 2013, constitutional reforms are conditional for the entering into force of the EU Stabilization and Association Agreement.[222] In 2014, the German and UK foreign ministers proposed to move on with the European integration process of Bosnia and Herzegovina without first implementing the constitutional amendments required by *Sejdić and Finci* as a precondition as long as there is commitment of the Government to implement the required reforms. Although various political and legislative efforts were taken since to make progress, the implementation of the *Sejdić and Finci* ECtHR decision is still pending.[223]

VI. Conclusion

US Ambassador Richard Holbrooke, who was one of the co-chairs of the Dayton peace conference, publicly admitted that the solution found was 'imperfect':

> I agree the agreement was deeply flawed. The country is one country divided into two or three administrations, it is an administrative mess and there were plenty of problems at Dayton …, but the underlying point is that our goal was to end a war.[224]

Holebrook commented that the three-headed 'presidency based on ethnicity is undemocratic'.[225] However, at that moment in time, the Dayton compromise appeared to be the most feasible option.

A. Human Rights and Temporal Limitations of Post-Conflict Transitions

In *Sejdić and Finci v Bosnia and Herzegovina*, the ECtHR restated that a justification of human rights restrictions must be assessed in relation to the public aim and proportionality of the measure under consideration. Particularly with

[220] 'Bosnia Edges Closer to State Government Deal' *Balkan Insight* (28 July 2011).
[221] 40th Report of the High Representative for Implementation of the Peace Agreement on Bosnia and Herzegovina to the Secretary-General of the United Nations, 15 November 2011.
[222] UN Doc S/2013/90, above n 5, para 4.
[223] Status January 2019.
[224] 'In Memoriam: Richard Holbrooke on Dayton Agreement', *Dayton Council of World Affairs*, Speech by Richard Holbrooke, 17 November 2005.
[225] 'A New Constitution for Bosnia', above n 3.

regard to peace processes, this acknowledgment of sometimes 'necessary discrimination' is realistic; it is a reasonable legal balance in transitional periods from conflict to consolidated peace. As the judgment demonstrates, what is problematic is not *whether* human rights restrictions can be justified, but *for how long*. It is significant that the ECtHR did not simply dismiss the attempt to justify ethnic-racial discrimination with the argument that international human rights law tends to be resistant to accepting differential treatment based on ethnic or racial grounds. The Court rather exemplifies that in the context of human rights and minority protection in states of transition the prohibition of ethnic-racial discrimination is temporarily softened. As the development of ECtHR jurisprudence shows, the aspect of time and temporality is increasingly gaining importance in the evaluation of human rights restrictions, which is also visible in the *Sejdić and Finci* case.[226] As the decision demonstrates, exceptional reasons can justify differential treatment for the sake of peace.[227] For instance, the restoration of peace can take precedence over equality and the prohibition of discrimination. However, measures in question must remain temporary in order to be proportionate. The commitment of a state to human rights law urges adherence to it, even in moments of enormous post-conflict uncertainty.[228]

B. The Prohibition of Discrimination as a Continuous Challenge

Beyond the context of post-conflict periods, the *Sejdić and Finci* case is a reminder of the fact that discrimination is a continuing challenge for states. In this regard, even states without a history of civil war are to a certain degree 'in transition' while they are constantly striving towards a better protection of human rights. The reality in Europe shows that ethnic-racial discrimination is regrettably not only an issue in temporary post-conflict constellations. In 2010, the EU Fundamental Rights Agency found in its Focus Report on Multiple Discrimination that ethnic minorities in EU Member States are on average almost five times more likely to experience multiple discrimination than those from the majority ethnicity.[229] 'Ethnicity or immigrant origin consistently emerges as the most significant ground for experiencing discrimination among ethnic minorities and immigrants ... more than other grounds such as age or gender', the report states.[230] In 2011, the Council

[226] For the prior conceptual debate about 'Transitional Jurisprudence' of the ECtHR regarding human rights in post-conflict state-transitions see Ch 2, Part VI.G.

[227] This approach in international practice reveals a legal complexity that exceeds Levitt's explanations about 'illegal peace' regarding post-conflict power-sharing agreements. See Jeremy I Levitt, *Illegal Peace in Africa: An Inquiry into the Legality of Power Sharing with Warlords, Rebels, and Junta* (Cambridge, Cambridge University Press, 2012).

[228] *Sejdić and Finci v Bosnia and Herzegovina*, above n 12, para 49.

[229] European Union Agency for Fundamental Rights, EU-MIDIS 5 Data in Focus Report: Multiple Discrimination, 2010, 4.

[230] ibid.

of Europe Commissioner for Human Rights wrote in his Report on Human Rights in Europe that 'there is a need to counter hypocrisy', since 'some governments belittle or cover up their own shortcomings while using human rights as a propaganda tool against other states'.[231] As he observed, 'national pride' often 'trumps', leading to a 'growing problem' in Europe: racism, xenophobia, Islamophobia, anti-Semitism, homophobia, transphobia and other phobias directed against others who are considered 'different' by the majority group.[232] In 2012, the Eurobarometer on perceptions of discrimination in the EU confirmed that discrimination is 'still considered to be common in the EU member states', while the 'most widely perceived ground is "ethnic origin"'.[233] With this in mind, overcoming ethnic-racial discrimination becomes imperative in any context. It explains that the abolishment of discrimination is eventually a continuous long-term effort. This circumstance puts the temporal factor into a wider perspective.

C. Constitutional Change, Peacemaking and the Role of Courts

Concerning the role of local and international judiciary for post-conflict state transitions, the ECtHR *Sejdić and Finci* decision and the prior judgments of Bosnia and Herzegovina's Constitutional Court reveal how judicial processes can be used to either protect conflict settlements or enable alterations to them. The *Sejdić and Finci* case highlights that international courts have a crucial function in pushing for change from the outside, when an internal stalemate is blocking reforms. At the same time, as explained in the analysis of the margin of appreciation, the ECtHR has been heavily criticised for taking the approach of a quasi-constitutional court.[234] In *Sejdić and Finci*, the dissenting judge Bonello went so far to say that the judgment disgraced the constitution, describing the decision as 'an exercise in star-struck mirage-building which neglects to factor in the rivers of blood that fertilised the Dayton Constitution'.[235] Similarly, Judge Borrego argued in his dissenting opinion in *DH and Others v the Czech Republic* that 'the hearing room of the Grand Chamber had become an ivory tower, divorced from the life and problems' of the concerned people.[236]

[231] Human Rights in Europe: No Grounds for Complacency, Viewpoints by Thomas Hammarberg Council of Europe Commissioner for Human Rights, April 2011, 10.
[232] ibid, 11.
[233] Discrimination in the EU in 2012, Eurobarometer, No 393, European Commission, November 2012, 5.
[234] See Part IV.F above.
[235] *Sejdić and Finci v Bosnia and Herzegovina*, above n 12, Dissenting Opinion of Judge Bonello.
[236] *DH and Others v the Czech Republic*, above n 52, Dissenting Opinion of Judge Borrego, para 10.

Ultimately, decisions about human rights are value judgements and a matter of choice.[237] As Robert Keeton wrote, 'people call judges good not because they are good at logic but because they are good at making hard choices'.[238] The *Sejdić and Finci* case illustrates that international court rooms are arenas for unsolved disputes of the greatest political gravity. Although constitutional adjustments cannot be imposed, they may be provoked from the court bench. Yet, judges have to be careful of turning into lawmakers when deciding questions of law.[239] International courts are maybe not the best places to decide about a state's constitutional design and its transition. Nonetheless, they are often the last resort to motivate dialogue and catalyse change.

[237] Egbert Willem Viergang, *The Concept of Discrimination in International Law: With Special Reference to Human Rights* (The Hague, Martinus Nijhoff Publishers, 1973) 15. For an overview of the scholarly debate on the matter, see Arnardóttir, above n 93, 13. See also Louise Mulder, 'How Positive Can Equality Measures Be?' in Titia Loenen and Peter R Rodrigues (eds), *Non-Discrimination Law: Comparative Perspectives* (The Hague, Kluwer Law International, 1999) 65.

[238] Robert E Keeton, *Judging* (St Paul, Minn, West Publishing Co, 1990) 2.

[239] Frederic Reynold, *The Judge as Lawmaker* (London, MacGibbon & Kee, 1967) 7. See also Patrick Delvin, *The Judge* (Oxford, Oxford University Press, 1979) 1.

4

Through the Lens of Human Rights Committees

Lebanese Political Confessionalism and Transitional Mechanism

I. State Stability, Sectarian Traditions and Socio-Political Change

Peace is still fragile in Lebanon. As much as political confessionalism aims to hold the country together, it also tears it apart.[1] While Lebanon has been a home for various religious groups, it remains a place of conflict at the crossroads of Europe, Africa and Asia. External political dynamics regularly impact on the state's stability, triggering internal friction and reactivating long-standing feuds. The signing of the Taif Peace Agreement marked the end of the Lebanese Civil War. Yet the 15-year-long armed conflict casts its shadow into the present, stoking fears of a renewed outbreak whenever heavy disagreements between political fractions arise. Although the peace accord declared a gradual phasing-out of confessionalism, the country is still far away from changing its existing structures. In 2008, the Doha Agreement Lebanese Dialogue Conference in Qatar showed that the vow of unity and sectarian balance is still perceived to be essential for the country's survival; however, it also appears to be its curse.

A. Demonstrations for Secularism (2010–2012)

Over the last few years, public calls for secularism as an alternative to sectarianism have been increasing. In 2010, a 'Laique Pride' brought thousands of people onto the streets of Beirut to demonstrate for a shift towards secularism.[2]

[1] For an introduction on power-sharing in Lebanon, see Ch 2, Part III.C.

[2] 'Lebanese Stage First Pro-secular Demonstration' *Al Arabiya News* (25 April 2010). See also 'Lebanese March in Beirut to Demand Secularism' *BBC News* (25 April 2010).

Demonstrators argued that Lebanon's sectarian system needs to be abolished as it is the root of national strife and breeds corruption.[3] In 2011, an estimated 20,000 people joined together for a protest against political sectarianism, which became the largest demonstration for secularism in Lebanon's history.[4] The gathering followed the wave of popular uprisings in the Arab region.[5] In 2012, activists revived the anti-sectarianism campaign, but only 400 people heeded the call to re-launch the anti-sectarian movement.[6] The developments show how difficult it is to overcome the political rules of a country, despite the aspiration to change.

B. First Civil Marriage in Lebanon (2013)

At the beginning of 2013, attention was drawn by the first civil marriage in Lebanon, which challenged the social side of the confessional system. Lebanon still lacks a civil personal status law.[7] Previously, reform proposals introducing civil marriage had been shelved due to the opposition of the country's religious authorities.[8] In November 2012, a Lebanese couple took the initiative to sign their civil marriage contract without registering the marriage at a Muslim religious tribunal.[9] Kholoud Succariyeh and Nidal Darwish crossed out the confessional affiliation from their identity cards to prove before the law that they were not affiliated with any sect. Finally, they submitted a request to the Consultations Committee at the Ministry of the Interior for acknowledgement of their secular marriage. Their application was initially dismissed, but was later approved.[10]

[3] Patrick Galey, 'Thousands March in Beirut to Promote Secularism in Politics' *The Daily Star (Lebanon)* (26 April 2010).

[4] Simona Sikimic, 'Laique Demonstrators Call for Secular State' *The Daily Star (Lebanon)* (16 May 2011).

[5] Brooke Anderson, 'Anti-sectarian Protesters Revamp Movement' *The Daily Star (Lebanon)* (26 June 2011). See also Emma Gatten, 'Anti-sectarian Spring Ended as Summer Began' *The Daily Star (Lebanon)* (2 November 2011).

[6] Emma Gatten, 'Activists Reawaken Anti-Sectarianism Campaign' *The Daily Star (Lebanon)* (27 February 2012).

[7] Traditionally, religious sects decide independently about their status laws. See Ch 2, Part III.C.

[8] For an overview, see 'Lebanon's Sleiman Calls for Legalizing Civil Marriage' *The Daily Star (Lebanon)* (23 January 2013). See also Marie Dhumieres, 'Civil Marriages on the Rise Amongst Lebanese' *The Daily Star (Lebanon)* (7 September 2011).

[9] Arwa Al-Husseini, 'Lebanon's First Civil Marriage' *NOW Lebanon* (18 January 2013).

[10] In February 2013, the Higher Committee for Consultations in the Justice Ministry deemed the concept of civil marriage legal. According to the Committee's ruling, a public notary is entitled to uphold the marriage of Lebanese citizens who do not belong to any sect, or who have removed sectarian affiliations from their official documents. In April 2013, Lebanon's Interior Minister Marwan Charbel approved the couple's application to register their marriage. See 'Charbel Insists Civil Marriage Couple Keep Sects' *The Daily Star (Lebanon)* (26 April 2013); 'Ministers, Judges Discuss Legalization of Civil Marriage' *The Daily Star (Lebanon)* (22 February 2013).

Lebanon's President called for a resumption of the debate about legalising civil marriage in Lebanon, seeing it as an 'important step in eradicating sectarianism and solidifying national unity'.[11] However, reform efforts failed, given the lack of consensus among political parties.[12] The debate demonstrates that a change of Lebanon's confessional power-sharing structures is still unattainable.

C. Electoral Law Reform Proposals (2013)

The discussion about the civil status law coincided with the ongoing talks about the reform of the electoral law prior to the general elections, which were scheduled for summer 2013. The aim was to find a modus that guarantees 'fair representation' while abolishing sectarian notions.[13] Prime Minister Mikati announced that an electoral law was needed 'that represents the unity of the Lebanese and not a law that creates a further divide among them'.[14]

Several reform drafts were discussed: One of the proposals was to divide Lebanon into 13 districts based on a proportional representation system.[15] Another draft law proposed by the March 14 bloc advocated 50 smaller districts based on a winner-takes-all system. The so-called 'Orthodox proposal', which has garnered the support of the four major Christian parties from within both the March 14 and March 8 coalitions, suggested that candidates should be voted for based on one electoral district for the whole country. Opponents to this proposal argued that it would only widen sectarian differences among the Lebanese. Which direction the electoral reform process will actually take is still unclear.

D. International Law, Human Rights and Legal Challenges

This chapter focuses on how international human rights monitoring bodies treat power-sharing provisions. The debate in the UN Committee on the Elimination of Racial Discrimination (CERD) about Lebanon illustrates that legal limitations on peacemaking entail ambiguities but also clear parameters. The practice of the

[11] 'Lebanon's First Request for Civil Marriage Rejected: Interior Minister' *Al Arabiya News* (21 January 2013).

[12] 'Mikati Says Debate on Civil Marriage Useless in Face of Political Paralysis' *The Daily Star (Lebanon)* (23 January 2013).

[13] 'Lebanon Committee Focusing on Boutros Electoral Law' *YaLibnan* (22 January 2013).

[14] 'Miqati Urges Politicians to be Reasonable: Says Electoral Law Takes Lebanon to Shores of Safety' *Naharnet* (16 January 2013).

[15] For an overview, see Arda Arsenian, *Confessional and Electoral Reform in Lebanon*, The Aspen Institute, Briefing Paper, July 2012, 3.

human rights bodies give directions about the standards of international law for states in transition.

The first part of this chapter gives an overview about the CERD reports submitted by Lebanon. The second part summarises the concluding observations of the Committee. The third part assesses conditions of racial discrimination and limits of confessional power-sharing. As comparative cases, the CERD considerations concerning Belgium, India and Switzerland are taken into consideration. The fourth part scrutinises the practice of transitional governments and quotas of high level posts in the light of the right to participation. The fifth part analyses the normative framework for justifying potential human rights restrictions. Finally, the chapter closes with a reflection on the current secular movements in the Middle East and Northern Africa, human rights and the imperfection of constitutional change.

II. Reports Submitted by Lebanon to the Committee on the Elimination of Racial Discrimination

Historically, CERD was among the first international human rights monitoring bodies. It consists of independent experts who review the implementation of the Convention in each of the signatory countries, based on country reports prepared every two years by the states parties.[16] Experts are supposed to serve impartially, in their personal capacity.[17] Although their concluding observations do not create international law, the recommendations of the expert Committee do give indications about the collective interpretation of international law.[18]

After signing the International Convention on the Elimination of All Forms of Racial Discrimination (ICERD) in 1971, Lebanon has submitted 17 reports to CERD.[19] Throughout its reports, the Government has said that the Taif Peace Agreement was 'a first step in the return to peace', but instability and regional tensions continued making confessionalism power-sharing necessary.[20]

[16] See ICERD, Art 8, para 1 and Art 9, para 1.

[17] CERD, General Recommendation No 9: Independence of Experts (Art 8, para 1), 23 August 1990.

[18] Michael O'Flaherty, 'The Concluding Observations of United Nations Human Rights Treaty Bodies' (2006) 6(1) *Human Rights Law Review* 27.

[19] See Tables 1 and 2. In its last concluding observations, the Committee recommended that Lebanon should prepare its next periodic report by December 2006. However, no further reports have yet been submitted.

[20] UN Doc HRI/CORE/1/Add.27, 12 May 1993, para 27. See also UN Doc HRI/CORE/1/Add.27/Rev.1, 3 October 1996.

Table 1 Lebanon's history of ratifying ICERD, ICCPR, ICESCR and CEDAW

Convention	Ratification by Lebanon	Entry into force	Declarations and reservations
ICERD (1965/1969)	12 November 1971	12 December 1971	Declaration regarding ICERD, Article 22: ICJ procedures in disputes of interpretation
ICCPR (1966/1976)	3 November 1972	23 May 1976	
ICESCR (1966/1976)	3 November 1972	3 January 1976	
CEDAW (1979)	16 April 1997	16 May 1997	Reservations regarding Article 9(2), and Article 16(1)(c), (d), (f) and (g) (right to choose a family name) Declaration regarding ICERD, Article 29, para 1: arbitration and ICJ procedures in disputes of interpretation

Table 2 CERD reports submitted by Lebanon (1972–2004)

Report	**UN Doc**	**Date**
1st report (initial report)	CERD/C/R.33/Add.4	5 December 1972
Addendum	CERD/C/R.33/Add.13	31 July 1975
2nd–5th reports	CERD/C/65/Add.4	12 December 1980
6th–13th reports	CERD/C/298/Add.2	6 November 1997
14th–16th reports	CERD/C/383/Add.2	18 November 2003
17th report	CERD/C/475/Add.1	25 February 2004
18th report	Not yet submitted	due December 2006
19th report	Not yet submitted	due December 2008
20th report	Not yet submitted	due December 2010
21st report	Not yet submitted	due December 2012

A. Summary of Lebanon's 1st–5th CERD Reports (1972–1980)

In 1972, Lebanon's first CERD report comprised merely two sentences, stating that Lebanese law 'prohibits racial and religious discrimination', and that the

Constitution 'guarantees the rights of all Lebanese citizens, irrespective of sect'.[21] Just a few months after the beginning of the Lebanese Civil War in 1975, an addendum was submitted that announced that Lebanon's past struggle made the country 'a land or even an "oasis" of freedom governed by a juridical order'.[22] In autumn 1980, Lebanon's second CERD submission came when the second phase of the armed conflict was at its peak.[23]

i. Lebanon: A Country of Religious Minorities

Perhaps euphemistically, the 1980 report claimed that Lebanon 'has always stood out as a haven of freedom'.[24] The report remarked that the 'predo2minant feature of the population of Lebanon is its pluralism'.[25] Lebanon needed to be understood as 'country of religious minorities which have decided to live together within the framework of a unitary State'.[26]

The Lebanese Government admitted that the confessional system 'could be interpreted as introducing inequalities between citizens depending on whether they belonged to a given religious community'.[27] However, confessional proportions should not be perceived as discrimination, but as 'special features' particular to the Lebanese regime, as this 'religious infrastructure' formed the basis of society in Lebanon.[28]

ii. Equal Access to Public Service Posts

Concerning the confessional distribution of public posts, the 1980 report upheld that the right to equal access to public service posts was formally guaranteed under the Constitution. Religious quotas were seen as 'necessary to observe a certain balance in the representation of religious communities'.[29] The Lebanese Government stressed that the Constitution explicitly stipulated confessional quotas 'as an interim measure'; all communities 'shall be equitably represented in public employment and in the composition of the Government, provided that the well-being of the State is not prejudiced thereby'.[30]

[21] UN Doc CERD/C/R.33/Add.4, 5 December 1972.
[22] UN Doc CERD/C/R.33/Add.13, 31 July 1975.
[23] UN Doc CERD/C/65/Add.4, 12 December 1980.
[24] ibid, para 2.
[25] ibid, para 3.
[26] ibid.
[27] ibid.
[28] ibid, paras 3–4.
[29] ibid, para 8.
[30] ibid.

B. Summary of Lebanon's 6th–13th CERD Reports (1997)

Given the Lebanese Civil War from 1975 to 1990 and its aftermath of interventions, the Lebanese Government had to delay the submission of its first consolidated CERD report until 1997.[31]

In the updated report, the central issue was whether Lebanon's system of political confessionalism constituted 'racial discrimination', as prohibited by the Convention.[32] Also discussed was whether power-sharing in Lebanon could be regarded as a 'special measure' under the ICERD.[33] As laid down in the Convention, special measures can be taken for the protection of certain racial or ethnic groups to secure adequate advancement of their rights.

Table 3 ICERD definition of discrimination and special measures

Issue	Article	Provision
Definition of 'racial discrimination'	ICERD, Article 1, para 1	'In this Convention, the term "racial discrimination" shall mean any distinction, exclusion, restriction or preference based on race, colour, descent, or national or ethnic origin which has the purpose or effect of nullifying or impairing the recognition, enjoyment or exercise, on an equal footing, of human rights and fundamental freedoms in the political, economic, social, cultural or any other field of public life'.
Definition of 'special measures'	ICERD, Article 1, para 4	'Special measures taken for the sole purpose of securing adequate advancement of certain racial or ethnic groups or individuals requiring such protection as may be necessary in order to ensure such groups or individuals equal enjoyment or exercise of human rights and fundamental freedoms shall not be deemed racial discrimination, provided, however, that such measures do not, as a consequence, lead to the maintenance of separate rights for different racial groups and that they shall not be continued after the objectives for which they were taken have been achieved'.

i. The Confessional System as a Transitional 'Special Measure'

In its report submitted in 1997, Lebanon's Government argued that the Lebanese community-based system neither creates a distinction related to descent nor

[31] UN Doc CERD/C/298/Add.2, 6 November 1997.
[32] ICERD, Art 1, para 1. See Table 3.
[33] ICERD, Art 1, para 4. See UN Doc CERD/C/298/Add.2, above n 31, para 21.

to national or ethnic origin, as mentioned in the wording of the Convention. Religious communities cannot be equated to ethnic groups. Distinctions 'created by the religious system were not meant, in the eyes of the founding fathers of the Lebanese Republic, to constitute discrimination', but 'originally intended both to protect all the groups making up the Lebanese people and to ensure them all equal chances of development and progress'.[34]

In 'the spirit of' a special measure, the equitable representation of religious communities was intended to be of transitional nature.[35] The elimination of confessionalism could only be achieved gradually, as 'many people have tended to view the system as a means of securing civil peace among the Lebanese'.[36]

ii. Promotion of Non-Discrimination, Freedom of Movement and Compliance with Other ICERD Obligations

With regard to the obligation in the ICERD, whereby state parties have to discourage anything which tends to strengthen racial division, the 1997 report claimed that the electoral division of Lebanon into the governorates, at the time, provided for a 'sufficiently broad spectrum of creeds'.[37] The Government stressed that Lebanese citizens were 'invited to vote not just for the candidates of their creed as in the past, but for other candidates as well'.[38]

Concerning the right to freedom of movement and residence, the report stated that the Lebanese Constitution guarantees that every citizen has the right to reside in any part of the territory.[39] The Government noted that it was implementing far-reaching programmes in order to remedy the enforced geographical distribution of the Lebanese population according to individual religious affiliation following the Lebanese Civil War.[40]

It was also found that at no point in its history had Lebanon promoted or permitted the propagation of racial or ethnic superiority.[41] The Lebanese Government reiterated that 'no provision of Lebanese law distinguishes between races or individuals on the grounds of colour or of national or ethnic origin'.[42]

iii. Right to Marriage and Non-Discrimination

The 1997 report also clarified that marriages 'between members of different branches of the same religion, Muslim or Christian, are [actually] common,

[34] ibid, para 21.
[35] ibid.
[36] UN Doc CERD/C/298/Add.2, above n 31, para 25.
[37] ibid, para 29.
[38] ibid.
[39] ibid, para 44.
[40] ibid, para 45.
[41] ibid, para 32.
[42] ibid, para 35.

except for the Druze community, which practices endogamy'.[43] The report went on to say that mixed Muslim-Christian marriages are generally discouraged by the family and so are de facto relatively rare; however, there is *de jure* no obstacle to the freedom of marriage. Although the concept of a civil marriage and civil personal status laws do not exist in Lebanon, civil marriages confirmed abroad are recognised by Lebanese authorities and Lebanese civil courts apply foreign personal status laws.[44]

C. Summary of Lebanon's 14th–17th CERD Reports (2002–2004)

Submitted in 2002, the combined 14th–16th reports were solely a copy of Lebanon's 1997 CERD submission.[45] Two years later in 2004, Lebanon's 17th report contained a few additional general remarks. The Lebanese Government vehemently reemphasised that the Christian-Muslim quota in place aimed 'to safeguard and strengthen national unity'.[46]

i. Confessionalism, Communities and Ethnicity

In its concluding remarks on the 1997 CERD report, the Committee stated that the recognition of Syrians, Greeks, Armenians, Copts, Kurds and Jews as communities and religions 'might constitute grounds for different treatment of these communities, including, in some instances, racial discrimination', as there is no 'recognition of the different ethnic origin of some of them'.[47] In its 2004 report, the Lebanese Government responded that the fact that no mention is made of the ethnic origin of other communities, by saying that it was actually 'the very opposite of racial discrimination'.[48] While some communities do have a distinct ethnic origin, this 'is not taken into consideration in the prevailing political and legislative system', and this focuses mainly on a balance between Christians and Muslims.[49]

The Lebanese Government stressed that, most importantly, the Constitution did not define any religion as the State religion. Instead, confessionalism did not give preference to any religious group. The purpose of political confessionalism in Lebanon was solely 'to provide reassurance to all groups' that 'none of them is excluded from the country's legislative and administrative life'.[50]

[43] ibid, para 49.
[44] ibid, para 51.
[45] UN Doc CERD/C/383/Add.2, 18 November 2003.
[46] UN Doc CERD/C/475/Add.1, 25 February 2004, para 4.
[47] UN Doc CERD/C/304/Add.49, 30 March 1998, para 12.
[48] UN Doc CERD/C/475/Add.1, above n 46, para 5.
[49] ibid.
[50] ibid, para 8.

ii. Questions of Time and the Duration of Transition

On the duration of confessionalism as a transitional measure, the Lebanese Government restated that the elimination of confessionalism 'is expected to take some time and must be done with care, since what is at stake is civil peace in the country'.[51] There 'can be no harm in waiting', insofar as the preservation of confessionalism aims to serve civil peace.[52] Yet, the Government conceded that political confessionalism should only be 'temporary'.[53]

III. Debate in the Committee on the Elimination of Racial Discrimination

CERD considered the reports on Lebanon in several sessions from 1991 to 2004, which led to heated debates between its members on the interpretation of discrimination, matters of equality and the temporary nature of special measures.

A. Consideration of the 1st–5th Periodic Reports (1991–1996)

In 1991, CERD scrutinised Lebanon's power-sharing system only tangentially. Rüdiger Wolfrum, who was the country rapporteur on Lebanon at that time, raised the concern that previous reports had only provided very general information about Lebanon's demographic composition, given that the last census had been held in 1932.[54] He questioned the confessional quota on the grounds that 'some communities had declined in number as a result of low birth rates and/or emigration, while others, including the Shiites, had been gaining because of very high birth rates'.[55] As the Government of Lebanon did not send a representative to the CERD hearing, the review was postponed.[56] Similarly, five years later in 1996, considerations of the report on Lebanon were deferred.[57]

B. Consideration of the 6th–13th Periodic Reports (1998)

The first comprehensive legal reflection in CERD on Lebanon was held in 1998. At the beginning of the meeting, Lebanon's representative restated that the

[51] ibid, para 12.
[52] ibid.
[53] ibid.
[54] UN Doc CERD/C/SR.923, 8 November 1991, para 8.
[55] ibid, para 3.
[56] ibid, para 32.
[57] UN Doc CERD/C/SR.1165, 24 October 1996, para 3.

recognition of religious communities did 'not constitute an infringement of the Convention because the intention was to protect the interests of all and not to deprive one group or another of its rights'.[58] The confessional system had 'ensured stability in the country and no one could blame the Lebanese for having adopted it'.[59] After all, confessionalism made it 'possible for the communities to take part in the political and administrative life of the country'.[60] Changes could 'not take place overnight, since they depended on the political and military situation in the country'.[61]

CERD members, such as Mahmoud Aboul-Nasr, agreed with the Lebanese Government, arguing that the established quotas in Lebanon should be seen as 'a way of ensuring the representation of minorities who would otherwise be systematically excluded from public life'.[62] CERD member Mario Jorge Yutzis concurred that confessional power-sharing might be preferable to domination by a single religion.[63] However, he warned that 'if changes were not made, political discrimination would inevitably occur in Lebanon insofar as the other communities would never be able to accede to power'.[64] The country rapporteur, Ivan Garvalov, summarised diplomatically that, given the 'political, economic, social and psychological difficulties' of the situation in Lebanon, it could not yet be expected that Lebanon meet 'all its obligations under the Convention at one time'.[65]

C. Concluding Observations (1998)

In its concluding observations, CERD acknowledged that Lebanon faced 'severe difficulties' as a 'result of almost 20 years of war and foreign intervention which have resulted in widespread destruction'.[66] Lebanon had had to go through the 'trauma of a civil war, two military invasions and subsequent occupation of part of its territory in the south'.[67] However, the Committee also expressed its concern about 'the insufficiency of the legal definition of ethnic groups and the protection given to them in domestic law'.[68] It lamented the continuing 'resistance to the progressive elimination of the political system of confessionalism' despite the political and legal efforts which had been undertaken.[69]

[58] UN Doc CERD/C/SR.1259, 1 April 1998, para 13.
[59] ibid.
[60] ibid, para 13.
[61] ibid.
[62] ibid, para 26.
[63] ibid, para 25.
[64] ibid.
[65] ibid, para 29.
[66] UN Doc CERD/C/304/Add.49, above n 47, para 3.
[67] ibid, para 4.
[68] ibid, para 9.
[69] ibid, para 10.

D. Consideration of the 14th–17th Periodic Report (2004)

Critique of Lebanon's political confessionalism continued in the Committee's debates. At the start of the considerations of the 14th–17th periodic report in 2004, the representative for Lebanon stressed once more that 'although the Lebanese legal and political systems were not perfect, efforts were continually being made to improve them'.[70] As the first commentator in the CERD debate, Patrick Thornberry advised that the Committee was 'respectful of individual identities within the social and political system in Lebanon'.[71] However, the confessional arrangement in the country raised concerns for individual rights, notably for the freedom of persons who do not wish to disclose their religious faith in order to participate in public affairs.[72] On the question of special measures, Thornberry recalled that there was a 'fine line between special measures and the recognition of minority rights, on the one hand, and the institutionalisation of a system of privileges' contrary to the Convention, on the other.[73]

Similarly, CERD member José Augusto Lindgren Alves wondered whether it was wise for the Committee to advise Lebanon to follow the trend of 'micro-communities' of identities, which 'might foster a form of segregation that could potentially lead to war'.[74] Other members of the Committee, such as Nourredine Amir, observed that Lebanon had actually 'managed to provide a safe haven for people of many religions and had been one of the first states in the region to lead the way to democracy'.[75] The point was raised that 'failing to draw distinctions could also foster discriminatory practices'.[76]

E. Concluding Observations (2004)

In its concluding observations, the Committee reiterated that Lebanon 'continues to be confronted with numerous challenges resulting from almost two decades of war, foreign intervention and partial occupation, which have resulted in wide-spread destruction'.[77] Yet, the lack of progress towards the gradual elimination of confessionalism remained problematic.[78] CERD recommended that the Lebanese Government should particularly review its legislation on citizenship to guarantee equal rights.[79]

[70] UN Doc CERD/C/SR.1628, 9 March 2004, para 2.
[71] ibid, para 13.
[72] ibid.
[73] ibid, para 14.
[74] ibid, para 22.
[75] ibid, para 24.
[76] ibid, para 40.
[77] UN Doc CERD/C/64/CO/3, 28 April 2004, para 4.
[78] ibid, para 10.
[79] ibid, para 13.

IV. Analysis: Confessionalism and Non-Discrimination

Whether political confessionalism falls under the category of racial discrimination in the sense of the ICERD is questionable. The following analysis shows that consociational power-sharing, as practised in Lebanon, partly infringes upon human rights. Yet, the assessment clarifies that the advocacy of some scholars, who argue that power-sharing conflict settlements tend to create 'illegal peace', needs to be treated with caution.[80] Similar to Bosnia and Herzegovina, the case of Lebanon exemplifies that maintaining stability in a multi-confessional state requires human rights compromises which make peace not necessarily illegal but imperfect.[81] The analysis also validates the principle that legal assessments of post-conflict constitutions and power-sharing arrangements need strict scrutiny.

A. Ordinary Meaning of 'Racial Discrimination'

According to its legal definition in the ICERD, 'racial discrimination' comprises:

> any distinction, exclusion, restriction or preference based on race, colour, descent, or national or ethnic origin which has the purpose or effect of nullifying or impairing the recognition, enjoyment or exercise, on an equal footing, of human rights and fundamental freedoms in the political, economic, social, cultural or any other field of public life.[82]

The ICERD lists a set of differential treatments (eg race, colour, descent, or national or ethnic origin), and religious affiliation was not included. Hence, it would be difficult to subsume confessionalism under the Convention's wording.[83]

B. Context of the ICERD: Comparison to Other Human Rights Law

In comparison, other international and regional human rights instruments address the protection of religious discrimination.[84] Systematically, the issue

[80] Jeremy I Levitt, *Illegal Peace in Africa: An Inquiry into the Legality of Power Sharing with Warlords, Rebels, and Junta* (Cambridge, Cambridge University Press, 2012).

[81] See also Part VIII.D below, and Ch 5, Part III.E.

[82] ICERD, Art 1, para 3.

[83] See also CERD, General Recommendation No 14: Definition of Discrimination (Article 1 para 1), 22 March 1993, UN Doc A/48/18, 15 September 1993, para 2.

[84] For an overview, see Table 4 below.

of political confessionalism and secularism is rather a matter of the freedom of religion and the prohibition of discrimination on grounds of religion or belief.[85] The Human Rights Committee clarified that theistic, non-theistic and atheistic beliefs are equally protected.[86] Whether, and if so to what extent, Lebanon's political confessionalism could actually be a violation of the freedom of religion and belief would need thorough assessment by the UN human rights monitoring bodies.[87] The matter would be relevant if political candidates running for Parliament or citizens applying for high-level positions in public service were rejected because of their religion or belief.[88] The Human Rights Committee has noted 'with concern that every Lebanese citizen must belong to one of the religious denominations officially recognised by the Government, and that this is a requirement in order to be eligible to run for public office'.[89]

Apart from freedom of religion, Lebanon's confessional system has been criticised regarding diminished women rights. Separately from CERD, the UN Committee on the Elimination of Discrimination against Women (CEDAW) has scrutinised Lebanon's sectarian structures concerning the inequality of religious status laws and discrimination against women.[90] Among others, CEDAW highlighted as problematic the fact that the confessional laws have different minimum age requirements for marriage and the existing religious courts vary in their compositions and appeals procedures. The Committee advised Lebanon to 'urgently adopt a unified personal status code which is in line with the Convention and would be applicable to all women in Lebanon, irrespective of their religion'.[91] The Committee urged Lebanon to ensure that the promotion and protection of women's human rights and gender equality becomes 'a central goal of all aspects of the transition process'.[92]

[85] See also Declaration on the Elimination of All Forms of Intolerance and of Discrimination Based on Religion or Belief, GA Res 36/55, 25 November 1981.

[86] CCPR, General Comment No 22: The Right to Freedom of Thought, Conscience and Religion (Article 18), UN Doc CCPR/C/21/Rev.1/Add.4, 30 July 1993, para 2.

[87] The UN Special Rapporteur on Freedom of Religion or Belief has not yet dealt comprehensively with Lebanon's system of political confessionalism. Previously, cases regarding Lebanon have only focused on attacks on Christian churches and the desecration of Christian cemeteries after the end of the Civil War in Lebanon in 1993 and 1994. See UN Doc A/HRC/19/60, 22 December 2011, para 4.

[88] So far, self-declared non-confessional politicians appear to be placed in the Christian or Muslim category following the confessional origin of their family.

[89] In the Committee's opinion, 'this practice does not … comply' with the requirements of ICCPR, Art 25. See UN Doc CCPR/C/42/Add.14, 22 November 1996, para 23.

[90] UN Doc CEDAW/C/LBN/3, 7 July 2006, paras 24, 326. See also UN Doc CEDAW/C/LBN/2, 11 February 2005; UN Doc CEDAW/C/LBN/1, 2 September 2004.

[91] UN Doc CEDAW/C/LBN/CO/3, 8 April 2008, para 19.

[92] ibid.

Table 4 Legal comparison of human rights discrimination prohibitions

	International				Regional			
	UDHR	**ICERD**	**ICCPR**	**ICESCR**	**ECHR**	**ACHPR**	**AmCHR**	**ArCHR**
	Article 2	Article 14	Article 2, para 1	Article 2, para 2	Article 14	Article 2	Article 1, para 1	Article 3, para 1
Race	+	+	+	+	+	+	+	+
Colour	+	+	+	+	+	+	+	+
Sex	+	–	+	+	+	+	+	+
Language	+	–	+	+	+	+	+	+
Religion	+	–	+	+	+	+	+	+
Political or other opinion/ thought	+	–	+	+	+	+	+	+
National or social origin	+	–	+	+	+	+	+	+
Ethnic origin	–	+	–	–	–	+	–	–
Association with 'national minority'	–	–	–	–	+	–	–	–
Property/ wealth/ economic status	+	–	+	+	+	+	+	+
Birth/ descent	+	+	+	+	+	+	+	+
Other status/ other social condition	+	–	+	+	+	+	+	–
Physical or mental disability	–	–	–	–	–	–	–	+

C. Object and Purpose of the ICERD

As shown in the comparison above, confessional or religious discrimination is omitted from the ICERD.[93] The object and purpose of the ICERD is to establish a

[93] See Table 4.

specialised human rights regime that specifically focuses on discrimination on the ground of race, colour or ethnic origin.[94] Other potential stigmatisation which could lead also to discrimination, such as wealth, education, health and status, or religion, were excluded. The ICERD aims to particularly strengthen the prohibition of racial discrimination. All this needs to be kept in mind by those who are trying to argue that Lebanon's confessional power-sharing is an infringement of the Convention.

D. Preparatory Work for the ICERD

The debate during the preparatory work for the ICERD reveals that the scope of the Convention was intended to be limited. Historically, the Convention formed part of a series of actions within the UN to raise awareness about racial discrimination in the post-World War II era, at a time of General Assembly resolutions and Security Council decisions on combatting the apartheid policies in South Africa.[95] The discussion during the preparation of the Convention revolved around the question of whether or not references to specific forms of racial discrimination should be included.[96] Some states wished to list, for instance, Fascism, Nazism, Zionism or Anti-Semitism as forms of racial discrimination, however, none could gain a majority for their proposals.[97] Accordingly, the Indian representative regretted that the Convention was 'a compromise'.[98] The Argentinian representative agreed that 'the text was by no means perfect'.[99] The statements during the discussion offer an insight into the fact that the composition of international law is itself imperfect. Based on this historical perspective, the intended narrow framework for the ICERD leads to the conclusion that only racially motivated power-sharing violates the Convention, which excludes religion-based arrangements such as political confessionalism in Lebanon.

E. Comparative Cases

In practice, Lebanon's approach of political confessionalism has been exceptional. Countries such as Iraq, Syria or Egypt feature some elements of societal confessionalism, but do not have a fully-fledged constitutional system based on political sectarian balances such as in Lebanon.[100] Arguing that Lebanon's political

[94] Preamble CERD, para 12. See also GA Res 1904 (XVIII), 20 November 1963.
[95] UN Doc A/C.3/SR.1374, 15 December 1965, para 34.
[96] UN Doc A/C.3/SR.1373, 14 December 1965, para 47.
[97] ibid, para 60.
[98] UN Doc A/C.3/SR.1374, above n 95, para 22.
[99] ibid, para 32.
[100] For Syria, see UN Doc CERD/C/304/Add.70, 19 March 1999. For Iraq, see UN Doc CERD/C/304/Add.80, 12 April 2001; UN Doc CERD/C/320/Add.3, 11 February 1999. For Egypt, see UN Doc CERD/C/384/Add.3, 11 April 2001.

confessionalism is racial discrimination would set a precedent. Three comparative cases to consider are Belgium, India and Switzerland, whose power-sharing systems have drawn the CERD's attention.

i. CERD Considerations Concerning Belgium (2002/2008): De Facto Segregation of Communities

Following constitutional reforms in 1994, Belgium's new power-sharing structure is based on the devolution of authority from the federal Government to communities and regions.[101] The federal state is comprised of three communities, namely the Flemish, French and German-speaking communities, and three regions: the Flemish Region (Flanders) and the Walloon Region (Wallonia), as well as the capital region around Brussels.[102]

In its considerations in 2002, the CERD was rather quiet about the internal structure of Belgium's political system. Primarily, it showed itself 'concerned about the increasing influence of xenophobic ideology on political parties, especially in Flanders'.[103] The Committee highlighted 'occurrences of racial acts against persons belonging to ethnic minorities, especially those of the Muslim faith'.[104] Difficulties 'of access to employment and housing of members of ethnic minorities' were another matter of concern.[105]

In 2008, CERD recommended strengthening measures to prevent and combat xenophobia and racial prejudice amongst politicians, public officials and the general public, as well as to promote tolerance between all ethnic and national groups.[106] The Committee was also concerned 'about the fact that ethnic minorities are often overrepresented in social urban housing – up to 90 per cent in some cases – which has resulted in de facto segregation in certain neighbourhoods of large cities'.[107]

ii. CERD Considerations Concerning India (2007): Caste-Based Discrimination

In terms reminiscent of the Lebanese situation, the Indian Government stresses that 'observance, promotion and protection of human rights are a complex task in a country of India's ethnic, religious, linguistic and economic diversity'.[108]

In 2007, CERD recognised as positive certain aspects India's comprehensive efforts to combat discrimination, particularly discrimination based on race

[101] UN Doc CEDAW/C/SR.300, 1 February 1996, para 2.
[102] UN Doc HRI/CORE/BEL/2012 F, 3 October 2012, para 21.
[103] UN Doc CERD/C/60/CO/2, 21 May 2002, para 14.
[104] ibid, para 20.
[105] ibid, para 18.
[106] UN Doc CERD/C/BEL/CO/15, 11 April 2008, para 11.
[107] ibid, para 15.
[108] UN Doc CERD/C/IND/19, 29 March 2006, para 6.

and caste. The Committee welcomed adopted special measures which aimed 'to advance the equal enjoyment of rights by members of scheduled castes and scheduled tribes, such as reservation of seats in Union and State legislatures and of posts in the public service'.[109]

However, legal questions endured over whether the remaining caste system should be seen as racial discrimination, which the Indian Government denies. Given the persistent 'de facto segregation' of the 'untouchables' (*Dalits*), CERD urged the Government to take effective measures to ensure equal access for them to places of worship, hospitals, water sources and any other places or services intended for use by the general public.[110]

Lastly, similar to confessionalism in Lebanon's, the Committee noted with concern that 'caste bias as well as racial and ethnic prejudice and stereotypes are still deeply entrenched in the minds of wide segments of Indian society, particularly in rural areas'.[111] The Committee advised India to strengthen its efforts to eradicate the social acceptance of caste-based discrimination, for example,

> by intensifying public education and awareness-raising campaigns, incorporating educational objectives of inter-caste tolerance … and ensuring adequate media representation of issues concerning scheduled castes, tribes and ethnic minorities, with a view to achieving true social cohesion among all ethnic groups, castes and tribes of India.[112]

iii. CERD Considerations Concerning Switzerland (2008): Discrimination due to Cantonal Power-Sharing

CERD member Mario Jorge Yutzis once called Lebanon the 'Switzerland of the Middle East'.[113] The concept of 'Swiss Democracy' has been often praised as the solution to conflict in multicultural societies.[114] Yet, Switzerland's power-sharing system has also raised concerns under the ICERD.

In 2008, CERD noted that although Switzerland claims that 'its federal system does not constitute an obstacle to the implementation of the Convention within its territory', the Committee was concerned about 'inconsistencies' in the application of the Convention.[115] It was critically noted that 'the laws, policies and decisions of cantons and communes could contradict the State Party's obligations under the Convention'.[116] CERD was also disconcerted by 'the hostility resulting from the negative perception of foreigners and certain minorities by part of the

[109] ibid, para 4.
[110] ibid, para 13.
[111] ibid, para 27.
[112] ibid.
[113] UN Doc CERD/C/SR.923, above n 54 para 16.
[114] Wolf Linder, *Swiss Democracy: Possible Solutions to Conflict in Multicultural Societies* (London, Palgrave Macmillan, 2010) 1.
[115] UN Doc CERD/C/CHE/CO/6, 23 September 2008, para 8.
[116] ibid.

population, which has resulted in popular initiatives questioning the principle of non-discrimination'.[117]

Just as there is no definition of ethnic groups in Lebanon, CERD noted 'with concern' that domestic legislation of Switzerland 'does not currently contain a definition of racial discrimination'.[118] Similar to the case of Bosnia and Herzegovina, Sinti and Roma were still 'subjected to numerous disadvantages and forms of discrimination', facing 'the persistence of racial stereotyping against them'.[119] CERD was disquieted by 'xenophobic and racist attitudes', the 'establishment of separate classes for foreign pupils in some cantons' and the lack of effort to 'recruit members of minority groups into the police and to provide sensitisation and training of police officers on issues of racial discrimination'.[120]

As highlighted in the previous chapter, discrimination remains a contemporary challenge even outside the post-conflict context.[121] The CERD considerations concerning Belgium, India and Switzerland demonstrate that power-sharing is unproblematic under international human rights law as long as ethnic minorities are protected and potential for racial prejudices is actively reduced.

F. Fine-Tuning the Parameters of Racial Discrimination

Placing the Lebanese confessional system per se in the category of racial discrimination would be a misinterpretation of the Convention. The wording, context, objective and purpose, preparatory work and subsequent interpretation represent a distinct understanding of the ICERD. The pressing lesson learnt is that judgements about the compliance of power-sharing and state transitions with international human rights law require precision.

i. The Challenge of Providing Legal Precision

In 2007, Asma Jahangir, the then Special Rapporteur on the Freedom of Religion or Belief, spoke at CERD about the overlapping of religious and ethnic discrimination in the context of 'intersectionality' between race and religion.[122] She advocated caution in order to prevent overbroad definitions and inclusions. Regis de Gouttes, then President of UN CERD, agreed that the Committee's

[117] ibid, para 7.
[118] ibid, para 11.
[119] ibid, para 19.
[120] UN Doc CERD/C/60/CO/14, 21 May 2002, paras 10–12.
[121] ibid; see Ch 3, Part VI.B.
[122] Committee on the Elimination of Racial Discrimination, 71st Session, Discussion with Asma Jahangir, Special Rapporteur on Freedom of Religion or Belief, Human Rights Monitoring Series (International Service for Human Rights), 6 August 2007, 1.

mandate is indeed becoming increasingly broad.[123] Noureddine Amir, CERD's vice-chairman, advised leaving discussions of religion out of the subject of race, as the treaty body would otherwise turn into 'an anthropology seminar'.[124] This discussion within CERD on religious discrimination illustrates how important it is to keep the application of human rights conventions narrow in order to maintain their credibility.

The CERD reports on Belgium in this chapter have shown that one of the focus areas of the Committee is occurrences of racial acts against persons belonging to ethnic minorities. Based on the experience of Switzerland, the impetus is to combat racist and xenophobic attitudes. The comparative case of India showed that vulnerable groups such as tribal people need to be given legal recognition in the national laws of states. Lebanon's confessional system needs to be judged along these lines. Religious and racial issues have to be separated in this context.

ii. Understanding the Difference between Religious and Ethnic Groups

As described above, the Lebanese Government mainly argued that confessionalism does not entail a distinction related to descent, national or ethnic origin.[125] In response, CERD members emphasised that while Syrians, Greeks, Armenians, Copts, Kurds and Jews are recognised as communities and religions, there is no recognition of the different ethnic origin of other confessions.[126] In their view, this might constitute grounds for racial discrimination.

The two sides appear to be talking at cross purposes. First, that a distinction in the Lebanese confessional system is made on religious and not on ethnic grounds speaks against the conclusion of racial discrimination and the application of the ICERD. Again, religious discrimination is not covered by this Convention. Indeed, the need to disclose one's religious faith for public services and personal status issues could be indirectly discriminatory, if secularists are deliberately excluded. A well founded decision about whether this is factually the case requires sufficient empirical data. This still needs to be collected and provided by the Lebanese state.

Second, the fact that some confessions relate in their descriptions to certain ethnicities does not imply racial discrimination against those ethnicities which are not acknowledged. The mention of the prefix 'Greek' or 'Armenian', for instance, in the confessional listing (eg Greek Catholic, Greek Orthodox) is not an automatic

[123] ibid.
[124] ibid, 2.
[125] See Part II.C.i above.
[126] UN Doc CERD/C/304/Add.49, above n 47.

recognition of ethnicity but primarily a description of the confession.[127] The term 'Greek Orthodox', for example, refers historically to the Byzantine Empire, which was oriented towards Greek culture and language rather than Latin culture, as in the Western Roman Empire.[128] Hence, the Greek Orthodox confession is often related to Greek ethnicity and an ethnic self-identification with being Greek, but people of other ethnicities may also become members of the Greek Orthodox Church.[129] As for the Armenian Orthodox Church, the title 'Armenian Orthodox' refers to the fact that the liturgy is celebrated in classical Armenian. However, although the Armenian Orthodox Church has been labelled as an 'ethnic church' and its members are mainly ethnic Armenian, people who are of other ethnicity are not excluded.[130]

As mentioned, some CERD members have warned that this issue could lead to an endless anthropological debate. And indeed, in the case of Lebanon, the attempt to link religion and ethnicity appears prone to error.

iii. Absence of Minority Protection in the Arab World

Nonetheless, the Committee's call for dedicated minority protection mechanisms in Lebanon needs to be heard. The actual question is not whether Lebanese political confessionalism is discriminatory, but whether there are solid and efficient guarantees for ethnic or religious minority groups in place.[131] Shifting this notion in the debate could eventually untangle the knotted relationship between religion and ethnicity.

After the Arab uprisings, it has increasingly been suggested that there should be a 'new vision' for minorities in the region.[132] In this context, vulnerable groups include religious minorities such as Christians and Jews in all parts of the Arab world, and ethnic minorities such as Kurds, Turkmen, Armenians, Circassians and other minorities. The Arab Charter on Human Rights of 2004 enshrines that '[p]ersons belonging to minorities shall not be denied the right to enjoy their

[127] Herbert J Gans, 'Symbolic Ethnicity and Symbolic Religiosity: Towards a Comparison of Ethnic and Religious Acculturation' (1994) 17(4) *Ethnic and Racial Studies* 577.

[128] Joan M Hussey, *The Orthodox Church in the Byzantine Empire* (Oxford, Oxford University Press, 2010) iv.

[129] As anthropological studies reveal, the preservation of Greek national identity has been a challenge for the Greek Orthodox Church outside of Greece: Vasilikie Demos, 'Maintenance and Loss of Traditional Gender Boundaries in Two Greek Orthodox Communities' (1989) 16(1) *Journal of the Hellenic Diaspora* 77. See also Alice Scourby, 'Three Generations of Greek Americans: A Study in Ethnicity' (1980) 14 *International Migration Review* 43.

[130] Jeremy Morris, *The Church in the Modern Age: The History of the Christian Church* (London, IB Tauris, 2007) 169. For details, see also Betty Jane Bailey and J Martin Bailey, *Who Are the Christians in the Middle East?* (Michigan, Eerdmans, 2010) 68.

[131] See also David Keane and Joshua Castellino, 'Transcending Sectarianism through Minority Rights in Iraq' (2012) 5(3) *International Journal of Contemporary Iraqi Studies* 387.

[132] Dina Al-Shibeeb, 'Prominent Yemeni Novelist Defends Minority Rights in Arab World' *Al Arabiya News* (18 September 2012).

own culture, to use their own language and to practice their own religion', and that the 'exercise of these rights shall be governed by law'.[133] However, national legislation for the protection of religious and ethnic minorities is still limited in most states of the Arab world. A comprehensive regional minority rights regime, similar to the Council of Europe system, that could acknowledge minority rights while maintaining specific cultural customs, does not yet exist.[134]

V. Transitional Power-Sharing, Unity Governments, Proportions of High-Level Posts and the Right to Participation

Jeremy Levitt concluded in his book *Illegal Peace* that international human rights law recognises the right of every citizen to take direct part in the conduct of public affairs, whereas political power-sharing arrangements are considered 'incompatible' with human rights, when 'citizens are denied meaningful participation in their creation'.[135] In Lebanon's CERD report, the Lebanese Government mentioned only briefly that the right to equal access to public service posts was guaranteed under the Constitution.[136] Analysing the issue in more depth, this section focuses on the normative framework and practice of the right to political participation during phases of state transitions.

A. Normative Framework: The Right to Participation

The legal framework of the right to participation in the conduct of public affairs or concerning equal access to public service poses various 'difficult interpretative questions', as Gregory Fox once noted.[137] In essence, it guarantees 'minimum standards of procedural fairness'.[138] However, as the following overview will show, there are limits to participation in the conduct of public affairs and access to public service.

[133] Arab Charter on Human Rights, Article 25, League of Arab States (adopted 22 May 2004, entered into force 15 March 2008) (2005) 12 *International Human Rights Reports* 893.
[134] Elizabeth Picard, 'Nation-Building and Minority Rights in the Middle East' in Anh Nga Longva and Anne Sofie Roald (eds), *Religious Minorities in the Middle East: Domination, Self-empowerment, Accommodation* (Leiden, Brill, 2012) 230.
[135] Levitt, above n 80, 151.
[136] UN Doc CERD/C/65/Add.4, above n 23.
[137] Gregory H Fox, 'The Right of Political Participation in International Law' in Gregory H Fox and Brad R Roth (eds), *Democratic Governance and International Law* (Cambridge, Cambridge University Press, 2000) 50, 55.
[138] ibid, 90.

i. Complementary Rights: Participation in Conduct of Public Affairs, the Right to Vote and Access to Public Service

Normatively, the right to political participation and equal access to public service is protected by international and regional human rights instruments.[139] Citizens have the right and the opportunity, without any distinction, to take part in the conduct of public affairs and to have access to public service.[140] Moreover, the right to vote, the right to stand for election and the guarantee that genuine periodic elections express the will of the electors are guaranteed.[141] Limitations are only permitted to a certain extent, as long as they are not 'unreasonable'.[142]

ii. Practice of the Human Rights Committee

In the past, the Human Rights Committee affirmed that states have a certain margin in how they design their internal state structure.[143] The Human Rights Committee emphasised that international human rights law 'does not impose any particular electoral system', as long as it is compatible with the protected rights and it respects the free expression of the will of the electors.[144] Elections must be conducted fairly on a periodic basis.[145] The right and the opportunity to stand for elective office must ensure that persons entitled to vote have a free choice of candidates. Among others, it is also important that the drawing of electoral boundaries and the method of allocating votes do 'not distort the distribution of voters or discriminate against any group and should not exclude or restrict unreasonably the right of citizens to choose their representatives freely'.[146] As the Human Rights Committee highlighted, persons should not be excluded by discriminatory requirements such as education, residence or descent, or by reason of political affiliation. In the case of restrictions, states should indicate and explain the legislative provisions which exclude any group or category of persons from elective office. Any restrictions 'must be justifiable on objective and reasonable criteria'.[147]

[139] UDHR, Art 21, paras 1–2; ICCPR, Art 25, paras (a), (c); ICERD, Art 5, para (c); CEDAW, Art 7(b); AmCHR, Art 23, para 1(a); ACHPR, Art 13, para 1.

[140] ICPPR, Art 25, para (a); ICPPR, Art 25, para (c).

[141] ICPPR, Art 25, para (b).

[142] ICPPR, Art 25 includes that the mentioned right shall be safeguarded 'without unreasonable restrictions'.

[143] CCPR, General Comment No 25: The Right to Participate in Public Affairs, Voting Rights and the Right of Equal Access to Public Service, 7 December 1996, para 5.

[144] ibid, para 21.

[145] ibid, para 19.

[146] ibid.

[147] ibid, para 15.

B. Comparative Cases: Permitted Limitation of Participation Rights

In the cases *Mikmaq People v Canada* (1991), *Kall v Poland* (1997) and *Vladimir Raosavljevic v Bosnia and Herzegovina* (2007), the UN Human Rights Committee established a set of criteria and conditions for the limitation of human rights in the context of constitutional change and access to public service in post-conflict settings.

i. Mikmaq People v Canada *(1991)*

In *Mikmaq People v Canada*, members of the Mikmaq tribe complained that they were not included in a series of constitutional conferences on aboriginal matters which were convened by the Prime Minister of Canada to discuss amendments in the Constitution on self-government of aboriginal peoples.[148] Only four national associations were invited to represent the interests of approximately 600 aboriginal groups.

The Mikmaq tribe argued that the exclusion denied them their right of self-determination and also infringed their right to take part in the conduct of public affairs. The Government of Canada countered that the invitation of aboriginal groups had to be limited, as the main participants were the elected members of Parliament. The Government argued that restrictions were 'not unreasonable', underlining that the conduct of public affairs does not require direct input from every citizen, as long as there is a properly elected government.[149] In its opinion, the right to participation is fulfilled when freely chosen representatives make decisions on the affairs with which they are entrusted by the constitution.

The UN Human Rights Committee agreed that the right to take part in the conduct of public affairs cannot mean that every citizen can choose whether to either take part directly in the conduct of public affairs or to leave it to freely chosen representatives.[150] It concluded that the right of participation 'cannot be understood as meaning that any directly affected group, large or small, has the unconditional right to choose the modalities of participation in the conduct of public affairs'.[151]

ii. Kall v Poland *(1997)*

In the case *Kall v Poland*, Polish citizen Wieslaw Kall alleged a violation of his right to have access, on general terms of equality, to public service in

[148] *Mikmaq People v Canada*, Communication No 205/1986, UN Doc CCPR/C/43/D/205/1986, 3 December 1991.
[149] ibid, para 4.1.
[150] ibid, para 5.4.
[151] ibid, para 5.5.

his country.[152] Until 1990, he was employed in various positions in the civic militia of the Ministry of Internal Affairs, lately at senior inspector level. Following constitutional and legislative changes after the end of the Cold War, reforms dissolved the security police and replaced it with a new department. A vetting process was introduced to review the applications for new positions of former members of the security police. Kall's re-employment at the provincial police was rejected.

He argued that he should not have been subjected to the verification proceedings. Kall claimed that he was denied access to public service only because of his political opinions, since he had been an active member of the Polish United Workers Party.[153] The Government responded that public employment decisions were at its discretion.

The UN Human Rights Committee concluded that the right of access to public service 'does not entitle every citizen to obtain guaranteed employment in the public service'.[154] Access to public service is only guaranteed 'on general terms of equality'.[155] The comprehensive reorganisation of the Ministry of Internal Affairs and the associated vetting process had to been seen as part of restoring democracy and the rule of law in the country.[156]

iii. Vladimir Raosavljevic v Bosnia and Herzegovina *(2007)*

Vladimir Raosavljevic v Bosnia and Herzegovina concerned the distribution of public posts in Bosnia and Herzegovina after the Dayton Accords.[157] Following successful appeals against two of his court decisions, Vladimir Raosavljevic was refused reappointment as a judge to the Supreme Court of the Republika Srpska, where he had presided over the criminal department for 20 years.

In his submission to the UN Human Rights Committee, Raosavljevic claimed that the non-renewal of his appointment was discriminatory, amounted to a denial of his right to equal access to public service, interfered with his independence as a judge and damaged his reputation.[158] He argued that he had received higher scores in the evaluation process than all other candidates who were appointed to the Supreme Court. The Government of Bosnia and Herzegovina responded that Raosavljevic received a low ranking among the judges of Serbian ethnicity.[159]

[152] *Wieslaw Kall v Poland*, Communication No 552/1993, UN Doc CCPR/C/60/D/552/1993, 29 September 1997.

[153] ibid, para 3.

[154] ibid, para 13.2.

[155] ibid, para 13.6.

[156] ibid, para 13.4.

[157] *Vladimir Raosavljevic v Bosnia and Herzegovina*, Communication No 1219/2003, UN Doc CCPR/C/89/D/1219/2003, 28 March 2007.

[158] ibid, para 3.1.

[159] Under the State and Republika Srpska Constitutions, the composition of the Supreme Court reflects the ethnic visions in the country, whereby the nomination panel proposed eight Serbs, two Bosniaks, two Croats and one candidate from 'other' minorities. For details, see also Ch 2, Part III.B.

The Government stressed that the selection process gave every applicant '"a fair opportunity" to run for the post of judge'.[160]

The UN Human Rights Committee noted that, in principle, access to public service needs to be based on general terms of equality, which obliges states to not discriminate against anyone. The rating system used to determine the eligibility and suitability of judges was itself 'complex and based on objective criteria'.[161] As Raosavljevic had the opportunity to access and remain in public service, his rights were not violated.

C. Limits of the Right to Participation

The conclusions of the UN Human Rights Committee in *Mikmaq People v Canada* explain that the conduct of elections is key for the legitimacy of constitutional change processes. The cases *Kall v Poland* and *Vladimir Raosavljevic v Bosnia and Herzegovina* make clear that the right to participation does primarily protect access to public service positions on general terms of equality. The proportional distribution of high level posts in governments or public service is not barred by international human rights law.[162] A 'clear-cut breach' of human rights occurs when participation in public affairs is arbitrarily denied.[163]

i. Temporary Unity Coalitions and Transitional Governments

Arrangements that contravene participation rights have to be temporary. In practice, power-sharing has been widely supported as long as transitional governments lead to elections or unity coalitions are limited for the time between ballot votes.[164] As previously touched upon in Chapter 2 of this study, unity governments are common mechanisms for breaking political stalemates by establishing interim solutions through the inclusion of all major political parties.[165]

In the case of Lebanon, the UN Security Council welcomed the Doha Agreement between political leaders in 2008, which, in its view, constituted 'an essential step towards the resolution of the current crisis, the return to the normal functioning of Lebanese democratic institutions, and the complete restoration of Lebanon's

[160] UN Doc CCPR/C/89/D/1219/2003, above n 157, para 5.2.

[161] ibid, para 7.6.

[162] 'Article 25' in Manfred Nowak (ed), *UN Covenant on Civil and Political Rights: CCPR Commentary* (Kehl, NP Engel, 2005) para 12.

[163] Sarah Joseph, 'Rights of Political Participation' in David Harris and Sarah Josesph (eds), *The International Convenant on Civil and Political Rights and United Kingdom Law* (Oxford, Oxford University Press, 1995) 539.

[164] For example, the Security Council encouraged transitional institutions in Burundi to assume responsibility for the organisation and successful completion of the electoral process. See SC Res 1545, 21 May 2004. On the post-election unity government in Kenya, see UN Doc S/PRST/2008/4, 6 February 2008.

[165] See Ch 2, Table 1. See also Appendix, Table 1.

unity and stability'.[166] After the parliamentary elections in Lebanon in 2009, the UN Secretary General 'welcomed the formation of a national unity government and expressed his hope that Lebanese political leaders would continue to work steadfastly in the spirit of unity, dialogue and cooperation'.[167]

More recently, transitional power-sharing arrangements in Yemen und Libya after the uprisings were internationally endorsed to bridge the period of political instability and insecurity until the completion of elections.[168] In the case of Libya, the UN Security Council emphasised as a principle that transitional governments need to be 'inclusive' and 'representative', while they also need to promote 'the equal and full participation of women and minority communities in the discussions related to the political process in the post-conflict phase'.[169]

ii. Change of Democratic Governments by Unconstitutional Means

Indeed, international critique of interim power-sharing arrangements for the settlement of armed conflict has remained marginal among states within international human rights entities. This is exactly why Levitt raised his concerns in protection of the 'small man', the 'ordinary citizen', arguing that power-sharing 'does not serve the good of the public'.[170] His nightmare scenario is that a rebel group coerces a democratically constituted government into a power-sharing arrangement through force.[171]

However, Levitt fails to acknowledge that there is a fundamental difference between power-sharing as a way to obtain peace and *coups d'état* as the source of state instability. *Coups d'état* are the actual cause of state instability and potential human rights violations, not power-sharing as a means for settling conflict.

In comparison to power-sharing, *coups d'état* are explicitly denounced. The African Union (AU), for instance, condemned 'all types of unconstitutional change of Government as anachronistic and in contradiction of its commitment to the promotion of democratic principles and constitutional rule'.[172] Similarly, the UN Security Council has made clear on several occasions that the military overthrow of a democratically elected government is not tolerated.[173]

[166] UN Doc S/PRST/2008/17, 22 May 2008.

[167] UN Doc S/PV.6223, 24 November 2009.

[168] UN Doc S/PV.6725, 28 February 2012; UN Doc S/PV.6595, 28 July 2011.

[169] SC Res 2009, 16 September 2011, paras 2–3.

[170] Levitt, above n 80, 7.

[171] ibid, 3.

[172] Decision on Unconstitutional Changes of Government in Africa, Doc. AHG/Dec. 141 (XXXV), UN Doc A/54/424, 5 October 5 1999, Annex II, para 2. See also Decision on Unconstitutional Changes of Government in Africa, Doc. CM/2166 (LXXII), UN Doc A/55/286, 15 August 2000, Annex II; African Charter on Democracy, Elections and Governance, African Union, 30 January 2007.

[173] On the condemnation of unconstitutional changes of governments in Africa, see UN Doc S/PRST/2009/11, 5 May 2009. On the case of the Ivory Coast, see SC Res 1479, 13 May 2003. On the case of the *coup d'état* in Mauritania, see UN Doc S/PRST/2008/30, 19 August 2008.

Indeed, changes of governments 'by unconstitutional means' are at the threshold between human rights violation or protection, depending on the side from which one argues. For example, while revolutions can be perceived as revolts against the legitimate institutional order of a state, they can also be seen as liberations.[174] For their own sake, states understandably tend to oppose *coups d'état* as a factor of disorder, but welcome means to re-establish stability. This explains why power-sharing arrangements are mostly praised rather than condemned, as long as they lead to a continuation of state order resulting in regional peace and security. At the other end of the scale, in contrast to Levitt, an alternative to power-sharing is a brutal suppression of uprisings with even greater human rights infringements. Such a state reaction is clearly even less desirable.

iii. Encouraging Genuine, Regular and Democratic Elections

Following the Arab uprisings in 2011, the UN General Assembly reiterated that all citizens, without distinction of any kind, should have the right and the opportunity to take part in the conduct of public affairs, directly or through freely chosen representatives.[175] Organising, conducting and ensuring free and fair electoral processes in countries undergoing democratisation has been declared central for achieving a 'successful transition to long-term sustainable democracies'.[176] Elections are seen as a peaceful means for contributing to national and regional stability. The role of the international community is to establish 'conditions which could foster stability and security throughout the pre-election, election and post-election periods in transitional and post-conflict situations'.[177]

Hence, as long as genuine, regular and democratic elections are held, interim coalitions and other transitional power-sharing arrangements are accepted, even if compliance with human rights might appear imperfect. In the worst case, unity governments become a habit and perpetuate elite monopolies of some groups, for which Lebanon has been criticised. However, even then, power-sharing remains a better alternative than the exclusion of opposition groups who are willing to take power by force at the cost of human lives.

VI. Proportionality and Time Limitations

As described above, the Lebanese Government argued in its reports to UN CERD that confessionalism could be justified as a 'special measure' for a time

[174] Ben Saul, 'Criminality and Terrorism' in Ana María Salinas de Frias et al (eds), *Counter-Terrorism: International Law and Practice* (Oxford, Oxford University Press, 2012) 162.
[175] GA Res. 66/163, 10 April 2012.
[176] ibid.
[177] ibid.

of transition.[178] Distinctions created by the sectarian system were not meant to constitute discrimination but intended both to protect all confessional groups and ensure equal chances of development and progress. As in the case *Sejdić and Finci v Bosnia and Herzegovina*, the pivotal question has been what timeframe is legitimate for state transitions.[179]

A. Normative Framework and Principles for 'Special Measures'

Under international human rights law 'special measures' may be taken for the purpose of securing adequate advancement of certain racial or ethnic groups or individuals in order to ensure such groups or individuals equal enjoyment of human rights.[180] Temporary special measures may be needed in order 'to bring disadvantaged or marginalized persons or groups of persons to the same substantive level as others' and 'attenuate or suppress conditions that perpetuate discrimination'.[181] The condition is that if these measures 'are necessary to redress de facto discrimination and are terminated when de facto equality is achieved, such differentiation is legitimate'.[182]

Whether Lebanese confessionalism can be considered as a special measure is debatable. On the one hand, the Human Rights Committee noted that it 'is for the States parties to determine appropriate measures to implement the relevant provisions', as long as the Committee is 'informed about the nature of such measures'.[183] This gives states leeway in the adoption of special measures. On the other hand, the Committee emphasised that special measures must themselves conform with 'principles of non-discrimination and equality'.[184] In this sense, special measures have to be distinguished from 'unjustifiable preferences'.[185] They also have to be differentiated from 'specific rights', such as minority rights, which correspond to this context better.[186]

[178] See Part II.B.ii above.

[179] On temporal aspects in the case of Bosnia and Herzegovina, see Ch 3, Part IV.D.ii, Part IV.E.iii and Part VI.A.

[180] ICERD, Art 1, para 4; CEDAW, Art 4. In comparison, the UDHR, ICCPR and ICESCR do not mention special measures explicitly, but they have accepted them in practice. See Daniel Moeckli, 'Equality and Non-Discrimination' in Daniel Moeckli et al (eds), *International Human Rights Law* (Oxford, Oxford University Press, 2010) 104, 189.

[181] CESCR, General Comment No 16: The Equal Right of Men and Women to the Enjoyment of All Economic, Social and Cultural Rights (Art 3 of the International Covenant on Economic, Social and Cultural Rights), UN Doc E/C.12/2005/4, 11 August 2005, para 15.

[182] CCPR, General Comment No 18: Non-discrimination, 11 October 1989, para 15, UN Doc HRI/GEN/1/Rev. 9 (Vol I) 195, 27 May 2008.

[183] ibid, para 4.

[184] ibid.

[185] CERD, General Recommendation No 32: The Meaning and Scope of Special Measures in the International Convention on the Elimination of All Forms of Racial Discrimination, UN Doc CERD/C/GC/32, 24 September 2009, para 7.

[186] ibid, para 15. See also Part IV.F.iii above.

Concerning the aspect of temporality, national policies and strategies have to include appropriate benchmarks and specific time frames in order to measure the progressive realisation of the right to equality.[187] Temporary special measures 'should be distinguished from permanent policies and strategies undertaken to achieve equality'.[188] However, there can be exceptions which allow special measures to become permanent.[189] It is important that the measures taken are 'reasonable, objective and proportional means' to redress de facto discrimination and are 'discontinued when substantive equality has been sustainably achieved'.[190]

B. Defining Justifiable Time Periods: The Case of *Gillot v France* (2002)

International human rights law practice applies flexibility in the determination of time frames for the justification of human rights restrictions.[191] An insightful case is *Gillot v France* (2002), in which the UN Human Rights Committee concluded that temporal limits for justifications need to be interpreted on a case-by-case basis and can take into consideration the right to self-determination.[192]

In *Gillot v France*, French overseas citizens contested the way in which the electorates for referenda on the self-determination of New Caledonia were determined. The referenda formed part of the Noumea Accord, which was signed between the Government of France and two local liberation movements. The Accord established a framework for the future development of New Caledonia. As a result, a constitutional amendment derogated certain constitutional principles, such as the principle of equality of political rights. Under the title 'Transitional provisions concerning New Caledonia' in the Constitution, the amendment specified certain criteria for participation in the referenda, such as 20 years of continuous residence. The complainant, Marie-Hélène Gillot, argued that the required length of residence constituted discriminatory treatment between French citizens.[193] The Government of France maintained that the procedures for determining the electorate for the referendum were based on reasonable criteria. The length of the residence requirements was fixed in order to ensure that the referendums would reflect the will of the population

[187] CESCR, General Comment No 20: Non-Discrimination in Economic, Social and Cultural Rights (Art 2, para 2), UN Doc E/C.12/GC/20, 10 June 2009, para 39.
[188] ibid.
[189] ibid, para 9.
[190] ibid.
[191] See *Ms Marie-Hélène Gillot v France*, Communication No 932/2000, UN Doc CCPR/C/75/D/932/2000, 26 July 2002; *Wieslaw Kall v Poland*, above n 152; *Jorge Landinelli Silva v Uruguay*, Communication No R.8/34, 30 May 1987.
[192] *Ms Marie-Hélène Gillot v France*, above n 191, para 2.1.
[193] ibid, para 3.5.

concerned and ensure that the results could not be undermined by a massive vote by people who had recently arrived in the territory without proven, strong ties to it.[194]

The UN Human Rights Committee concluded that the right to vote is not an absolute right and that restrictions may be imposed on it provided they are not discriminatory or unreasonable. The Committee considered that the evaluation of any restrictions must be effected 'on a case-by-case basis, having regard in particular to the purpose of such restrictions and the principle of proportionality'.[195] In the case of New Caledonia, the Noumea Accord reflected 'the common destiny chosen' in providing the basis for restrictions on the electorate.[196] Concerning the residence criteria, the Committee concluded that it was 'not in a position to determine the length of residence requirements', but it noted that the length of time was not excessive. The temporal cut-off points adopted did 'not have a disproportionate effect, given the nature and purpose of the referendums in question'.[197] The Committee highlighted that, in the present case, the time length was 'justified by the time frame for self-determination'.[198]

C. Timeframes for Transitions

This section has outlined that the question about the legitimate timeframe for transition periods is answered by procedures and qualitative indicators rather than quantitative constraints.[199] The case law regarding temporal aspects in the justification of human rights restrictions suggests that international human rights law practice tends to avoid fixed time limits in order to accommodate specific circumstances.[200] As established in *Gillot v France*, long periods and 'cut-off points' in time are not disproportionate if they relate to self-determination.[201] The decisive point is whether the measure taken has the purpose of establishing different rights, or aims to balance equality.[202] The sectarian system of Lebanon falls into the second category, as quotas are intended as a mechanism for inter-confessional equalisation and not as an instrument for exclusion. In this regard, it is also not too far-fetched to argue that the practice of political confessionalism in Lebanon relates to internal self-determination.[203] As described in Chapter 2, the

[194] ibid, para 8.31.
[195] ibid, para 13.2.
[196] ibid, para 13.16.
[197] ibid, para 14.15.
[198] ibid, para 14.6.
[199] See Part VII.A above.
[200] See also 'Article 25', above n 162, para 12. On the practice that the assessment of proportionality turns on the specific facts of a given case, see Moeckli, above n 180, 201.
[201] *Ms Marie-Hélène Gillot v France*, above n 191, para 14.7.
[202] ibid, para 13.11.
[203] Similarly, see ibid, para 14. On confessional power-sharing in Lebanon, see Ch 2, Part III.C.

Taif Agreement expressed the political will to phase out confessionalism; however, the implementation of the Taif Agreement continued to be challenging, as confessional quota and the fixed allocations of seats in the Government continued to be perceived as the key to stability and inter-communal balance.[204] As noted at the beginning of this chapter, increased calls for secularism have won more public support, but could not yet mobilise a critical mass of a clear and significant majority of people to push further for a transition of the state system.[205] All this evidence makes a larger timeframe for the phasing-out of human rights constraints in the case of Lebanon permissible.

i. The Quantitative Approach: Peacebuilding in the Immediate Aftermath of Conflict

An alternative would be to follow tight and rigorous time limits for transition periods. Taking such a quantitative approach, the UN Secretary General's initial Report on Peacebuilding in the Immediate Aftermath of Conflict (2009) defined 'the first two years after conflict' as the temporal milestone for state transitions.[206] Setting fixed time limits for human rights constraints in post-conflict periods is certainly one way of drawing temporal boundaries.

However, as the latest report of the UN Secretary General on Peacebuilding in the Aftermath of Conflict (2012) emphasised, reforms can prove detrimental when they are 'pursued too quickly and without national ownership, or prematurely by authorities that lack legitimacy'.[207] As admitted in the report, the end of conflict 'tends to create high expectations for the delivery of concrete political, social and economic dividends', whereas the political will, commitment and consensus among the main national protagonists is often too weak to bring about long-term peace immediately after an end to violence.[208] While 'immediate work to restore basic functionality' of a state should not be impeded, it is necessary to allow 'sufficient time for longer-term policy solutions to emerge'.[209] Balancing long-term support for institution-building with the need to achieve early and tangible outcomes through the restoration of core government functions and service delivery, institutional reform programmes should be paced and sequenced.[210] Based on those considerations, temporal frames for state transitions are given leeway in practice.

[204] On past and recent developments in Lebanon, see Ch 2, Part III.
[205] See Part I.A above.
[206] Report of the Secretary-General on Peacebuilding in the Immediate Aftermath of Conflict, UN Doc A/63/881–S/2009/304, 11 June 2009, para 4.
[207] Report of the Secretary-General on Peacebuilding in the Immediate Aftermath of Conflict, UN Doc A/67/499-S/2012/746, 8 October 2012, para 44.
[208] UN Doc A/63/881–S/2009/304, above n 206, para 4.
[209] UN Doc A/67/499-S/2012/746, above n 207, para 44.
[210] ibid.

ii. The Qualitative Approach: Emergency Derogations as Temporal Indicators

Further guidance for the notion in international human rights law that the temporal scope of human rights restrictions is defined qualitatively can be borrowed from the concept of derogation in human rights law.[211] Derogations allow states to pause their human rights obligations in order to re-establish peace and order in times of public emergencies, as long as they are 'required by the exigencies of the situation'.[212] The UN Human Rights Committee emphasised that those phases 'must be of an exceptional and temporary nature'.[213]

In practice, the line between emergencies and the state of normalcy can be blurry. One reason for this is that states might formally impose emergency laws, when the conditions are de facto absent.[214] As the UN Special Rapporteur on Human Rights and States in Emergency noted, 'many cases states of emergency merely became the legal means of "legalizing" the worst abuses and the most pernicious forms of arbitrariness'.[215] National security doctrines have been often exploited to justify the seizure or maintenance of power and use of repressive measures.[216] This experience in human rights law warns that the qualitative approach for defining temporal limits is error-prone.

For how long post-conflict situations could be treated as emergency periods has never been comprehensively assessed by the UN Human Rights Committee.[217] In any case, international practice tends to give states a wide margin of appreciation for defining derogation periods.[218] Finally, the permitted

[211] See also Gro Nystuen, *Achieving Peace or Protecting Human Rights: Conflicts between Norms Regarding Ethnic Discrimination in the Dayton Peace Agreement* (Leiden, Martinus Nijhoff Publishers, 2005) 186.

[212] ICCPR, Art 4, para 1; ECHR, Art 15, para 1; ACHR, Art 27, para 1; ArCHR, Art 4, para 1.

[213] CCPR, General Comment 29: States of Emergency (Article 4), UN Doc CCPR/C/21/Rev.1/Add.11, 31 August 2001, para 4. See also The Paris Minimum Standards of Human Rights Norms in a State of Emergency, 1984, para (A)3(a), reprinted in (1985) 79 *American Journal of International Law* 1072. See also The Siracusa Principles on the Limitation and Derogation Provisions in the International Covenant on Civil and Political Rights, Commission on Human Rights, UN Doc E/CN.4/1985/4, Annex, 28 September 1984, para 53.

[214] Laura K Donohue, 'Temporary Permanence: The Constitutional Entrenchment of Emergency Legislation' (1999) 1 *Stanford Journal of Legal Studies* 60.

[215] The Administration of Justice and the Human Rights of Detainees, Question of Human Rights and States of Emergency, Commission on Human Rights, Sub-Commission on Prevention of Discrimination and Protection of Minorities, UN Doc E/CN.4/Sub.2/1997/19, 23 June 1997, para 3.

[216] Colm Campbell, 'Wars on Terror and Vicarious Hegemons: The UK, International Law, and the Northern Ireland Conflict' (2005) 54 *International and Comparative Law Quarterly* 337.

[217] Besides 'armed conflict', the General Comment 29 of the UN Human Rights Committee referrers to natural catastrophes, mass demonstrations including instances of violence, or a major industrial accident as possible causes. However, the UN Human Rights Committee also clarified for the regime of the ICCPR that not every disturbance or catastrophe qualifies as a public emergency. See CCPR, General Comment 29, above n 213, paras 3–5. So far, none of the notified derogations between 1992–2004 ever related to power-sharing. See Nowak, above n 162, 984–1041.

[218] Peter Rowe, 'The Application of the European Convention on Human Rights during an International Armed Conflict' in Richard Burchill et al (eds), *International Conflict and Security Law: Essays in Memory of Hilaire McCoubrey* (Cambridge, Cambridge University Press, 2005) 186.

time length for human rights limitations depends on the concrete circumstances of the case at hand, while, in principle, they have to be short-term and transitory.[219] Against this legal background, rules of international human rights law urge that the phasing out of political confessionalism in Lebanon must be sincerely limited in time.[220]

iii. The Need for Flexible Timeframes and Steady Efforts

To sum up, there are no static parameters for time limits of state transitions in international law. Indeed, a blueprint of a general timetable for post-conflict developments would be arbitrary. The principle of proportionality requires that restrictions are: first, 'appropriate to achieve their protective function'; second, 'the least intrusive instrument amongst those which might achieve the desired result'; third, 'proportionate to the interest to be protected'.[221] It is important that the objectives pursued 'outweigh the damage that would be caused through the violence'.[222] Time limits and measures need to be 'carefully tailored to meet the particular needs of the groups or individuals concerned'.[223]

In the case of Lebanon, an argument by the Government has been that sectarian power-sharing is needed to prevent a collapse of the state's unity and maintain civil peace in the face of foreign threats.[224] And in fact, apart from a cessation of hostilities, the relations between Lebanon and Israel are still unsettled.[225] The United Nations Interim Force in Lebanon (UNIFIL) continues to be stationed in the region to monitor the disputed boundary. Disputes about disarmament have heated up since 2011 as a result of the ongoing crisis in Syria.[226] The destiny of Lebanon's stability is closely tied to the unsolved Palestine question and the region's overall development. In February 2013, the UN Secretary General noted that progress towards a long-term solution to the conflict is lacking, and that the situation remains 'fragile'.[227]

The CERD country rapporteur on Lebanon, Ivan Garvalov, commented once that the situation in Lebanon needs to be given the 'benefit of the doubt'.[228]

[219] CCPR, General Comment 29, above n 213, paras 2, 4.

[220] About the transitory nature of human rights limitations, see also Antônio Augusto Cançado Trindade, 'Co-Existence and Co-Ordination of Mechanisms of International Protection of Human Rights (At Global and Regional Levels)' (1987) 202 *RdC* 104.

[221] Report of the Special Rapporteur on the Promotion and Protection of Human Rights and Fundamental Freedoms while Countering Terrorism, Martin Scheinin, UN Doc A/HRC/13/37, 28 December 2009, para 17.

[222] Report of the Special Rapporteur on Extrajudicial, Summary or Arbitrary Executions, Christof Heyns, UN Doc A/HRC/17/28, 23 May 2011, para 49.

[223] CERD, General Recommendation No 32, above n 185, para 27.

[224] UN Doc CERD/C/298/Add.2, above n 31.

[225] UN Doc S/2013/120, 27 February 2013, para 2.

[226] ibid, paras 2, 36.

[227] ibid, para 59.

[228] UN Doc CERD/C/SR.1259, above n 58, para 33.

It is precisely this benefit of the doubt which could encourage states to continue to participate in human rights monitoring procedures and the dialogue which arises from them, instead of perceiving recommendations as paternalism. The latter may otherwise lead to a rejection of change and a loss of trust in the value of human rights discourses.

VII. Conclusion

Lebanon's confessionalism is a riddle which poses many difficult questions. At the heart of international law lies the challenge of guaranteeing universal human rights, while safeguarding the right to internal self-determination. In particular, the relation between the right to equality and the prohibition of discrimination vis-à-vis the right to religious freedom holds the potential for serious normative collisions. The animated debates in the UN human rights monitoring bodies described in this chapter prove that the process of crafting consensus among states about human rights standards in post-conflict transitions often lacks unanimity and remains ongoing.

A. Secularism Movements, State Structures and Human Rights

Currently, Arab countries in transition, such as Libya, Egypt and Tunisia, are increasingly struggling with whether to protect secular state structures or permit a stronger role for religion in policy-making. In October 2012, for instance, secularist protesters accused Tunisia's Government of undermining the transition to democracy, after a secular politician was violently killed.[229] Since then, the struggle over what role, if any, religion can or should play in the state has polarised politics in Tunisia.[230] Prior to the revolution, Tunisia's constitution named Islam as the religion of state, but did not include the Sharia as a source of law-making. Pro-secular protesters expressed their rejection of growing calls by conservative Salafi Islamists to transform post-revolutionary Tunisia into an Islamic state.[231] Similar calls for religious tolerance have been directed towards the Governments in Egypt and Libya.[232] Pro-secular demonstrations also took place in Turkey. A fear

[229] 'Thousands of Tunisian Secularists Protest against Islamist Rulers' *The Daily Star (Lebanon)* (23 October 2012).

[230] Justin Hyatt, 'The Secular Fret in New Tunisia' *IPS News Agency* (26 November 2012).

[231] Tarek Amara, 'Tunisian Protesters Reject Calls for Islamic State' *Al Arabiya News* (20 March 2012).

[232] 'USA: Egypt Needs to Do More on Religious Tolerance' *The Huffington Post* (17 January 2013).

is that an overtly Muslim government could endanger the country's tradition of separating religious and state matters.[233]

These events, among others, suggest that the freedom of religion and belief continue to be significant guarantees. At the current time of transition in the Middle East and Northern Africa, the protection of the religious rights of all groups and of the rights of non-believers appears to be important more than ever before. As this chapter has detailed, states are not obliged to be secular. They can have strong religious outlooks. However, international human rights law demands provisions for the freedom of religion and, with it, mechanisms for non-sectarian citizens. Special protection for vulnerable groups needs to be considered, such as for minorities, women and indigenous people. Confessional power-sharing is permissible, yet the rights to equality and prohibition of discrimination create boundaries for sectarian policies and state structures.

B. Formal Equality versus Informal Inequality

It is critical for the credibility of state transitions that human rights principles are not only acknowledged, but also implemented. With regard to Saudi Arabia, for instance, CERD highlighted that although the 'Basic Law, and provisions of Royal Decrees, regulations and codes, as well as the Islamic Shariah, guarantee equality', the 'mere statement of the general principle of non-discrimination in these laws is not a sufficient response to the requirements of the Convention'.[234] In addition, the expert group commented that guarantees of non-discrimination laid down in law need mechanisms to monitor their application.

In the case of Lebanon, lifting its reservations to CEDAW would be a breakthrough for inter-confessional relations and the recognition of secularists. However, this would not automatically remove deep-rooted confessional clientelism within society. A revocation of the Christian-Muslim quota might bring about more legal equality between all citizens regardless of their confession or their secular views. Yet, factual equality in the appointment of posts and societal acceptance would require additional effort by the state.

Indeed, ending the confessional system too rapidly might accelerate conflict, which political parties play on to keep sectarian representation alive. Under international law, the responsibility for deciding how to phase out existing power-sharing structures lies with the state. Although the executive, legislative and judicative are entrenched in confessional arrangements, any imposition of change from the outside has only limited impact. As this chapter on Lebanon

[233] Arash Dabestani et al, 'Is Turkey's Secular System in Danger?' *BBC News* (24 October 2012). See also Jonathon Burch, 'Turkish Police Fire Tear Gas at Banned Secularist March' *Reuters* (29 October 2012).

[234] UN Doc CERD/C/62/CO/8, 21 March 2003, para 10.

and the previous chapter on Bosnia and Herzegovina have detailed, human rights monitoring bodies can suggest reforms, but they cannot impose or enforce them.

C. Options and Strategies

State practice offers a variety of options for transition processes which could hold promise for the Lebanese context.

In the case of India, for instance, institutions responsible for the implementation of anti-discrimination legislation and the monitoring of acts of discrimination and violence against members of scheduled castes and scheduled tribes were established.[235] CERD also noted with appreciation the Indian Prime Minister's declaration at the International Dalit and Minorities Conference and his renewed commitment to addressing discriminatory practice and promoting equality.[236] In Switzerland, a Federal Commission against Racism was founded to work on the prevention of racial discrimination and promote inter-ethnic dialogue.[237] In the case of Belgium, CERD noted approvingly that a draft general law on racial discrimination was under consideration by the Parliament.[238] In its concluding observations on Germany, CERD welcomed the creation of the Secretariat for Minorities, which strengthened the visibility of minority rights at the federal level and offered opportunities for minorities to voice their concerns to the federal executive and legislative bodies.[239] These experiences show that what matters is whether states are pro-active in introducing institutions and legislation in order to gradually increase their human rights compliance.

Regarding Lebanon, the UN Human Rights Committee encouraged the creation of a post of national human rights ombudsman or of an independent national human rights commission, which would have the authority to investigate human rights violations and to make recommendations on remedial action to the Government.[240] CEDAW has urged the Lebanese Parliament to adopt and implement a 'National Plan of Action for Human Rights' with clear time frames.[241]

Even if progress towards the abolishment of confessionalism is delayed because of political disagreement, Lebanon will at least need to explain how it intends to steer the process of modifying discriminatory state practices and enhance equality among citizens. Following the legal principle of good faith, small steps can be sufficient to demonstrate that progress is sought.[242]

[235] UN Doc CERD/C/IND/19, above n 108, para 3.
[236] ibid, para 6.
[237] UN Doc CERD/C/CHE/CO/6, above n 115, para 10.
[238] UN Doc CERD/C/60/CO/2, above n 103, para 12.
[239] UN Doc CERD/C/DEU/CO/18, 21 August 2008, para 9.
[240] UN Doc CPR/C/79/Add.78, 14 April 1997, para 9.
[241] UN Doc CEDAW/C/LBN/CO/3, above n 91, para 17.
[242] CESCR, General Comment No 20, above n 187, para 14.

D. Imperfection and Constitutional Change

During the preparation of the ICERD, it was regretted that the Convention was a compromise and 'by no means perfect'.[243] Achieving a flawless international legal framework is impossible and would perhaps even be counter-productive, as it could result in apodictic assumptions about how international human rights standards must be, without appropriately accommodating particular cases and the individual needs of states.

As this chapter has shown, flexible timeframes and steady efforts are needed cumulatively.[244] This could enable a continuing discourse about human rights obligations and protections in states of transition: about their limits but also about the opportunities they offer.

[243] UN Doc A/C.3/SR.1374, above n 95, para 22.
[244] UN Doc A/67/499-S/2012/746, above n 207, para 44.

5

On the Law of Peace: Parameters, Challenges and Limits

'O Muse, pour into my ear that tale of law of peace which men have too long neglected, that this sorely afflicted generation of ours may see its reflection in that peerless mirror and learn its lesson'.[1]

Cornelis Van Vollenhoven, *The Law of Peace*, 1936

'The more enduring peace is not to be implemented in halting expedients, or bought with dollars, or even enforced with arms. Increasingly it must be waged in execution of a well-planned and embracing strategy. Increasingly it must be waged with law. It is in progress thus conceived and persistently advanced that we may hope to glimpse such horizons'.[2]

Edwin D Dickinson, *Law and Peace*, 1951

'Conflicts ... are not resolved simply by legal rules, for these conflicts have causes and it is only by the elimination of these causes that the conflicts can ultimately be resolved. However, all societies face the need to impose limits on the methods which parties may use to promote their interests which are at variance with the interests of others'.[3]

Derek Bowett, *The Search for Peace*, 1972

I. The Quest for Absolute Limitations in Peacemaking

Peace requires compromises, which entail human rights concessions.[4] The ongoing constitutional change processes in the Arab world and the Balkans demonstrate that ethnic and sectarian diversity remains a challenge for international law. The quest for absolute legal limitations for peace agreements and constitutions poses difficulties in identifying the exact threshold between legality and illegality.

[1] Cornelis van Vollenhoven, *The Law of Peace* (London, MacMillian and Co, 1936) 1.

[2] Edwin D Dickinson, *Law and Peace* (Philadelphia, University of Pennsylvania Press, 1951) 147.

[3] Derek Bowett, *The Search for Peace* (London, Routledge & Kegan Paul, 1972) 1.

[4] As Hersch Lauterpacht put it, peace sometimes involuntarily involves 'the sacrifice of justice on the altar of stability and security': Hersch Lauterpacht, *The Function of Law in the International Community* (Oxford, Oxford University Press, 2003) 446.

During the Kosovo conflict, some commentators tried to make a distinction between illegality and illegitimacy, arguing that NATO's use of force was incompatible with international law but nonetheless morally justified.[5] In the case of peacemaking, a semantic nuance has been made by diplomats in speaking of an *imperfect peace* to value the end or prevention of devastating hostilities.[6]

However, this begs the question about what kind of *peace* is desired. It is hard to argue that peace should be reached at any price, particularly if the absence of armed violence means the suppression and discrimination of some groups for the disproportionate benefit of others.

This chapter reflects on the prior findings and case studies, closing the circle of thoughts on state transitions, power-sharing and international law begun in the first chapter. The chapter takes a step back to reconsider the relation between the just war and just peace concepts. Following on from the analysis of the European Court of Human Right's (ECtHR) decision in *Sejdić and Finci v Bosnia and Herzegovina*, and the debates about Lebanon's confessional system in the UN human rights monitoring bodies, a closer look will be taken at the category of peremptory norms as a red line that should not be crossed in peacemaking. Subsequently, a conceptual model is proposed for systematising dilemmas in the *law of peace* debate. The chapter concludes with suggested further research questions and final remarks.

A. From Just War to Just Peace: Human Rights as the Foundations for Peace

It remains significant that international law entails an explicit normative approach towards controlling and restraining warfare, but appears to be less categorical about how to control or restrain peacemaking, beyond arguing for the fulfilment of human rights.[7]

Authors have written extensively about the concept of war, the *perfect war*, the use of force and the ethics of destruction.[8] Historically, for instance, while Grotius deliberately entitled his treatise *De Jure Belli Ac Pacis* in order to emphasise equally the law of war and the law of peace, he mainly focused on the manner

[5] Anthea Roberts, 'Legality vs Legitimacy: Can Uses of Force be Illegal but Justified?' in Philip Alston and Euan MacDonald (eds), *Human Rights, Intervention, and the Use of Force* (Oxford, Oxford University Press, 2008) 179.

[6] For more detail, see Ch 1.

[7] The amount of legal literature on warfare is striking. For a selection, see Onuma Yasuaki (ed), *A Normative Approach to War: Peace, War, and Justice in Hugo Grotius* (Oxford, Clarendon Press, 1993) 1; David Kennedy, *Of War and Law* (Princeton, Princeton University Press, 2006) 1. In the field of political philosophy, see Michael Walzer, *Just and Unjust Wars: A Moral Argument with Historical Illustrations* (New York, Basic, 1977) 3.

[8] Ward Thomas, *The Ethics of Destruction: Norms and Force in International Relations* (Ithaca, NY, Cornell University Press, 1999) 1. On the *perfect war*, see Henry Wheaton, *Elements of International Law* (New York, Baker, Voorhis & Co, 1916) 518–19.

and justification of warfare.[9] Grotius defines war, explains 'who may lawfully make war', elaborates on the 'difference between the real and pretended causes of war', and even the 'dubious causes of war', 'rules of prudence, directing our choice of what is good', and 'the miseries of war', but does not go into equivalent detail about peace.[10] Those parts of Grotius' treatise which do address peace, stipulate how to breach it rather than how to maintain it.[11]

The 1899 and 1907 Hague Conventions and subsequent Geneva Protocols are an example of international law for meticulous limits regarding the employment of force and the correct behaviour of soldiers, as well as the rights and duties of states.[12] In comparison, although legal scholars have tried to grasp the essence of peace and continually discuss mechanisms for effective constitutional designs, specific rules for peacemakers are rare.[13]

Indeed, the very first Hague Convention of 1899 focuses on the 'Pacific Settlement of International Disputes' (Hague I), whereas the second Convention introduces 'Laws and Customs of War on Land'.[14] Symbolically, this gives hope that humanity aims for peace instead of war. Hague I encourages recourse to instruments such as good offices, mediation, inquiry and international arbitration, which were included in Article 33 of Chapter VI of the UN Charter. Nonetheless, dispute settlement mechanisms in international law have been mainly tailored to settle disputes between states, whereas the vast majority of current conflicts appears within states. In 1977, Protocol II extended the rules of warfare to the protection of victims of non-international armed conflicts.[15] Yet, rules for the pacific settlement of intra-state conflicts have not been annexed to Hague I, keeping the issue a matter of state sovereignty.[16]

[9] Hugo Grotius, *The Rights of War and Peace: Including the Law of Nature and of Nations* first published in 1624, ed Jean Barbeyrac (Indianapolis, Liberty Fund, 2005) 133.

[10] ibid, 134, 384, 1096, 1140, 1148.

[11] Only a few of his writings actually scrutinise peace in particular. See ibid, 1558 (XI A General Rule for the Interpreting Articles of Peace), 1567 (XXVII That There is a Distinction between Giving New Occasions of War, and Breaking the Peace), 1568 (XXVIII How a Peace May be Broke by Doing Contrary to What is Supposed to be in Every Peace), 1572 (XXXIV How a Peace May be Broken by Doing Contrary to What is Expressed in the Peace), 1574 (XXXVIII The Peace Shall Stand Firm, If the Injured Party be Willing to It), 1574 (XXXIX How a Peace May be Broken, by Doing What is Contrary to the Nature of every Peace), 1606 (XI A Truce Broken on one Side, the other May Renew the War).

[12] See, eg, Convention (IV) Respecting the Laws and Customs of War on Land and its Annex: Regulation concerning the Laws and Customs of War on Land, 18 October 1907, 187 CTS 227; Protocol Additional to the Geneva Conventions of 12 August 1949, and relating to the Protection of Victims of Non-International Armed Conflicts (Protocol II), 8 June 1977.

[13] See Chs 1 and 2.

[14] Convention (I) for the Pacific Settlement of International Disputes, 29 July 1899; Convention (II) with Respect to the Laws and Customs of War on Land and its Annex: Regulations concerning the Laws and Customs of War on Land, 29 July 1899.

[15] Protocol II, above n 12.

[16] For a contemporary view of the historical effects of the Second Hague Peace Conference, see Christine Chinkin et al, 'Panel Discussion: Has International Law Civilized Conflicts Since 1907?' in Thomas Giegerich and Ursula E Heinz (eds), *A Wiser Century?: Judicial Dispute Settlement, Disarmament and the Laws of War 100 Years After the Second Hague Peace Conference* (Berlin, Duncker & Humblot, 2009) 509.

i. The Missing Piece of the Perfect War: Towards a 'Jus in Pace'?

The role of foreign third parties in the settling of intra-state conflicts became critical comparatively recently.[17] In parallel, the growing emphasis on responsibility in international law developed gradually, leading to the present legal discourse about *Humanity's Law, lex pacificatoria* and *jus post bellum*.[18] Alongside this evolution within the legal field, scholars of ethics, public policy, global governance and anthropology have begun theorising about a *jus in pace* ('law in peace') and a *jus ad pacem* ('law after peace') in the post-Cold War context.[19] They aim at supplementing the laws of war with a 'new law in peace' under the umbrella of 'human security'.[20] This notion is connected to the aforementioned 'culture of peace' debate in the General Assembly, bringing together aspects of peace, security, foreign interventions and post-conflict peace-building.[21]

Among other authors, Gwyn Prins asked whether 'the quality of the peace' and 'who made the peace and how' matter.[22] Focusing on contemporary intra-state conflicts, he concluded that the 'legitimation of the peace in fraught circumstances is less often a dogmatic judgement than a question of choosing the lesser evil'.[23] Meanwhile, Mary Kaldor argued that a 'new ethical approach is needed', grounded 'in the notion that the rights of individuals supersede the rights of states and that, therefore, international law that applies to individuals overrides the law'.[24] Christine Chinkins encouraged in this context an 'articulation of a more specific "law of peace" that encompasses the concept of security in interventions and post-conflict societies'.[25] She commented that the

> time appears to be ripe to clarify and conceptualize practice round the security continuum of conflict prevention, management, resolution (and attempted resolution) and post-conflict reconstruction in order to develop an international legal framework that identifies that legal obligations and duties applicable to the diverse actors.[26]

[17] Meredith Reid Sarkees, Frank Whelon Wayman and J David Singer, 'Inter-State, Intra-State, and Extra-State Wars: A Comprehensive Look at their Distribution over Time, 1816–1997' (2003) 47(1) *International Studies Quarterly* 49.

[18] See Ch 1. Larry May revitalised Aristotle's concept of 'meionexia', the disposition to accept less than one is due, to describe the dilemmas after the end of a war from a legal-philosophical perspective: see Larry May, *After War Ends: A Philosophical Perspective* (Cambridge, Cambridge University Press, 2012) 8.

[19] George R Lucas, 'From Jus ad Bellum to Jus ad Pacem: Re-thinking Just-War Criteria for the Use of Military Force of Humanitarian Ends' in Deen K Chatterjee and Don E Scheid (eds), *Ethics And Foreign Intervention* (Cambridge, Cambridge University Press, 2003) 74.

[20] ibid.

[21] See Ch 1, Part I.B.ii.

[22] Gwyn Prins, 'Conditions for Jus in Pace in the Face of the Future' in Charles Reed and David Ryall (eds), *The Price of Peace Just War in the Twenty-First Century* (Cambridge, Cambridge University Press, 2007) 236.

[23] ibid, 239.

[24] Mary Kaldor, 'From Just War to Just Peace' in Monica Den Boer and Jaap De Wilde (eds), *The Viability of Human Security* (Amsterdam, Amsterdam University Press, 2008) 21.

[25] Christine Chinkin, 'An International Law Framework with Respect to International Peace and Security' in Marlies Glasius and Mary Kaldor (eds), *A Human Security Doctrine for Europe: Project, Principles, Practicalities: Project, Principles and Practicalities* (Oxford, Routledge, 2006) 173, 193.

[26] ibid.

However, although at present there may be a 'blurring of the distinction between external and internal, state and non-state, combatant and non-combatant' which implies a 'blurring of the distinction between war and peace', international law remains clear.[27] As this study has shown, the relevant question for international law is whether peace agreements and constitutional designs infringe human rights. Potential derogations and justifications need careful consideration, while peremptory norms must be respected. Instead of inventing new concepts, refocusing the debate on human rights could help to sharpen the view on peacemaking through the lens of international law.

ii. Peacemaking and Legal Restrictions

An explanation for why peacemaking is, as yet, less restricted than warfare, may be borrowed from the thinking of Walter Benjamin, who conceptualised the relationship between law, justice and violence.[28] In Benjamin's view, law becomes imperative when violence needs to be tamed or executed, which explains the concentration on the laws of war.[29] As he understands it, violence has a dual function: it creates law (*rechtsetzend*) and preserves law (*rechtserhaltend*); this might explain why the absence of violence is less regulated.[30] In other words, on the condition that peacemaking ends violence, legal restrictions are unnecessary.

Concerning conflict resolution in the private law or national public law context, mediation associations and advocacy groups have increasingly called for a code of conduct for mediators.[31] The main rationale behind this movement is to guarantee standards for the behaviour of third parties. Internationally, organisations such as the United Nations have released guidance notes for Special Envoys and Special Representatives of the Secretary General, among others, instructing them about the limits of their actions.[32] Yet, although such internal guidelines can reflect institutional practice, accepted or tolerated by states, they are not binding on state action and remain solely an in-house directive when third-party mediators are sent.[33]

[27] Kaldor, above n 24, 21.

[28] Walter Benjamin, 'Zur Kritik der Gewalt' in Walter Benjamin, *Zur Kritik der Gewalt und andere Aufsätze* (Frankfurt am Main, Suhrkamp, 1990) 45.

[29] ibid.

[30] On the impact and role of Walter Benjamin's thinking in the field of peace and conflict studies, see also Johannes Schwerdtfeger, 'Zu Theorien und Methoden in der Friedensforschung' in Bernhard Moltmann (ed), *Perspektiven der Friedensforschung* (Baden-Baden, Nomos, 1988) 48. See also Diane Morgan, 'Why "Perpetual Peace" is Almost a Pleonasm' (2013) 25(1) *Peace Review: A Journal of Social Justice* 9.

[31] Penny Brooker, 'Towards a Code of Professional Conduct for Construction Mediators' (2011) 3(1) *International Journal of Law in the Built Environment* 24. For an introduction, see Nadja Alexander, 'Mediation and the Art of Regulation' (2008) 8 *Queensland University of Technology Law and Justice Journal* 1.

[32] See Ch 1.

[33] See, eg, William Edeson, 'The Role of Technical Bodies' in Rüdiger Wolfrum and Volker Röben (eds), *Developments of International Law in Treaty Making* (Berlin, Springer, 2005) 63, 83.

iii. Do Peacemakers Need Specific Normative Rules?

In 2000, the UN Brahimi Report took an important step in recommending that:

> before the Security Council agrees to implement a ceasefire or peace agreement with a United Nations-led peacekeeping operation, the Council assure itself that the agreement meets threshold conditions, such as consistency with international human rights standards and practicability of specified tasks and timelines.[34]

Adopting parts of the report, the Security Council urged

> parties to prospective peace agreements, including regional and subregional organizations and arrangements, to coordinate and cooperate fully with the United Nations from an early stage in negotiations, bearing in mind the need for … compliance with the rules and principles of international law, in particular international humanitarian, human rights and refugee law.[35]

One decade later in 2010, the UN Secretary General's guidance note on the UN's approach to transitional justice stressed 'compliance with international norms and standards when designing and implementing transitional justice processes and mechanisms', as these set 'the normative boundaries of UN engagement'.[36]

In 2012, the UN Guidance for Effective Mediation emphasised that mediators have to

> conduct their work within the framework constituted by the rules of international law that govern the given situation, most prominently global and regional conventions, international humanitarian, human rights and refugee laws and international criminal law, including, where applicable, the Rome Statute of the International Criminal Court.[37]

The UN guidance acknowledges that mediators 'frequently have to grapple with the urgency of ending violence' and weigh up 'the demands of conflict parties with the normative and legal frameworks'.[38] It recommends that mediators should balance 'the need to adhere to international norms without overtly taking on an advocacy role'.[39] Although the guidance states that peace agreements that provide for certain amnesties cannot be endorsed, no further concrete normative rules for thematic issues are provided.

As described above, the debate about responsibility of UN peacemakers developed alongside the promotion of the ICC Rome Statute and Transitional Justice, which explains why the guidance note provides more details in these areas.

[34] Report of the Panel on United Nations Peace Operations, UN Doc A/55/305–S/2000/809, 21 August 2000, para 64(a).

[35] SC Res 1327, 13 November 2000, Annex, para I.

[36] Guidance Note of the Secretary-General: United Nations Approach to Transitional Justice, March 2010, para A.1.

[37] Guidance for Effective Mediation, Strengthening the Role of Mediation in the Peaceful Settlement of Disputes, Conflict Prevention and Resolution, Report of the Secretary-General, 25 June 2012, Annex, para 40.

[38] ibid, para 40.

[39] ibid.

The UN also have a close eye on women's issues related to peace and security.[40] Legal limitations for power-sharing peace agreements or other specific thematic areas of conflict settlements have been addressed only in general terms so far.[41]

The question of whether peacemaking needs rules is ultimately not a legal one, but a political and diplomatic matter. The problem is not the drafting of codes of conduct, but the decision about what rules should be in place. Seen purely from the perspective of international law, legal practice and state consent specify the normative framework of operation in the absence of agreed laws and codification.[42] As analysed in this book, the decisions of regional human rights courts and statements by international human rights monitoring bodies shed light on the legal boundaries of conflict settlements.

Forcing peacemakers into normative straitjackets should, if advisable at all, not extend beyond the requirement to be conscious of 'minimum conditions' of international law in order to maintain flexibility.[43] Ultimately, peacemakers do not need new rules, but more systematic legal reflection, reminding them of the nuances in international human rights law while comprehending the end to armed violence as a prerequisite for peace.

B. The Illusion of a 'Perfect Peace'

Legal dilemmas are, in any case, unavoidable. Diplomats and heads of states appear to have already accepted that peacemaking renders an *imperfect peace* superior to *perfect victories*. In the 1980 debate in the Security Council about Rhodesia, the UK Representative, Sir Anthony Parsons, remarked pragmatically that it 'would have been too much to expect … to return to perfect peace within a few weeks of the end of a harsh and long drawn out civil war'.[44] In 1991, Botswana's foreign minister, Gaositwe Chiepe, commented on the peace process in South Africa in the UN General Assembly that expecting 'the establishment of perfect peace … as a prelude to the commencement of the negotiations' is 'expecting the impossible'.[45]

Perhaps peacemaking needs to accept and appreciate imperfection as a value instead of seeing it as a flaw. Waiting for *perfect peace* while facing continued suffering and killings would be more irresponsible than signing a legally flawed peace agreement when there is no time to waste in order to save lives, even if peace proves

[40] ibid. See also SC Res 1325, 31 October 2000.

[41] See Guidance for Mediators: Addressing Conflict-Related Sexual Violence in Ceasefire and Peace Agreements, United Nations, Department of Political Affairs, 2012.

[42] Hersch Lauterpacht, *International Law: The Collected Papers* vol 2 (The Law of Peace), ed Elihu Lauterpacht (Cambridge, Cambridge University Press, 2004) 271.

[43] For the debate, see also Christine Bell, 'Peace Agreements and Human Rights: Implications for the UN' in Nigel D White and Dirk Klaasen (eds), *UN, Human Rights and Post-Conflict Situations* (Manchester, Manchester University Press 2005) 241.

[44] UN Doc. S/PV.2192, 30 January 1980, para 56.

[45] UN Doc. A/46/PV.25, 15 October 1991.

to be only temporary.[46] Namibia's Permanent Representative to the UN, Martin Andjaba, one put this dilemma in a nutshell during a Security Council meeting:

> [I]t is unrealistic to expect a perfect peace … The English say 'The perfect is the enemy of the good'. If we wait for perfection …, we will lose everything that has been achieved in the … peace process.[47]

In the end, not only peace, but international law too tends to be imperfect, which reinstates the aforementioned nexus between law and peace.[48] At the beginning of the Iraq war in 2003, Singapore's Minister for Foreign Affairs, Shunmugam Jayakumar, summarised this tension between the imperfect, but yet aspiring, order of international law and the maintenance of peace:

> International legal regimes and norms are imperfect in their efficiency and observance. Some international norms are hotly contested. Still, the conduct of international relations today does not take place in a vacuum, but within that framework of laws, rules, standards and norms. Nevertheless, there is no escaping the fact that the maintenance of international peace and security is first among the purposes of the United Nations, and the most contested and controversial of its roles.[49]

The cases studies of Bosnia and Herzegovina and Lebanon have shown that the legal answer to the question whether peace should be sought at any price entails an array of legal considerations.[50] Affirming or negating this question too quickly would ignore the nuances of international law, which require the obligation to evaluate alternatives and keep the period of human rights restrictions proportional.

C. The Supremacy of Peace or Human Rights at Any Price?

Compromises in peacemaking do not necessarily imply a contest of the supremacy of *peace versus human rights*, or *peace versus justice*, since peace and human rights correlate.[51]

[46] See also UN Doc S/2000/54, 26 January 2000, Annex VII (Comment by Phakiso Mochochoko, Chargé d'affaires ad interim Lesotho: 'With memories of Srebrenica and Rwanda, in particular, as well as other unsuccessful United Nations stories still fresh in our minds, and given the complexity of the situation in the Democratic Republic of the Congo, we appreciate warnings not to throw caution to the wind and that delay may be preferable to error. At the same time, we cannot wait for perfect peace in the face of continued suffering and killing of Congolese people who want peace now …').

[47] UN Doc S/PV.4083, 16 December 1999, Comment by Mr Andjaba (Namibia). The expression 'The perfect is the enemy of the good' actually appears to derive back to Italy, as Voltaire wrote in his poem *La Bégueule* in 1772: 'Dans ses écrits, un sàge Italien dit que le mieux est l'ennemi du bien': Marie-Jean-Antoine-Nicolas Caritat, marquis de Condorcet, *Œuvres complètes de Voltaire* vol II (Paris, Carez, Thomine et Fortic, 1822) 706.

[48] On the imperfection of international law, see Bruno Simma and Andreas Th Müller, 'Exercise and Limits of Jurisdiction' in James Crawford and Martti Koskenniemi (eds), *The Cambridge Companion to International Law* (Cambridge, Cambridge University Press, 2012) 148.

[49] UN Doc A/58/PV.16, 29 September 2003.

[50] See Chs 3 and 4.

[51] Hurst Hannum, 'Peace Versus Justice: Creating Rights as Well as Order Out of Chaos' (2006) 13(4) *International Peacekeeping* 582.

Historically, the ostracism of war and the prohibition of the use of force were historical achievements in international law prior to the language of human rights.[52] A major accomplishment in international law was the aforementioned Convention Hague I and the Kellogg-Briand Pact in 1928, both of which emphasise the supremacy of peace, without referencing individual or group rights.[53] The UN Charter reiterates that the purposes of the UN are to maintain international peace and security, acknowledging human rights only after the need for developing friendly relations between states.[54] The UN Charter includes mechanisms for responding to a breach of peace, but not explicitly for a breach of human rights.[55] This absence of a normative rule for human rights enforcement is why the justification of interventions by the international community under the concept of *responsibility to protect* is complicated.[56]

On the other hand, many human rights documents, such as the Universal Declaration of Human Rights, recognise human rights as 'the foundation for freedom, justice and peace in the world'.[57] A decisive factor in this debate is what definition of 'peace' one applies, as the concept of peace can take on a narrow or wide meaning, which can range from the end to hostilities to the conclusive solving of conflict causes.[58] As this study has discussed, the first is a necessary precondition for enabling human rights.

In the end, peace and human rights are interwoven. As the experience of the Arab uprisings confirms, conflict will arise if human rights are not protected, whereas the full exercise of rights is impossible without an end to violence. The case studies Bosnia and Herzegovina and Lebanon revealed that full compliance with human rights can be deferred in order to grasp any prospect of peace.[59] This may be a 'bitter pill', but it remains a necessity in practice, opting first for the end of

[52] In this regard, Lauterpacht stated that the purpose of international law is 'first, to protect and secure the independence of States by the prohibition of the use of force' and only 'thirdly, to give effect, through appropriate limitations and international supervision of sovereignty of States, to the principle that the protection human personality and its fundamental freedoms is the ultimate purpose of all law': Lauterpacht, above n 42, 47.

[53] Convention (I), above n 14, Preamble ('Animated by the sincere desire to work for the maintenance of general peace …'). See also General Treaty for the Renunciation of War, signed in Paris, 27 August 1928 ('Persuaded that the time has, come when a frank renunciation of war as an instrument of national policy should be made to the end that the peaceful and friendly relations now existing between their peoples may be perpetuated …').

[54] UN Charter, Art 1.

[55] See UN Charter, Chapter VII ('Action with Respect to Threats to Peace, Breaches of the Peace, and Acts of Aggression'). See also UN Charter, Art 39 ('The Security Council shall determine the existence of any threat to the peace, breach of the peace, or act of aggression …').

[56] Carsten Stahn, 'Responsibility to Protect: Political Rhetoric or Emerging Legal Norm?' (2007) 101(1) *American Journal of International Law* 99, 106.

[57] Universal Declaration of Human Rights, GA Res 217A (III), 10 December 1948, Preamble ('Whereas recognition of the inherent dignity and of the equal and inalienable rights of all members of the human family is the foundation of freedom, justice and peace in the world …').

[58] Bruno Simma (ed), *The Charter of the United Nations: A Commentary* vol I (Oxford, Oxford University Press, 2002) Art 1, para 9, Art 39, paras 6, 11.

[59] See Chs 3 and 4.

armed conflict and the protection of the right to life, and second for a compliance with other human rights as a reward in the long-run.[60]

As the Ambassador of Botswana, Legwaila Joseph Legwaila, once put it in a debate about peace in Bosnia and Herzgeovina, there is no doubt that the scars of the deep wounds that people inflicted upon one another during war 'will remain visible for a long time to come', yet peace settlements offer the possibility of sustainable peace.[61] The end of hostilities provides an opportunity to create conditions conducive to a secure and durable peace, which may allow a turning-point for starting 'a journey on the road to national reconciliation and healing and a peaceful future'.[62]

II. Peremptory Norms and Peacemaking

In *Sejdić and Finci v Bosnia and Herzegovina*, the legal counsel of the applicants argued that direct and explicit racial discrimination is considered amongst the 'most egregious types of discrimination, the prohibition of which is widely accepted as customary international law and even *jus cogens*' ('the compelling law').[63] The ECtHR did not address the argument; however, various other legal scholars have continued to call for using peremptory norms (*jus cogens*) as a red line that should not be crossed in peacemaking.[64]

Although sometimes criticised for being against the principle of state consent, peremptory norms are increasingly seen as instructive about the normative meaning of global justice and human security.[65] *Jus cogens* norms 'evolve from the common value fund cherished by all nations'.[66] In this regard, *jus cogens* is seen

[60] Bill Clinton, *My Life* (New York, Alfred A Knopf, 2004) 644. On the relationship between the right to life and right to peace, see Paul de Waart, 'The Inter-Relationship Between the Right to Life and the Right to Peace' in Bertrand G Ramcharan (ed), *The Right to Life in International Law* (The Hague, Martinus Nijhoff Publishers, 1985) 90.

[61] UN Doc S/PV.3607, 15 December 1995.

[62] ibid.

[63] Applicants' Written Submission to the Grand Chamber, ECtHR App Nos 27996/06 and 34836/06, 28 April 2009, para 84.

[64] For the debate, see also Gro Nystuen, *Achieving Peace or Protecting Human Rights: Conflicts between Norms Regarding Ethnic Discrimination in the Dayton Peace Agreement* (Leiden, Martinus Nijhoff Publishers, 2005) 130–34; and Serena Forlati, 'Coercion as a Ground Affecting the Validity of Peace Treaties' in Enzo Cannizzaro (ed), *The Law of Treaties Beyond the Vienna Convention* (Oxford, Oxford University Press, 2011) 320, 329 ('It deems … to be the most appropriate way to restore peace, as long as the content of that treaty is not inconsistent with *jus cogens* …').

[65] See also Ruti Teitel, *Humanity's Law* (Oxford, Oxford University Press, 2011) 17. For a plea for caution, see Rosalyn Higgins, *Problems and Process: International Law and How We Use It* (Oxford, Clarendon Press, 1994) 267 ('There is a contemporary trend of mindless invocation of the fashionable concepts – self-determination, rights *erga omnes*, *uti possidetis*, etc., etc. But these are not *mantras*, the mere chanting of which is sufficient in itself. We have to see, rigorously, what exactly these legal concepts mean, and when they are appropriately applicable …'). See also Andrea Bianchi, 'Human Rights and the Magic of Jus cogens' (2008) 19(3) *European Journal of International Law* 491.

[66] Christian Tomuschat, 'Obligations Arising for States Without or Against Their Will' (1993) 241.IV *Recueil des Cours* 209, 307

as international law's 'higher ethical norms' and the 'bedrock of the international law order'.[67] The UN Guidance on Effective Mediation highlightes that 'there is a growing international consensus on some norms', despite the fact that 'not all norms are equally applied in different national contexts and there can be different interpretations within a given society'.[68] And although the UN Guidance does not explicitly mention the technical terms 'peremptory norms' or 'jus cogens', as both are usually utilised in the particular context of the validity of international treaties, the concept of universal norms shines through as a starting point for defining absolute minimum standards in international law for peacemaking.[69]

A. Normative Foundations of Peremptory Norms

After decades of political and legal debate, peremptory norms have been acknowledged in the Vienna Convention on the Law of Treaties (VCLT).[70] In the course of its work on the codification of the law of treaties, the International Law Commission (ILC) commented that there are rules in international law 'from which States cannot at their own free will contract out'.[71]

In 1996, the International Court of Justice (ICJ) endorsed the existence of *jus cogens* norms.[72] The ICJ noted that whether a norm is part of *jus cogens* depends on 'the legal character of the norm'.[73] In 2012, the Court's decision on the *Jurisdictional Immunities of the State (Germany v. Italy)* provided an application of *jus cogens*.[74] Scrutinising the relationship between *jus cogens* and the rule of state immunity, the ICJ ruled that 'against the background of a century of practice in … almost every peace treaty or post-war settlement', it

> is difficult to see that international law contains a rule requiring the payment of full compensation to each and every individual victim as a rule accepted by the

[67] Mary Ellen O'Connell, 'Jus cogens: International Law's Higher Ethical Norms' in Donald Earl Childress III (ed), *The Role of Ethics in International Law* (Cambridge, Cambridge University Press, 2011) 78. See also Karl Zemanek, 'The Metamorphosis of Jus cogens: From an Institution of Treaty Law to the Bedrock of the International Legal Order?' in Cannizzaro, above n 64, 381.

[68] Guidance for Effective Mediation, above n 37.

[69] As Christian Tomuschat noted: 'One thing is certain … the international community accepts today that there exists a class of legal precepts which is hierarchically superior to "ordinary" rules of international law, precepts which cannot even be brushed aside, or derogated from, by the sovereign will of two or more States as long as the international community upholds the values encapsulated in them': Christian Tomuschat, 'Reconceptualizing the Debate on Jus Cogens and Obligations Erga Omnes: Concluding Observations' in Christian Tomuschat and Jean Marc Thouvenin (eds), *The Fundamental Rules of the International Legal Order: Jus Cogens And Obligations Erga Omnes* (The Hague, Martinus Nijhoff Publishers, 2006) 425.

[70] VCLT, Arts 53, 64 and 71, 27 January 1980, 1155 United Nations Treaty Series 331, 8 International Legal Materials 679.

[71] Draft Articles on the Law of Treaties, and Commentary, Report of the International Law Commission, 4 May–19 July 1966, Art 50, para 1.

[72] Legality of the Threat or Use of Nuclear Weapons, ICJ Advisory Opinion, 8 July 1996, para 83.

[73] ibid.

[74] Jurisdictional Immunities of the State (Germany v. Italy; Greece intervening), ICJ Judgment, 3 February 2012, paras 92–97.

international community of States as a whole as one from which no derogation is permitted.[75]

The VCLT establishes that a norm belongs to *jus cogens* if the enshrined right or prohibition is 'accepted and recognized by the international community of States as a whole as a norm from which no derogation is permitted and which can be modified only by a subsequent norm of general international law having the same character'.[76] This has led to the conclusion that the establishment of *jus cogens* norms is 'less a constitutive than a declaratory process'.[77] Hence, the consensus in state practice needs to be analysed in order to decide whether certain provisions in peace settlements are allowed or prohibited under international law.[78]

B. Acknowledged *Jus Cogens* Norms

During the drafting process of the Vienna Convention, the ILC decided against including any examples of *jus cogens*.[79] In the debate, legal scholars mentioned some of the acknowledged peremptory norms: the prohibition of the use of force; the prohibition of slavery, piracy or genocide; human rights; the equality of states; and the principle of self-determination.[80] The ILC Commentary on the Draft Articles on the Responsibility of States for Internationally Wrongful Acts highlight: the prohibitions of aggression, genocide, slavery, racial discrimination, crimes against humanity and torture, and the right to self-determination.[81] In 2006, the ILC Study Group on the Fragmentation of International Law under the chairmanship of Martti Koskenniemi summarised in its report the 'most frequently cited candidates for the status of *jus cogens*', which are summarised in Table 1 below.[82]

[75] ibid, para 94.

[76] VCLT, Art 53. Technically, not all non-derogable rights are necessarily peremptory norms. Non-derogable rights are a starting point for *jus cogens*. However, non-derogable rights more narrowly require a status of emergency, whereas *jus cogens* norms apply at any time. See Draft Articles on the Law of Treaties, and Commentary, above n 71, Art 50, para 2, which states that it would be not correct 'to say that a provision in a treaty possesses the character of *jus cogens* merely because the parties have stipulated that no derogation from that provision is to be permitted, so that another treaty which conflicted with that provision would be void'. See also, eg, Ian D Seiderman, *Hierarchy in International Law: The Human Rights Dimension* (Antwerp, Intersentia, 2001) 84, 88.

[77] Tomuschat, above n 69, 307.

[78] For the importance of analysing state practice and the rulings of national cours, see also Jurisdictional Immunities of the State, above n 74, para 85.

[79] Draft Articles on the Law of Treaties, and Commentaries, Art 50, above n 71, para 3.

[80] ibid.

[81] Draft Articles on Responsibility of States for Internationally Wrongful Acts, and Commentary, Art 26, para 5, Report of the International Law Commission, 23 April–1 June and 2 July–10 August 2001.

[82] See Table 1, paras 1–9. Fragmentation of International Law, Difficulties Arising from the Diversification and Expansion of International Law, Report of the Study Group of the International Law Commission, UN Doc A/CN.4/L.682, 4 April 2006, para 374. For Table 1, paras 10–11, see also Report of the Study Group of the International Law Commission, Addendum, UN Doc A/CN.4/L.682/Add.1, 2 May 2006, para 35. In comparison to the first document mentioned, which speaks of the 'prohibition of aggressive use of force', the Addendum only mentions the 'prohibition of the use of force'.

In 2011, the ILC affirmed the same set of peremptory norms as in the Draft Articles on Responsibility of States when it produced its Commentary on the Draft Articles on the Responsibility of International Organisations, which reflects that there is a growing certainty about the determination and volume of *jus cogens* norms.[83]

Table 1 Summary of peremptory norms mentioned by the ILC

1	Prohibition of aggression and the use of force
2	Right of self-defence
3	Prohibition of genocide
4	Prohibition of torture
5	Prohibition of crimes against humanity
6	Prohibition of slavery and slave trade
7	Prohibition of piracy
8	Prohibition of racial discrimination and apartheid
9	Prohibition of hostilities directed at a civilian population ('basic rules of international humanitarian law')
10	Rights protecting the basic rights of the human person
11	Rights of self-determination

C. The Prohibition of Racial Discrimination as a Peremptory Norm

With regard to state transitions, power-sharing and international law, the prohibition of racial discrimination becomes relevant. A general prohibition of discrimination is not covered by practice and state consent.[84]

In 1971, the ICJ addressed wider aspects of non-discrimination in its advisory opinion on the *Legal Consequences for States of the Continued Presence of South Africa in Namibia (South West Africa)*.[85] The ICJ stated that 'distinctions,

[83] Draft Articles on the Responsibility of International Organizations, and Commentary, Art 26, para 2, Report of the International Law Commission, 26 April–3 June and 4 July–12 August 2011. On the matter, see also Nina Jørgensen, 'The Responsibility to Protect and the Obligations of States and Organizations under the Law of International Responsibility' in André Nollkaemper and Julian Hoffman (eds), *The Responsibility to Protect: From Principle to Practice* (Amsterdam, Amsterdam University Press, 2012) 127, 125.

[84] William E Conklin, 'The Peremptory Norms of the International Community' (2012) 23(3) *European Journal of International Law* 837.

[85] In this case, the ICJ held by 13 to 2 votes that the continued presence of South Africa in Namibia was illegal. Criticism was particularly levelled at South Africa's official governmental policy in Namibia of aiming 'to achieve a complete physical separation of races and ethnic groups in separate areas within the territory'. Legal Consequences for States of the Continued Presence of South Africa in Namibia (South West Africa) notwithstanding Security Council Resolution 276 (1970), ICJ Advisory Opinion, 21 June 1971, para 131.

exclusions, restrictions and limitations exclusively based on grounds of race, colour, descent or national or ethnic origin which constitute a denial of fundamental human rights is a flagrant violation of the purposes and principles of the Charter'.[86] However, the ICJ abstained from declaring the prohibition of discrimination as *jus cogens*.[87]

In comparison, the Inter-American Commission on Human Rights (IACHR) has explicitly stated that the prohibition of discrimination should be considered part of *jus cogens*.[88] In 2003, the IACHR stated that

> the principle of equality before the law, equal protection before the law and non-discrimination belongs to jus cogens, because the whole legal structure of national and international public order rests on it and it is a fundamental principle that permeates all laws.[89]

The Commission stressed that 'discriminatory treatment of any person, owing to gender, race, color, language, religion or belief, political or other opinion, national, ethnic or social origin, nationality, age, economic situation, property, civil status, birth or any other status is unacceptable' and that at 'the existing stage of the development of international law, the fundamental principle of equality and non-discrimination has entered the realm of *jus cogens*'.[90]

The IACHR endorsed a broad definition of the prohibition of discrimination as *jus cogens*, yet international state practice has never confirmed this extensive interpretation.[91] As detailed in this study, regional understandings of equality differ greatly.[92] The ECtHR included ethnic discrimination within the general prohibition of discrimination for the regime of the European Convention on

[86] ibid, para 130.

[87] In 1970, the ICJ previously stated in its decision *Barcelona Traction, Light and Power Company Ltd* that 'outlawing of acts of aggression, and of genocide, as also from the principles and rules concerning the basic rights of the human person, including protection from slavery and racial discrimination' are obligations *erga omnes*, declaring that these are rights 'all States can be held to have a legal interest in their protection'. In the Namibia Advisory decision, the ICJ revitalised its *erga omnes* concept. However, although the ICJ has characterised the prohibition of racial discrimination as an obligation *erga omnes*, it has not qualified it as *jus cogens* yet. See Barcelona Traction, Light and Power Company, Limited, ICJ Judgment, 5 February 1970, para 34. On differences and similarities between *erga omnes* obligations and *jus cogens* norms, see Paolo Picone, 'The Distinction between Jus Cogens and Obligations Erga Omnes' in Cannizzaro, above n 64, 411.

[88] Juridical Condition and Rights of Undocumented Migrants, IACHR, Advisory Opinion OC-18/03, 17 September 2003, para 101.

[89] ibid.

[90] ibid.

[91] Only 25 countries have accepted the IACHR's contentious judgement. The UN Human Rights Commission has also partially invoked the advisory decision. As Sarah Cleveland highlighted, 'the decision represents a significant milestone in the development of international protections' relating to non-discrimination. However, the Court's analysis still needs to be confirmed 'in future cases before that and other tribunals': Sarah H Cleveland, 'Legal Status and Rights of Undocumented Workers: Advisory Opinion OC-18/03' (2005) 99(2) *American Journal of International Law* 460, 465. See also UN Doc E/CN.4/RES/2004/53, 20 April 2004.

[92] See also Christopher McCrudden, 'International and European Norms Regarding National Legal Remedies for Racial Inequality' in Sandra Fredman et al (eds), *Discrimination and Human Rights: The Case of Racism* (Oxford, Oxford University Press, 2001) 251.

Human Rights (ECHR), but did not comment on a *jus cogens* consensus among European states.[93] The UN human rights monitoring bodies recommended a phasing-out of the political confessional system for Lebanon, but expressed its understanding of exceptional transitory phases.[94]

Gro Nystuen noted in her assessment of the Dayton Peace Agreement that the scope of non-discrimination 'is far from clear'.[95] She highlighted that there is 'a widespread practice among states not to engage in ethnic discrimination, as well as to consider ethnic discrimination as unlawful (*opinion juris*)'.[96] Nonetheless, state practice accepts that, although 'it is clearly prohibited to discriminate on racial or ethnic grounds in general, there may be situations in which such discrimination seems justified'.[97] As Javaid Rehman observed, an overly 'generous view of *jus cogens* might stretch the concept to unacceptable limits so as to risk its indelibility'.[98] The conclusion that ethnic or confessional power-sharing violate peremptory norms has not been explicitly recognised by the international community. Neither the Security Council nor the General Assembly has declared the general prohibition of discrimination to be *jus cogens*.[99] Only the prohibition of racial discrimination and apartheid has been considered *jus cogens*, which has been criticised as a weak point in the international protection of minority rights.[100] The absence of a clear practice declaring that discriminatory power-sharing arrangements are in contradiction to peremptory norms indicates that the international community tolerates them under certain conditions. The narrow scope of *jus cogens* implies that peacemaking is only constrained by international law to a limited extent.

D. Responsibility in International Law

A brief word of caution has to be sounded concerning the discussion about the responsibility under international law for human rights violations in the context

[93] See Ch 3.

[94] See Ch 4.

[95] Nystuen, above n 64, 134.

[96] She concludes that a 'prohibition against ethnic or racial discrimination figures prominently in most human rights instruments, and could for this reason also be considered an expression of state practice together with *opinion juris*, and thus deemed to have status of general customary law on this basis': ibid, 135.

[97] As an example, Nystuen mentions discrimination based on 'national origin', which makes 'internment of potential enemy nationals' permissible in 'times of emergency'. She refers to a similar opinion expressed by Hannikainen, who argues that it 'may be reasonable for the belligerent State to take temporary discriminatory measures against all the adult members of that national minority': ibid, 135–36. See also Lauri Hannikainen, *Peremptory Norms (Jus cogens) in International Law: Historical Development, Criteria, Present Status* (Helsinki, Finnish Lawyers' Publishing Company, 1988) 476.

[98] Javaid Rehman, *The Weaknesses in the International Protection of Minority Rights* (The Hague, Kluwer Law International, 2000) 121.

[99] Alexander Orakhelashvili, 'The Impact of Peremptory Norms on the Interpretation and Application of United Nations Security Council Resolutions' (2005) 16(1) *European Journal of International Law* 59, 81.

[100] Rehman, above n 98, 120.

of peace negotiations and post-conflict settlements.[101] As touched on in the Introduction to this study, the intersection of responsibility, human rights and peace has been increasingly scrutinised.[102] Among others, the matter primarily concerns three categories of actors in peace processes: states and their representatives, non-state actors, and peacemakers of international organisations such as UN envoys.[103] Should opposition groups be worried when they sign conflict settlements that contradict international human rights standards? Can UN diplomats be held accountable when they facilitate legally questionable peace agreements?

Regarding the latter, the development of international law is still in its infancy. In 2011, the ILC proposed in its Draft Articles responsibility of international organisations for internationally wrongful acts by their agents.[104] In addition to the current focus on UN peacekeeping missions, this could in the long run also raise attention for the UN's role in peacemaking and the compliance of UN-brokered peace agreements with human rights.[105] So far, peacemakers and their international organisations only bear responsibility according to their self-imposed internal obligations, such as the UN Guidance for Effective Mediation and other guidance notes of the Secretary General for UN envoys.[106]

The responsibility and accountability of non-state actors, as militias and armed insurgent groups, for the violation of international law during peace negotiations is limited.[107] Especially with regard to international humanitarian law, armed

[101] See also Caroline Holmqvist, 'Engaging Non-state Actors in Post Conflicts Settings' in Alan Bryden and Heiner Hänggi (eds), *Security Governance and Post-conflict Peacebuilding* (Berlin, Geneva Centre for the Democratic Control of Armed Forces, Lit Verlag, 2005) 49, 45.

[102] See Ch 1, Part I.C.i. On peacemaking and legal restrictions, see also Part I.A.ii above.

[103] On the discussion about whether or not peacemakers need specific normative rules, see Part I.A.iii above.

[104] Draft Articles on the Responsibility of International Organizations, above n 83, Art 6. The General Assembly took note of the articles and decided to return to the topic at its 69th session in September 2014. See GA Res 66/100, 9 December 2011.

[105] See also Matteo Tondini, 'Putting an End to Human Rights Violations by Proxy: Accountability of International Organizations and Member States in the Framework of Jus Post Bellum' in Carlos Villán Durán, *International Law for Humankind: Towards a New Jus Gentium* (The Hague, Martinus Nijhoff Publishers, 2010) 103–104. On the issue of human rights as limits to the authority of the UN, see Christian Tomuschat, 'International Organizations as Third Parties under the Law of International Treaties' in Cannizzaro, above n 64, 206, 222.

[106] See Guidance for Effective Mediation, above n 37. See also Guidance Note of the Secretary-General: United Nations Approach to Transitional Justice, above n 36; Guidance for Mediators: Addressing Conflict-Related Sexual Violence in Ceasefire and Peace Agreements, above n 41; Guidelines for UN Representatives on Certain Aspects of Negotiations for Conflict Resolution, United Nations, Department of Political Affairs, 1999 (updated 2006), printed in (2006) *UNJY* Ch 6, 495.

[107] The term 'non-state actor' in this context means all entities, individuals or groups that are not part of official state structures. See Draft Articles on the Responsibility of International Organizations, above n 83, Arts 4–5 and 10. For the debate of the terminology 'non-state actor', see Math Noortmann and Cedric Ryngaer, 'Introduction: Non-State Actors: International Law's Problematic Case' in Math Noortmann and Cedric Ryngaer (eds), *Non-State Actor Dynamics in International Law: From Law-Takers to Law-Makers* (Farnham, Burlington: Ashgate, 2010) 1.

non-state actors have been urged to comply with international minimum standards.[108] Since the establishment of the International Criminal Court, individuals have increasingly become addressees of international criminal responsibility.[109] Lobbying initiatives have also encouraged armed groups to adhere to international human rights.[110] However, despite this expanding debate about the role of armed non-state actors, transnational corporations and non-governmental organisations, the international legal system continues to focus predominantly on states.[111] Regarding human rights law, states are held exclusively responsible at an international level in human rights monitoring bodies and human rights courts for wrongful acts if they breach their human rights obligations under international law.[112] Finally, non-state actors participating in peace negotiations, especially opposition groups and armed fractions, should stay well-informed about legal rules of international human rights law and the legal limitations of conflict settlements; once they become members of transitional governments and new state structures their conduct is considered an act of that State under international law. This should urge them to take human rights seriously at any time.[113]

E. Consequences for Peace Accords and Peace Processes

It may be encouraging for peacemakers that war is not necessarily resumed if a peace settlement is in violation of international law. It is important to differentiate between legal and factual consequences. While peace agreements may be rendered void if they violate peremptory norms, this does not necessarily change the factual status of peace.

[108] Jonathan Somer, 'Engaging Armed Non-State Actors to Protect Children from the Effects of Armed Conflict: When the Stick Doesn't Cut the Mustard' (2012) 4(1) *Journal of Human Rights Practice* 106. For the argument that human rights have to be increasingly of concern to non-state actors in conflict situations, see also Andrew Clapham, 'Human Rights Obligations of Non-state Actors in Conflict Situations' (2006) 88.863 *International Review of the Red Cross* 491.

[109] Andrew Clapham, *Human Rights Obligations of Non-State Actors* (Oxford, Oxford University Press, 2006) 562.

[110] Ron Dudai and Kieran McEvoy, 'Thinking Critically about Armed Groups and Human Rights Praxis' (2012) 4(1) *Journal of Human Rights Practice* 1. See also David Petrasek, 'A Road Less Travelled: International Human Rights Advocacy and Armed Groups' (2012) 4(1) *Journal of Human Rights Practice* 128.

[111] Russell Miller, 'Paradoxes of Personality: Transnational Corporations, Non-Governmental Organizations and Human Rights in International Law' in Russell Miller and Rebecca Bratspies (eds), *Progress in International Law* (The Hague, Martinus Nijhoff Publishers, 2008) 381. For a comprehensive overview of the discourse, see Kate Parlett, *The Individual in the International Legal System: Continuity and Change in International Law* (Cambridge, Cambridge University Press, 2010) 38.

[112] Lisa Yarwood, *State Accountability under International Law: Holding States Accountable for a Breach of Jus cogens Norms* (New York: Routledge, 2011) 161.

[113] As the Draft Articles on Responsibility of States for Internationally Wrongful Acts suggest: 'The conduct of an insurrectional movement which becomes the new government of a State shall be considered an act of that State under international law'. See Draft Articles on Responsibility of States for Internationally Wrongful Acts, above n 81, Art 10, para 1.

Legally, the VCLT stipulates that a 'treaty is void if, at the time of its conclusion, it conflicts with a peremptory norm of general international law'.[114] As a result, the treaty's provisions 'have no legal force'.[115] In the case of peremptory norms, void treaty provisions cannot be separated.[116] Some commentators have argued that peace treaties contain complex provisions whereby clauses can be isolated while the rest of the agreement continues to have effect.[117] On the contrary, the ILC suggested that it is 'inappropriate' to consider a validity of the remaining agreement in the case of *jus cogens* violations.[118] Nonetheless, as long as the peace agreement produces an end to armed hostilities, it would appear to be a damaging formality to declare the unaffected parts void, if they are reinforced by the parties' mutual consent.[119] In this regard, the rules of the Vienna Convention require a teleological reduction. The legal nullity of a peace treaty does not *ipso jure* restore the state of war between the former belligerents.[120] As provided in VCLT, Article 43, any obligation existing independently from the treaty is not impaired by its invalidity.[121] The prohibition of the use of force is exactly such a general obligation under the UN Charter; even in the absence of peace treaty obligations, international law demands an end to military hostilities.[122]

Factually, neither the adoption nor the annulment of a conflict settlement automatically reinstates the status of an armed conflict or peace.[123] An end of hostilities can be formally manifested by the signing of a peace agreement as a legal document, but nonetheless the actual status of peace is defined through actions.[124] Conversely, the actual status of peace is impacted by – but not dependent on – a valid

[114] VCLT, Art 53. If a new peremptory norm of general international law emerges, 'any existing treaty which is in conflict with that norm becomes void and terminates'. See VCLT, Art 64. The VCLT applies primarily to treaties between states, such as peace treaties, but can also be considered a legally non-binding framework of interpretation for intra-state peace agreements. Most parts of the VCLT embody customary international law which can give guidance for intra-state peace agreements. See also Christine Bell, *On the Law of Peace: Peace Agreements and the Lex Pacificatoria* (Oxford, Oxford University Press, 2008) 127.

[115] VCLT, Art 69, para 1.

[116] VCLT, Art 44, para 5.

[117] Art 44 (1969) in Olivier Corten and Pierre Klein (eds), *The Vienna Conventions on the Law of Treaties* vol II (Oxford, Oxford University Press, 2011) para 22.

[118] Draft Articles on the Law of Treaties, and Commentaries, above n 71, Art 42, para 5.

[119] This ultimately supports the principle of *pacta sunt servanda*, which aims to keep contracts in force for the sake of stability. See Art 11, 26 VCLT. See also Art 71, para 1(b) VCLT and Draft Articles on the Law of Treaties, and Commentary, above n 71, Art 39, para 1 ('The Commission accordingly considered it desirable, as a safeguard for the stability of treaties, to underline … that the validity and continuance in force of a treaty is the normal state of things …').

[120] Yoram Dinstein, *War, Aggression and Self-Defence* (Cambridge, Cambridge University Press, 2011) 41, 91.

[121] Art 43 VCLT.

[122] Art 2, para 4 UN Charter.

[123] On the legal effects of the war-peace dichotomy, see also Robert Layton, 'The Effect of Measures Short of War on Treaties' (1962) 30(1) *University of Chicago Law Review* 96, 97.

[124] As, for instance, the UN General Assembly definition of 'aggression' states, the decisive factor is the 'use of armed force', regardless of whether there is a declaration of war. See GA Res 3314 (XXIX), 14 December 1974, Annex.

peace agreement. As touched on in the Introduction (Chapter 1) regarding the difference between 'imperfect peace' and 'illegal peace', the factual situation is conclusive for the condition of peace.[125] Although peace has multiple legal consequences and might be understood pre-eminently as a 'legal postulate', its occurrence or absence is real.[126]

III. A Conceptual Model for Reflections about the *Law of Peace* Debate

The analysis of this study proposes the consideration of three dimensions in the context of state transitions, conflict settlements and international law: first, questions about the process regarding how and with whom a transitional or permanent arrangement is reached; second, concerns about the actual conflict settlement mechanism in place; and third, aspects about time, relating to the duration, review and termination of peace settlements.[127]

A. Process Dimension

The process of peace settlements includes such factors as representation in peace negotiations, the authority of signatories and the scale of participation. As outlined in Chapter 2 on theory and practice, what underpins the debate between consociationalists and majoritarians is the question of what model of democracy is more inclusive.[128] Consequently, it is also critical whether the actual process leading to the arrangement has been participatory.

As explained, a point which has been raised concerning Bosnia and Herzegovina is that an internationally-steered transformation process risks limiting self-determination.[129] Chapter 3, which examined the ECtHR case *Sejdić and Finci*, highlighted that the difference between legislative and executive power-sharing impacts on the judgment of proportionality.[130]

In Chapter 4, the analysis of state practice regarding interim governments underlined that the establishment of consultative transition processes are crucial for creating legitimate constitutional change.[131] Elections are essential for the right to participation.[132]

[125] See Ch 1, Part I.B.iii.
[126] See Myres S McDougal, 'Peace and War: Factual Continuum with Multiple Legal Consequences' (1955) 49 *American Journal of International Law* 63. See also Lauterpacht, above n 4, 446.
[127] See Appendix, Table 8.
[128] See Ch 2, Part II.A.
[129] See Ch 2, Part IV.F.
[130] See Ch 3, Part IV.E.iii.c.
[131] See Ch 4, Part VI.C.i.
[132] See Ch 4, Part VI.C.iii.

All this shows that process aspects should be borne in mind in the evaluation of state transitions and peace agreements under international law.

B. Content Dimension

As seen in the practice of international courts and international human rights monitoring bodies, the central dimension of legal analysis is the actual mechanism of the conflict settlement. For a legal assessment, it is important to define precisely what type of power-sharing is employed.[133]

As summarised in the synopsis in Chapter 2, the spectrum includes diverse forms of political, territorial, economic and military power-sharing.[134] International law can appears as both a blessing and a burden in peacemaking.[135] As explained in the conclusions of Chapters 3 and 4, ethnic and confessional quotas result in different legal consequences. The case studies of Bosnia and Herzegovina and Lebanon demonstrated that the restoration of peace is a challenge for human rights protection.[136]

Following international practice, states can justify differential treatment based on objective and reasonable grounds.[137] The assessment of proportionality is problematic.[138] If options exist which would infringe human rights to a lesser extent, a state must pursue those alternatives. The fulfilment of international human rights is a significant indicator of the credibility of state transitions: they serve as a key reference point for rating the success of post-conflict change.

C. Time Dimension

Temporal aspects form the third dimension.[139] Proportionality demands a gradual modification of those elements in peace settlements that restrict human rights. Certain arrangements may be necessary for an immediate end to deadly hostilities, yet in the long run, rigid power-sharing can also make conflicts intractable.[140] Ideally, consociationalism with pre-defined shares of power builds trust among elites so that majority rule of democracy becomes acceptable. However, this is often not the case.[141]

As stated by the ECtHR in *Sejdić and Finci v Bosnia and Herzegovina* and by the UN human rights monitoring bodies regarding Lebanon, states need to

[133] See Ch 2, Part V.A.
[134] See Ch 2, Part III.A.
[135] See Ch 2, Part V.C.
[136] See Ch 3, Part IV.C.iii and Ch 4, Part I.D.
[137] See Ch 3, Part IV and Ch 4, II.A.
[138] See Ch 3, Part V and Ch 4, VII.
[139] See Ch 3, Part IV.E and Ch 4, Part VI.C.
[140] See Ch 2, Part II.C.
[141] See Ch 2, Part II.B.

phase out discrimination.[142] Legislative and constitutional change might not come overnight, but a sincere will has to be visible. States have to prove that they are trying to adhere to international human right law.[143] A periodic review and the initiation of dialogue about constitutional change is decisive.[144]

Evidently, all three dimensions (process, content and time) are closely interlinked. For example, whether the content of an agreement generates legal tension also depends on the setting of the process. The more inclusive peace negotiations are, the less their substance can be debated from the outside by other states, given the right of internal self-determination. Likewise, whereas a short-term ceasefire agreement can be exclusive between certain sides, a long-term comprehensive peace agreement will need a larger base for its legitimacy. The longer a peace agreement is in force, the more its re-evaluation is necessary in order to protect the *pouvoir constituant*. Considering all three dimensions could strengthen thinking about normative limits of peacemaking.

IV. Open Questions and Future Research Agenda

As this study could address only some aspects of state transitions, power-sharing and international law, three suggestions are offered for future research in this field.

First, one possibility could be to explore further case studies in order to deepen the understanding of regional differences and universal legal commonalities in human rights law. A crucial case in Asia could be Nepal, a country that is still struggling with developing a new constitution which could entail federalism based on ethnicity or determined on the grounds of identity, economic viability, administrative accessibility, geographic situation and historic orientation, built on the principle of secularism.[145] The case of Nepal could shed light on regional fragmentation in international law.

Second, peace settlements and transitional power-sharing with listed terrorist groups give rise to a range of additional legal questions, as terrorism is said to disrupt existing categories of international law.[146] As mentioned in Chapter 1, a transitional power-sharing pact with moderate Taliban in Afghanistan may materialise.[147] The UN has guidelines on terrorism for peace mediators, which describe the legal basis for negotiations, but are rather general and lack detail

[142] See Ch 3, Part IV.E.ii and Ch 4, Part III.C.

[143] See Ch 3, Part IV.D.iv.d and Ch 4, Part VII.C.iii.

[144] See Ch 4, Part VIII.C.

[145] For the debate, see Tulshi Ram Pandey, 'Culture and Politics of Caste in the Himalayan Kingdom' (2005) 9 *Occasional Papers in Sociology and Anthropology* 65. For the course of developments, see also 'Nepal Exercising Partyocracy' *The Himalayan* (14 February 2013); Shyam Prasad Mainali, 'Boundaries in Federalism' *The Himalayan* (5 January 2011).

[146] Antonio Cassese, 'Terrorism is also Disrupting some Crucial Legal Categories of International Law' (2001) 12 *European Journal of International Law* 993.

[147] See Chapter 1, nn 13–14.

concerning peace settlements.[148] Linkages between human rights, counter-terrorist measures, power-sharing and peace agreements have not yet been researched comprehensively.[149]

Third, another area which is seemingly unmapped within the contemporary context of intra-state conflict is the potential connection between conflict prevention, power-sharing and international law, which could fall into the category of a *jus pre-ad bellum*.[150] Instead of reacting to armed conflict, it could be worthwhile to investigate legal mechanisms for the prevention of conflict more thoroughly.[151] In relation to the debate about a '*human right to peace*', further research on preventive measures could provide crucial answers for the law and peace discourse.[152]

V. Concluding Remarks

The state of peace is evidently imperfect. However, the aspiration of trying to achieve perfection should not be abandoned.[153] Two decades ago, mass atrocities in the Balkans reminded the international community of the dilemma resulting from the attempt to strike a balance between state stability, responsibility, human rights and flexibility.[154] Currently, the ongoing armed conflict in Syria exemplifies how difficult it is to achieve a cessation of hostilities under this confluence of conditions. Those who suggest that peace settlements must always fulfil the highest standards of international human rights law have yet to witness the pain and suffering of innocent victims with every additional day spent awaiting a

[148] Guidelines for UN Mediators: Terrorism, United Nations, undated [copy with the author], para 2 ('UN envoys and representatives … should be guided by relevant legal bases which … General Assembly and Security Council resolutions developed over the past fifteen years, with direct implications for peace negotiations. These decisions constitute a normative framework for various aspects of the UN counter-terrorism effort … ').

[149] See also Sahla Aroussia and Stef Vandeginstea, 'When Interests Meet Norms: The Relevance of Human Rights for Peace and Power-sharing' (2013) 17(2) *International Journal of Human Rights* 183.

[150] See also Hanne Cuyckens and Philip De Man, 'The Responsibility to Prevent: On the Assumed Legal Nature of Responsibility to Protect and its Relationship with Conflict Prevention' in Julia Hoffmann and André Nollkaemper (eds), *Responsibility to Protect: From Principle to Practice* (Amsterdam, Amsterdam University Press, 2012) 111.

[151] For the debate, which has been of greater intensity over a decade ago, see Steven R Ratner, 'Does International Law Matter in Preventing Ethnic Conflict?' (1999–2000) 32 *NYU Journal of International Law and Politics* 591. See also John Packer, 'Making International Law Matter in Preventing Ethnic Conflict: A Practitioner's Perspective' (1999–2000) 32 *NYU Journal of International Law and Politics* 715.

[152] On the 'human right to peace' debate, see Ch 1, Part I.C.

[153] Van Vollenhoven stated encouragingly that international law 'can only be crowned with success if it is sustained by a burning conviction that success is possible … That faith, if anywhere, will find its inspiration in the history of the "law of peace" as it has developed in the course of the past eight hundred years': Van Vollenhoven, above n 1, 1.

[154] See Appendix, Table 9.

ceasefire.[155] Equally, lives should not be lost in vain: agreements between former belligerents that lead to discrimination and suppression do not bear much hope for lasting peace.

For some scholars, human rights may appear to be an illusion and peace an empty notion; and indeed, legal methodology and interpretation leave room for questions.[156] Human rights serve idealistic purposes, depending on 'confidence and persuasion'.[157] International courts and human rights monitoring bodies can help to catalyse change, but they cannot replace action by those directly concerned.[158] Particularly in the time after conflict, states can be overwhelmed by too high expectations to guarantee human rights before order is restored and when reforms have just been introduced.[159] Nevertheless, self-determination is 'necessarily accompanied by an assumption of responsibility'.[160] The imperfection of peace can never be an excuse for postponing state efforts, but should be a stimulus for progress.

In practice, rights and responsibility need to be balanced with flexibility.[161] Euphemistically, one can call this compromise the 'necessary evil' or the 'collateral damage of peacemaking'; both are unwanted but mostly unavoidable.[162] The challenge for peace settlements is to create adaptable legal instruments that provide both short-term benefits, which hold hostilities in abeyance pending conflict transformation, as well as keep the potential to comply with international law in the long run. In this endeavour, international human rights law has to be taken seriously, but needs to be seen in perspective.[163]

[155] On the matter of justice, human rights and global imperatives, see Amartya Sen, *The Idea of Justice* (London, Allen Lane, 2009) 355.

[156] Koskenniemi, for instance, argues provocatively that human rights 'are like love, both necessary and impossible … We cannot live without them, but we cannot have them, either … As soon as we are safely installed in a social order that promises to guarantee our rights, that order starts to appear oppressively totalitarian'. For him, peace 'too may be an empty notion, perfectly capable of coexisting with economic deprivation and suppression of human rights': Martti Koskenniemi, *The Politics of International Law* (Oxford, Hart Publishing, 2011) 153, 261.

[157] Christian Tomuschat, *Human Rights: Between Idealism and Realism* (Oxford, Oxford University Press, 2008) 387.

[158] As Christian Tomuschat put it, while human rights need to be 'vigorously defended' by the international community, it is, in the last resort, 'the society concerned that must come to terms with its fate': ibid, 389.

[159] As Edwin Dickinson phrased it, where 'frustrations have been encountered, the law must await more favorable opportunities for an expanded service': Dickinson, above n 2, 130.

[160] Tomuschat, above n 157, 389.

[161] In essence, in the words of Henkin: 'What is called for is the flexibility of diplomacy, not the strait jacket of law': Louis Henkin, *How Nations Behave: Law and Foreign Policy* (New York, Columbia University Press, 1979) 24.

[162] For the first quote, see Mark Freeman, *Necessary Evils: Amnesties and the Search for Justice* (Cambridge, Cambridge University Press, 2011) 180. The second comment was made by Georg Nolte in a Seminar at Humboldt University, 27 September 2012.

[163] Ideally, rights trump state power, see Ronald Dworkin, *Taking Rights Seriously* (Cambridge, MA, Harvard University Press, 1977) 184.

The signing of peace agreements is about gaining time. They cannot guarantee an end to conflict, but can put in motion mechanisms for transition. Human rights are not an optional feature in the waging of peace, as both depend on each other. Accompanied by trial and error, human rights protection as well as peacemaking are 'a process which cannot be finalized once and for all at some point in time'.[164] In conclusion, there is no alternative but to cherish peace as an imperfect but continuing effort.

[164] Tomuschat, above n 157, 387. See also Dickinson: 'There might be a good deal of trial and error in the process, but the trends are constructive … What cannot be won today in the more dramatic contests may be won tomorrow by assuring broader and firmer foundations', above n 2, 129.

APPENDIX

Table 1 Synopsis of power-sharing mechanisms

Type	Mechanism	Form	Example	Explanation
Political power-sharing	*Coalitions*	*Unity government*	Switzerland	• Coalition between all parties
		Collective Presidency	Iraq	• National partnership of major political parties
		Grand coalition	Germany (eg, 2005–2009)	• Coalition between two major parties
		Inter-party coalition	Germany (eg, 2009–2013)	• Coalition between major party and smaller party to maintain legislative majority
	Proportional representation	*Quota for executive, legislative and judiciary*	Sierra Leone	• Fixed governmental appointment for armed group (1999 Lomé Peace Agreement)
	Consensus	*Parallel consent/ mutual veto*	Northern Ireland	• Mutual veto rights for Unionist and Nationalists (1998 Good Friday Agreement)
	Minority veto	*Vital interest veto*	Macedonia	• Veto for constitutional amendments relating to self-government and culture, language and education laws (2001 Ohrid Agreement)
		Reasoned motion	Belgium	• Motion by 3/4 of a linguistic group prior to the final vote possible

Territorial power-sharing	*Autonomy*	*Autonomous region*	Trentino-South Tyrol region; Autonomous Region of Bougainville (Papua New Guinea); Aceh (Indonesia)	• Local control for autonomous region of Northern Italy, composed of the autonomous provinces of South Tyrol and Trentino
		Autonomous province	Trentino, South Tyrol	• Autonomous legislative and administrative competencies
		Temporary autonomy	Sudan	• Temporary autonomy of South Sudan until referendum (2005 Comprehensive Peace Agreement)
	Unitary state		United Kingdom	• Several constituent countries (England, Scotland, Wales and Northern Ireland) united under one supreme central government
	Federalism	*Symmetrical federalism: federation*	Germany; USA; United Arab Emirates	• Equal rights between states of the federation
		Symmetrical federalism: confederation	German Confederation	• Loose association of Central European states (1815 Vienna Congress Act)
		Asymmetrical federalism	India	• Federal union of 28 states and 7 union territories which are ruled directly by the government
			Malaysia	• 13 states (Negeri) and 3 federal territories
		Asymmetrical federalism: federal district	Malaysia	• Sarawak and Sabah entered the federation as states on special terms and conditions (1963 Malaysia Act)

		Asymmetrical federalism: federal territory	Malaysia	• Kuala Lumpur (national capital), Putrajaya (federal government administrative centre) and Labuan Island (international offshore financial centre) governed directly by the federal government of Malaysia
		Asymmetrical federalism: union territory	India	• Ruled directly by the federal government (President appoints an Administrator or Lieutenant-Governor), but also have special rights (own elected legislative assemblies and the executive councils of ministers)
		Federal region	Region of Kurdistan (Iraq)	• Other provinces have right to become regions as a part of the federal system
Economic power-sharing/ wealth-sharing	*Distribution of public enterprises*		Liberia	• Major state corporations, agencies and state-owned enterprises distributed between war-waging parties (2003 Accra Peace Agreement)
	Preliminary distribution of public enterprises on percentage base		Burundi	• Armed group granted 20-percent of public enterprises, exact distribution to be negotiated subsequently (2003 Pretoria Protocol)
	Divide natural resource revenues on percentage base		Sudan	• Net oil revenues allocated between the South and the North on a 50:50 basis (2005 Naivasha Comprehensive Peace Agreement)

	Commission for the Management of Strategic Resources, National Reconstruction and Development		Sierra Leone	• Joint board of the government, civil society and representatives of armed groups (1999 Lomé Peace Agreement)
	Contract and Monopolies Commission		Liberia	• Oversight of the state's contractual, financial and budgetary commitments (2003 Accra Peace Agreement)
	Broad-based socio-economic forum		Sierra Leone	• Formulation of policy proposals for the socio-economic sector (1996 Abidjan Peace Agreement)
Military power-sharing	*Integration of former non-state belligerents into the state's army*		Angola	• Partial integration into armed forces and partial disarmament of non-state forces (2002 Luanda MoU)
	Joint command structure		Burundi	• Joint command centre based on ethnic 50:50 balance (2003 Pretoria Protocol)
	Area Joint Military Committee		Sudan	• Separate armies in specific territorial regions and joint army for disputed territories (2005 Comprehensive Peace Agreement)
	Joint Defense Board		Sudan	• Structured on a parity basis and taking its decisions by consensus (2005 Comprehensive Peace Agreement)
	Joint Technical Committee		Sudan	• Formed by senior officers of the main armed groups and undertaking coordination between the former belligerents

Table 2 Synopsis of power-sharing provisions in the Constitution of Bosnia and Herzegovina

Article	**Provision**
Preamble *Constituent Peoples*	'Bosniacs, Croats, and Serbs, as constituent peoples (along with Others) …'
Territorial composition of Bosnia and Herzegovina Art 1, para 3	'3 Composition Bosnia and Herzegovina shall consist of the two Entities, the Federation of Bosnia and Herzegovina and the Republika Srpska (hereinafter "the Entities").
Responsibilities of and Relations Between the Institutions of Bosnia and Herzegovina and the Entities Art 3, paras 2–4	'2 Responsibilities of the Entities a) The Entities shall have the right to establish special parallel relationships with neighboring states consistent with the sovereignty and territorial integrity of Bosnia and Herzegovina. b) Each Entity shall provide all necessary assistance to the government of Bosnia and Herzegovina in order to enable it to honor the international obligations of Bosnia and Herzegovina, provided that financial obligations incurred by one Entity without the consent of the other prior to the election of the Parliamentary Assembly and Presidency of Bosnia and Herzegovina shall be the responsibility of that Entity, except insofar as the obligation is necessary for continuing the membership of Bosnia and Herzegovina in an international organization. c) The Entities shall provide a safe and secure environment for all persons in their respective jurisdictions, by maintaining civilian law enforcement agencies operating in accordance with internationally recognized standards and with respect for the internationally recognized human rights and fundamental freedoms referred to in Article II above, and by taking such other measures as appropriate. d) Each Entity may also enter into agreements with states and international organizations with the consent of the Parliamentary Assembly. The Parliamentary Assembly may provide by law that certain types of agreements do not require such consent. 3. Law and Responsibilities of the Entities and the Institutions a) All governmental functions and powers not expressly assigned in this Constitution to the institutions of Bosnia and Herzegovina shall be those of the Entities.

	b) The Entities and any subdivisions thereof shall comply fully with this Constitution, which supersedes inconsistent provisions of the law of Bosnia and Herzegovina and of the constitutions and law of the Entities, and with the decisions of the institutions of Bosnia and Herzegovina. The general principles of international law shall be an integral part of the law of Bosnia and Herzegovina and the Entities. 4. Coordination The Presidency may decide to facilitate inter-Entity coordination on matters not within the responsibilities of Bosnia and Herzegovina as provided in this Constitution, unless an Entity objects in any particular case. 5. Additional Responsibilities a) Bosnia and Herzegovina shall assume responsibility for such other matters as are agreed by the Entities; are provided for in Annexes 5 through 8 to the General Framework Agreement; or are necessary to preserve the sovereignty, territorial integrity, political independence, and international personality of Bosnia and Herzegovina, in accordance with the division of responsibilities between the institutions of Bosnia and Herzegovina. Additional institutions may be established as necessary to carry out such responsibilities. b) Within six months of the entry into force of this Constitution, the Entities shall begin negotiations with a view to including in the responsibilities of the institutions of Bosnia and Herzegovina other matters, including utilization of energy resources and cooperative economic projects.'
Membership and Election of the House of Peoples Art 4, paras 1–4	'The Parliamentary Assembly shall have two chambers: the House of Peoples and the House of Representatives. 1. House of Peoples The House of Peoples shall comprise 15 Delegates, two-thirds from the Federation (including five Croats and five Bosniacs) and one-third from the Republika Srpska (five Serbs). a. The designated Croat and Bosniac Delegates from the Federation shall be selected, respectively, by the Croat and Bosniac Delegates to the House of Peoples of the Federation2. Delegates from the Republika Srpska shall be selected by the National Assembly of the Republika Srpska. b. Nine members of the House of Peoples shall comprise a quorum, provided that at least three Bosniac, three Croat, and three Serb Delegates are present.

	2. House of Representatives The House of Representatives shall comprise 42 Members, two-thirds elected from the territory of the Federation, one-third from the territory of the Republika Srpska. a. Members of the House of Representatives shall be directly elected from their Entity in accordance with an election law to be adopted by the Parliamentary Assembly. The first election, however, shall take place in accordance with Annex 3 to the General Framework Agreement. b. A majority of all members elected to the House of Representatives shall comprise a quorum. 3. Procedures a. Each chamber shall be convened in Sarajevo not more than 30 days after its selection or election. b. Each chamber shall by majority vote adopt its internal rules and select from its members one Serb, one Bosniac, and one Croat to serve as its Chair and Deputy Chairs, with the position of Chair rotating among the three persons selected. c. All legislation shall require the approval of both chambers. d. All decisions in both chambers shall be by majority of those present and voting. The Delegates and Members shall make their best efforts to see that the majority includes at least one-third of the votes of Delegates or Members from the territory of each Entity. If a majority vote does not include one-third of the votes of Delegates or Members from the territory of each Entity, the Chair and Deputy Chairs shall meet as a commission and attempt to obtain approval within three days of the vote. If those efforts fail, decisions shall be taken by a majority of those present and voting, provided that the dissenting votes do not include two-thirds or more of the Delegates or Members elected from either Entity. e. A proposed decision of the Parliamentary Assembly may be declared to be destructive of a vital interest of the Bosniac, Croat, or Serb people by a majority of, as appropriate, the Bosniac, Croat, or Serb Delegates selected in accordance with paragraph l (a) above. Such a proposed decision shall require for approval in the House of Peoples a majority of the Bosniac, of the Croat, and of the Serb Delegates present and voting. f. When a majority of the Bosniac, of the Croat, or of the Serb Delegates objects to the invocation of paragraph (e), the Chair of the House of Peoples shall immediately convene a Joint Commission comprising three Delegates, one each selected by the Bosniac, by the Croat, and by the Serb Delegates, to resolve the issue. If the Commission fails to do so within five days, the matter will be referred to the Constitutional Court, which shall in an expedited process review it for procedural regularity.

	g. The House of Peoples may be dissolved by the Presidency or by the House itself, provided that the House's decision to dissolve is approved by a majority that includes the majority of Delegates from at least two of the Bosniac, Croat, or Serb peoples. The House of Peoples elected in the first elections after the entry into force of this Constitution may not, however, be dissolved. h. Decisions of the Parliamentary Assembly shall not take effect before publication. i. Both chambers shall publish a complete record of their deliberations and shall, save in exceptional circumstances in accordance with their rules, deliberate publicly. j. Delegates and Members shall not be held criminally or civilly liable for any acts carried out within the scope of their duties in the Parliamentary Assembly. 4. Powers The Parliamentary Assembly shall have responsibility for: a. Enacting legislation as necessary to implement decisions of the Presidency or to carry out the responsibilities of the Assembly under this Constitution. b. Deciding upon the sources and amounts of revenues for the operations of the institutions of Bosnia and Herzegovina and international obligations of Bosnia and Herzegovina. c. Approving a budget for the institutions of Bosnia and Herzegovina. d. Deciding whether to consent to the ratification of treaties. e. Such other matters as are necessary to carry out its duties or as are assigned to it by mutual agreement of the Entities.'
Membership and Election of the Presidency of Bosnia and Herzegovina Art 5, paras 1–2	'The Presidency of Bosnia and Herzegovina shall consist of three Members: one Bosniac and one Croat, each directly elected from the territory of the Federation, and one Serb directly elected from the territory of the Republika Srpska. 1. Election and Term a. Members of the Presidency shall be directly elected in each Entity (with each voter voting to fill one seat on the Presidency) in accordance with an election law adopted by the Parliamentary Assembly. The first election, however, shall take place in accordance with Annex 3 to the General Framework Agreement. Any vacancy in the Presidency shall be filled from the relevant Entity in accordance with a law to be adopted by the Parliamentary Assembly. b. The term of the Members of the Presidency elected in the first election shall be two years; the term of Members subsequently elected shall be four years. Members shall be eligible to succeed themselves once and shall thereafter be ineligible for four years.

	2. Procedures
	a. The Presidency shall determine its own rules of procedure, which shall provide for adequate notice of all meetings of the Presidency.
	b. The Members of the Presidency shall appoint from their Members a Chair. For the first term of the Presidency, the Chair shall be the Member who received the highest number of votes. Thereafter, the method of selecting the Chair, by rotation or otherwise, shall be determined by the Parliamentary Assembly, subject to Article IV § 3.
	c. The Presidency shall endeavor to adopt all Presidency Decisions (ie., those concerning matters arising under Article V § 3 (a)-(e)) by consensus. Such decisions may, subject to paragraph (d) below, nevertheless be adopted by two Members when all efforts to reach consensus have failed.
	d. A dissenting Member of the Presidency may declare a Presidency Decision to be destructive of a vital interest of the Entity from the territory from which he was elected, provided that he does so within three days of its adoption.
	Such a Decision shall be referred immediately to the National Assembly of the Republika Srpska, if the declaration was made by the Member from that territory; to the Bosniac Delegates of the House of Peoples of the Federation, if the declaration was made by the Bosniac Member; or to the Croat Delegates of that body, if the declaration was made by the Croat Member. If the declaration is confirmed by a two-thirds vote of those persons within ten days of the referral, the challenged Presidency Decision shall not take effect.
	3. Powers.
	The Presidency shall have responsibility for:
	a. Conducting the foreign policy of Bosnia and Herzegovina.
	b. Appointing ambassadors and other international representatives of Bosnia and Herzegovina, no more than two thirds of whom may be selected from the territory of the Federation.
	c. Representing Bosnia and Herzegovina in international and European organizations and institutions and seeking membership in such organizations and institutions of which Bosnia and Herzegovina is not a member.

	d. Negotiating, denouncing, and, with the consent of the Parliamentary Assembly, ratifying treaties of Bosnia and Herzegovina. e. Executing decisions of the Parliamentary Assembly. f. Proposing, upon the recommendation of the Council of Ministers, an annual budget to the Parliamentary Assembly. g. Reporting as requested, but not less than annually, to the Parliamentary Assembly on expenditures by the Presidency. h. Coordinating as necessary with international and nongovernmental organizations in Bosnia and Herzegovina. i. Performing such other functions as may be necessary to carry out its duties, as may be assigned to it by the Parliamentary Assembly, or as may be agreed by the Entities.'
Constitutional Court Art 6, para 1	'1. Composition The Constitutional Court of Bosnia and Herzegovina shall have nine members. a) Four members shall be selected by the House of Representatives of the Federation, and two members by the Assembly of the Republika Srpska. The remaining three members shall be selected by the President of the European Court of Human Rights after consultation with the Presidency.'
Central Bank Art 7, paras 2–3	'2. The first Governing Board of the Central Bank shall consist of a Governor appointed by the International Monetary Fund, after consultation with the Presidency, and three members appointed by the Presidency, two from the Federation (one Bosniac, one Croat, who shall share one vote) and one from the Republika Srpska, all of whom shall serve a six-year term. The Governor, who shall not be a citizen of Bosnia and Herzegovina or any neighboring state, may cast tie-breaking votes on the Governing Board. 3. Thereafter, the Governing Board of the Central Bank of Bosnia and Herzegovina shall consist of five persons appointed by the Presidency for a term of six years. The Board shall appoint, from among its members, a Governor for a term of six years.'
Finances Art 8, para 3	'3. The Federation shall provide two-thirds, and the Republika Srpska one-third, of the revenues required by the budget, except insofar as revenues are raised as specified by the Parliamentary Assembly.'

Table 3 Synopsis of power-sharing provisions in the Lebanese Constitution

Article	Provision
Preamble (Introduced by the Constitutional Law of September 21 1990)	'A) Lebanon is a sovereign, free, and independent country. It is a final homeland for all its citizens. It is unified in its territory, people, and institutions within the boundaries defined in this constitution and recognized internationally. B) Lebanon is Arab in its identity and in its affiliation. It is a founding and active member of the League of Arab States and abides by its pacts and covenants. Lebanon is also a founding and active member of the United Nations Organization and abides by its covenants and by the Universal Declaration of Human Rights. The Government shall embody these principles in all fields and areas without exception. C) Lebanon is a parliamentary democratic republic based on respect for public liberties, especially the freedom of opinion and belief, and respect for social justice and equality of rights and duties among all citizens without discrimination. D) The people are the source of authority and sovereignty; they shall exercise these powers through the constitutional institutions. E) The political system is established on the principle of separation of powers, their balance and cooperation. F) The economic system is free and ensures private initiative and the right of private property. G) The even development among regions on the educational, social, and economic levels shall be a basic pillar of the unity of the state and the stability of the system. H) The abolition of political confessionalism shall be a basic national goal and shall be achieved according to a staged plan. I) Lebanese territory is one for all Lebanese. Every Lebanese shall have the right to live in any part thereof and to enjoy the rule of law wherever he resides. There shall be no segregation of the people on the basis of any type of belonging, and no fragmentation, partition, or settlement of non-Lebanese in Lebanon. J) There shall be no constitutional legitimacy for any authority which contradicts the pact of mutual existence.'
The Lebanese, Their Rights and Duties Art 7	'All Lebanese shall be equal before the law. They shall equally enjoy civil and political rights and shall equally be bound by public obligations and duties without any distinction.'

Art 9	'There shall be absolute freedom of conscience. The state in rendering homage to the God Almighty shall respect all religions and creeds and shall guarantees, under its protection the free exercise of all religious rites provided that public order is not disturbed. It shall also guarantee that the personal status and religious interests of the population, to whatever religious sect they belong, shall be respected.'
Art 10	'Education shall be free insofar as it is not contrary to public order and morals and does not affect the dignity of any of the religions or sects. There shall be no violation of the right of religious communities to have their own schools provided they follow the general rules issued by the state regulating public instruction.'
Art 12	'Every Lebanese shall have the right to hold public office, no preference shall be made except on the basis of merit and competence, according to the conditions established by law. A special statute shall guarantee the rights of civil service in the departments to which they belong.'
Powers: General Provisions Art 19	'A Constitutional Council shall be established to supervise the constitutionality of laws and to arbitrate conflicts that arise from parliamentary and presidential elections. The President of the republic, the speaker of Parliament, the Prime Minister, along with any ten Members of Parliament, have the right to refer to this Council matters that relate to the constitutionality of laws. The officially recognized heads of religious communities have the right to refer to this Council laws relating to personal status, the freedom of belief and religious practice, and the freedom of religious education. The rules governing the organization, operation, composition of the Council and referral thereto shall be decided by a special law.'
Art 20	'The judicial power shall be exercised by courts of various degrees and jurisdictions. It shall function within the limits of an order established by the law and offering accordingly the necessary guarantees to judges and litigants. The law shall determine the conditions and limits of the judicial guarantees. The judges shall be independent in the exercise of their functions. The decisions and judgments of all courts shall be rendered and executed in the name of the Lebanese People.'
Art 21	'Every Lebanese citizen who has completed his twenty-first year is an elector provided he fulfills the conditions stated by the electoral law.'
Legislative Power Art 22	'With the election of the first Chamber of Deputies on a national, non-confessional basis, a Senate shall be established in which all the religious communities shall be represented. Its authority shall be limited to major national issues.'

Art 24	'The Chamber of Deputies shall be composed of elected members; their number and the method of their election shall be determined by the electoral laws in effect. Until such time as the Chamber enacts new electoral laws on a non-confessional basis, the distribution of seats shall be according to the following principles: a. Equal representation between Christians and Muslims. b. Proportional representation among the confessional groups within each of the two religious communities. c. Proportional representation among geographic regions. Exceptionally, and for one time only, the seats that are currently vacant, as well as the new seats that have been established by law, shall be filled by appointment, all at once, and by a two thirds majority of the Government of National Unity. This is to establish equality between Christians and Muslims as stipulated in the Document of National Accord. The electoral laws shall specify the details regarding the implementation of this clause.'
Art 34	'The Chamber shall not be validly constituted unless the majority of the total membership is present. Decisions shall be taken by a majority vote. Should the votes be equal, the question under consideration shall be rejected.'
Executive Power: The President of the Republic Art 49	'The President of the Republic is the head of the state and the symbol of the nation's unity. He shall safeguard the constitution and Lebanon's independence, unity, and territorial integrity. The President shall preside over the Supreme Defense Council and be the Commander-in-Chief of the Armed Forces which fall under the authority of the Council of Ministers. The President of the Republic shall be elected by secret ballot and by a two thirds majority of the Chamber of Deputies. After a first ballot, an absolute majority shall be sufficient. The President's term is six years. He may not be re-elected until six years after the expiration of his last mandate. No one may be elected to the Presidency of the Republic unless he fulfills the conditions of eligibility for the Chamber of Deputies. It is also not possible to elect judges, Grade One civil servants, or their equivalents in all public institutions to the Presidency during their term or office or within two years following the date of their resignation and their effective cessation of service, or following retirement.'

Art 50	'Upon assuming office, the President of the Republic shall take an oath of fidelity before the Parliament, to the Nation and the constitution, in the following terms: "I swear by Almighty God to observe the Constitution and the laws of the Lebanese Nation and to maintain the independence of Lebanon and its territorial integrity".'
Final and Temporary Provisions Art 95	'The Chamber of Deputies that is elected on the basis of equality between Muslims and Christians shall take the appropriate measures to bring about the abolition of political confessionalism according to a transitional plan. A National Committee shall be formed, headed by the President of the Republic, it include, in addition to the President of the Chamber of Deputies and the Prime Minister, leading political, intellectual, and social figures. The tasks of this Committee shall be to study and propose the means to ensure the abolition of confessionalism, propose them to the Chamber of Deputies and to the Ministers council of ministers, and to follow up the execution of the transitional plan. During the transitional phase: a. The sectarian groups shall be represented in a just and equitable manner in the formation of the Cabinet. b. The principle of confessional representation in public service jobs, in the judiciary, in the military and security institutions, and in public and mixed agencies shall be cancelled n accordance with the requirements of national reconciliation; they shall be replaced by the principle of expertise and competence. However, Grade One posts and their equivalents shall be excepted from this rule, and the posts shall be distributed equally between Christians and Muslims without reserving any particular job for any sectarian group but rather applying the principles of expertise and competence.'
Art 102	'All legislative provisions contrary to the present constitution shall be abrogated.'

Table 4 Confessional high level posts in Lebanon ('Grand One')[1]

Confession	Public Positions
Maronite	• President of the Republic • Commander of the Lebanese Army • Director General for Civil Defense • President of the Supreme Judicial Council • President of the Constitutional Council • Governor of the Central Bank • Director General of Finance • Director General of Customs • Director General of Tenders • Director General of Real Estate • Secretary General of Higher Council of Privatization • Director General of Water and Electricity • Director General of Petroleum • Director of Casino du Liban • Director General of Education • Director General of the National Employment Office • General Administrative Inspector
Greek Orthodox	• Governor of Beirut • President of the Supreme Disciplinary Authority • Director General of the Ministry of Public Works • Head of Staff Department of Civil Service Council • President of the Central Fund for the Displaced • Director General of the Departments and Local Councils
Catholic	• Governor of the North • Director General of National Security • Director General of Roads and Buildings • Director General of Agriculture • Director General of Industry • Chairman of the Commission of the Beirut Stock Exchange

[1] 'Sharing the Lebanese Government Apparatus' (2010) 100 *The Monthly* 6–10.

Armenian Orthodox	• Vice Governor of Central Bank of Lebanon • Director General of the Central Administration for Statistics • Director General of the Ministry of Environment
Sunni	• Prime Minister • Secretary General of the Ministry of Foreign Affairs • Secretary General of the Presidency of the Council of Ministers • Director General of Protocol and Public Relations at the Presidency of the Council of Ministers • Secretary General of the Legal and Administrative Affairs at the Presidency of the Republic • Governor of Mount Lebanon • Chairman of Civil Service Council • Director General of Justice • General Prosecutor • Director General of Touristic Affairs • Director General of Urban Planning • Director General of the Foundation for Promoting Investments • Director General of Civil Status • Director General of Higher Education • Director General of Culture • Director General of Land and Sea Transport • Director General of Aviation • Inspector General for Engineering • Vice Governor Central Bank of Lebanon • Chief of the Banking Control Commission • Chairman and Director General of Middle East Airlines
Shi'a	• Speaker of Parliament • Governor of Nabatieh • Director General of General Security • Director General, Chief of the Legal Affairs Branch Division at the Office of Council of Ministers • Director General of the National Social Security Fund • Director General of Social Affairs

	• Director General of Political Affairs and Refugees at the Ministry of Interior • Director General of Media • Director General of Youth and Sports • Director General of Emigrants • Vice Governor Central Bank of Lebanon • Secretary General of Scientific Research • General Inspector of Education • General Inspector at the Central Inspection Board • President of the Lebanese University • President of the Supreme Court of Customs • President and General Manager of the Administration for Tobacco and Tombacs • President and Director General of South Water Association • Chairman of Audit Bureau
Druze	• Governor of the South • Financial Auditor at the House of Parliament • Chairman and Director General of the Railway and Public Transportation Authority • Government Commissioner at the Council for Development and Reconstruction • Vice Governor of Central Bank of Lebanon • General Inspector of Finance • Director General of the Displaced • Director General of State Employees Cooperative • Director General for Parliamentary Sessions and Committees
Alawite	• Director General of Post

Table 5 Confessional distribution of posts in the Lebanese Government

Year (Prime Minister)	Maronite	Protestant	Greek Catholic	Greek Orthodox	Armenian Orthodox	Armenian Catholic	Druze	Sunni	Shi'a	Total
2011 (Mikati)	6	–	3	4	2	–	3	7	5	30
2009 (Hariri)	6	–	3	4	2	–	3	6	6	30
2005 (Siniora)	5	1	2	3	1	–	2	5	5	24
2005 (Mikati)	4	–	3	5	2	–	2	7	5	28
2004 (Karami)	6	–	3	4	2	–	3	6	6	30
2003 (Hariri)	6	–	3	4	2	–	3	6	6	30
2000 (Hariri)	6	1	3	4	1	–	3	6	6	30
1998 (Hoss)	3	–	1	2	1	–	2	4	3	16
1996 (Hariri)	7	–	2	4	1	1	4	5	6	30
1995 (Hariri)	6	–	3	4	1	1	3	5	5	28
1992 (Hariri)	6	–	3	4	1	1	3	6	6	30
1992 (Solh)	4	1	2	2	1	–	1	5	5	21
1990 (Karami)	6	–	3	4	1	1	3	5	5	28
1989 (Hoss)	3	–	1	2	1	–	1	3	3	14

Table 6 Synopsis of relevant universal rights affected by power-sharing

Prohibition of discrimination	• **Art 2 UDHR: Prohibition of discrimination** • **Art 2 ICERD: Prohibition of discrimination** ◦ **Art 1, paras 1–3 ICERD: Definition of 'racial discrimination'** ◦ **Art 1, para 4 ICERD: Necessity of special measures for adequate advancement of certain racial or ethnic groups** • **Art 3 ICERD: Prohibition of racial segregation and apartheid** • **Art 2, para 1 ICCPR: Prohibition of discrimination** • **Art 2, para 2 ICESCR: Prohibition of discrimination**
Universal Declaration of Human Rights (UDHR)	• Art 2 UDHR: Prohibition of discrimination 'Everyone is entitled to all the rights and freedoms set forth in this Declaration, without distinction of any kind, such as race, colour, sex, language, religion, political or other opinion, national or social origin, property, birth or other status. Furthermore, no distinction shall be made on the basis of the political, jurisdictional or international status of the country or territory to which a person belongs, whether it be independent, trust, non-self-governing or under any other limitation of sovereignty.'
International Convention on the Elimination of All Forms of Racial Discrimination (ICERD)	• Art 2 ICERD: Prohibition of discrimination '1. States Parties condemn racial discrimination and undertake to pursue by all appropriate means and without delay a policy of eliminating racial discrimination in all its forms and promoting understanding among all races, and, to this end: (a) Each State Party undertakes to engage in no act or practice of racial discrimination against persons, groups of persons or institutions and to en sure that all public authorities and public institutions, national and local, shall act in conformity with this obligation; (b) Each State Party undertakes not to sponsor, defend or support racial discrimination by any persons or organizations;

	(c) Each State Party shall take effective measures to review governmental, national and local policies, and to amend, rescind or nullify any laws and regulations which have the effect of creating or perpetuating racial discrimination wherever it exists; (d) Each State Party shall prohibit and bring to an end, by all appropriate means, including legislation as required by circumstances, racial discrimination by any persons, group or organization; (e) Each State Party undertakes to encourage, where appropriate, integrationist multiracial organizations and movements and other means of eliminating barriers between races, and to discourage anything which tends to strengthen racial division. 2. States Parties shall, when the circumstances so warrant, take, in the social, economic, cultural and other fields, special and concrete measures to ensure the adequate development and protection of certain racial groups or individuals belonging to them, for the purpose of guaranteeing them the full and equal enjoyment of human rights and fundamental freedoms. These measures shall in no case en tail as a con sequence the maintenance of unequal or separate rights for different racial groups after the objectives for which they were taken have been achieved.' • Art 1, paras 1–3 ICERD: Definition of 'racial discrimination' '1. In this Convention, the term "racial discrimination" shall mean any distinction, exclusion, restriction or preference based on race, colour, descent, or national or ethnic origin which has the purpose or effect of nullifying or impairing the recognition, enjoyment or exercise, on an equal footing, of human rights and fundamental freedoms in the political, economic, social, cultural or any other field of public life. 2. This Convention shall not apply to distinctions, exclusions, restrictions or preferences made by a State Party to this Convention between citizens and non-citizens.

	3. Nothing in this Convention may be interpreted as affecting in any way the legal provisions of States Parties concerning nationality, citizenship or naturalization, provided that such provisions do not discriminate against any particular nationality.' • Art 1, para 4 ICERD: Necessity of special measures for adequate advancement of certain racial or ethnic groups '4. Special measures taken for the sole purpose of securing adequate advancement of certain racial or ethnic groups or individuals requiring such protection as may be necessary in order to ensure such groups or individuals equal enjoyment or exercise of human rights and fundamental freedoms shall not be deemed racial discrimination, provided, however, that such measures do not, as a consequence, lead to the maintenance of separate rights for different racial groups and that they shall not be continued after the objectives for which they were taken have been achieved.' • Art 3 ICERD: Prohibition of racial segregation and apartheid 'States Parties particularly condemn racial segregation and apartheid and undertake to prevent, prohibit and eradicate all practices of this nature in territories under their jurisdiction.'
International Covenant on Civil and Political Rights (ICCPR)	Art 2, para 1 ICCPR: Prohibition of discrimination 'Each State Party to the present Covenant undertakes to respect and to ensure to all individuals within its territory and subject to its jurisdiction the rights recognized in the present Covenant, without distinction of any kind, such as race, colour, sex, language, religion, political or other opinion, national or social origin, property, birth or other status.'
International Covenant on Economic, Social and Cultural Rights (CESCR)	Art 2, para 2 ICESCR: Prohibition of discrimination 'The States Parties to the present Covenant undertake to guarantee that the rights enunciated in the present Covenant will be exercised without discrimination of any kind as to race, colour, sex, language, religion, political or other opinion, national or social origin, property, birth or other status.'

Right to political participation and equal access to public service	• **Art 21, paras 1–2 UDHR: Right to political participation and equal access to public service** • **Art 5, para c ICERD: Right to political participation and equal access to public service** • **Art 25, para a ICCPR: Right to political participation and equal access to public service**
Universal Declaration of Human Rights (UDHR)	• Art 21, paras 1–2 UDHR: Right to political participation and equal access to public service '(1) Everyone has the right to take part in the government of his country, directly or through freely chosen representatives. (2) Everyone has the right of equal access to public service in his country.'
International Convention on the Elimination of All Forms of Racial Discrimination (ICERD)	• Art 5, para c ICERD: Right to political participation and equal access to public service 'In compliance with the fundamental obligations laid down in article 2 of this Convention, States Parties undertake to prohibit and to eliminate racial discrimination in all its forms and to guarantee the right of everyone, without distinction as to race, colour, or national or ethnic origin, to equality before the law, notably in the enjoyment of the following rights: (c) Political rights, in particular the right to participate in elections-to vote and to stand for election-on the basis of universal and equal suffrage, to take part in the Government as well as in the conduct of public affairs at any level and to have equal access to public service ...'
International Covenant on Civil and Political Rights (ICCPR)	Art 25 ICCPR: Right to political participation and equal access to public service 'Every citizen shall have the right and the opportunity, without any of the distinctions mentioned in article 2 and without unreasonable restrictions: (a) To take part in the conduct of public affairs, directly or through freely chosen representatives; (b) To vote and to be elected at genuine periodic elections which shall be by universal and equal suffrage and shall be held by secret ballot, guaranteeing the free expression of the will of the electors; (c) To have access, on general terms of equality, to public service in his country.'

Freedom of movement and residence	• **Art 13, para 1 UDHR: Right to freedom of movement and residence** • **Art 5, para d(i) ICERD: Right to freedom of movement and residence** • **Art 12 ICCPR: Right to freedom of movement and residence**
Universal Declaration of Human Rights (UDHR)	• Art 13, para 1 UDHR: Right to freedom of movement and residence '(1) Everyone has the right to freedom of movement and residence within the borders of each state.'
International Convention on the Elimination of All Forms of Racial Discrimination (ICERD)	• Art 5, para d(i) ICERD: Right to freedom of movement and residence 'In compliance with the fundamental obligations laid down in article 2 of this Convention, States Parties undertake to prohibit and to eliminate racial discrimination in all its forms and to guarantee the right of everyone, without distinction as to race, colour, or national or ethnic origin, to equality before the law, notably in the enjoyment of the following rights: (d) Other civil rights, in particular: (i) The right to freedom of movement and residence within the border of the State …'
International Covenant on Civil and Political Rights (ICCPR)	• Art 12 ICCPR: Right to freedom of movement and residence '1. Everyone lawfully within the territory of a State shall, within that territory, have the right to liberty of movement and freedom to choose his residence.'

Minority rights	• **Art 1, para 4 ICERD: Necessity of special measures for adequate advancement of certain racial or ethnic groups** • **Art 27 ICCPR: Minority rights protection** • **Arts 1–4 UNDM: Minority rights protection** ◦ **Art 8, para 3 UNDM: Principle of equality** ◦ **Art 8, para 4 UNDM: Principle of sovereign equality, territorial integrity and political independence of States**
International Convention on the Elimination of All Forms of Racial Discrimination (ICERD)	• Art 1, para 4 ICERD: Necessity of special measures for adequate advancement of certain racial or ethnic groups '4. Special measures taken for the sole purpose of securing adequate advancement of certain racial or ethnic groups or individuals requiring such protection as may be necessary in order to ensure such groups or individuals equal enjoyment or exercise of human rights and fundamental freedoms shall not be deemed racial discrimination, provided, however, that such measures do not, as a consequence, lead to the maintenance of separate rights for different racial groups and that they shall not be continued after the objectives for which they were taken have been achieved.'

International Covenant on Civil and Political Rights (ICCPR)	• Art 27 ICCPR: Minority rights protection 'In those States in which ethnic, religious or linguistic minorities exist, persons belonging to such minorities shall not be denied the right, in community with the other members of their group, to enjoy their own culture, to profess and practise their own religion, or to use their own language.'
United Nations Declaration on the Rights of Persons Belonging to National or Ethnic, Religious and Linguistic Minorities (UNDM)	• Arts 1–4 UNDM: Minority rights protection 'Art 1 1. States shall protect the existence and the national or ethnic, cultural, religious and linguistic identity of minorities within their respective territories and shall encourage conditions for the promotion of that identity. 2. States shall adopt appropriate legislative and other measures to achieve those ends. Art 2 1. Persons belonging to national or ethnic, religious and linguistic minorities (hereinafter referred to as persons belonging to minorities) have the right to enjoy their own culture, to profess and practise their own religion, and to use their own language, in private and in public, freely and without interference or any form of discrimination. 2. Persons belonging to minorities have the right to participate effectively in cultural, religious, social, economic and public life. 3. Persons belonging to minorities have the right to participate effectively in decisions on the national and, where appropriate, regional level concerning the minority to which they belong or the regions in which they live, in a manner not incompatible with national legislation. 4. Persons belonging to minorities have the right to establish and maintain their own associations. 5. Persons belonging to minorities have the right to establish and maintain, without any discrimination, free and peaceful contacts with other members of their group and with persons belonging to other minorities, as well as contacts across frontiers with citizens of other States to whom they are related by national or ethnic, religious or linguistic ties.

	Art 3 1. Persons belonging to minorities may exercise their rights, including those set forth in the present Declaration, individually as well as in community with other members of their group, without any discrimination. 2. No disadvantage shall result for any person belonging to a minority as the consequence of the exercise or non-exercise of the rights set forth in the present Declaration. Art 4 1. States shall take measures when required to ensure that persons belonging to minorities may exercise fully and effectively all their human rights and fundamental freedoms without any discrimination and in full equality before the law. 2. States shall take measures to create favourable conditions to enable persons belonging to minorities to express their characteristics and to develop their culture, language, religion, traditions and customs, except where specific practices are in violation of national law and contrary to international standards. 3. States should take appropriate measures so that, wherever possible, persons belonging to minorities may have adequate opportunities to learn their mother tongue or to have instruction in their mother tongue. 4. States should, where appropriate, take measures in the field of education, in order to encourage knowledge of the history, traditions, language and culture of the minorities existing within their territory. Persons belonging to minorities should have adequate opportunities to gain knowledge of the society as a whole. 5. States should consider appropriate measures so that persons belonging to minorities may participate fully in the economic progress and development in their country.' • Art 8, para 3 UNDM: Principle of equality '3 Measures taken by States to ensure the effective enjoyment of the rights set forth in the present Declaration shall not prima facie be considered contrary to the principle of equality contained in the Universal Declaration of Human Rights.' • Art 8, para 4 UNDM: Principle of sovereign equality, territorial integrity and political independence of States '4. Nothing in the present Declaration may be construed as permitting any activity contrary to the purposes and principles of the United Nations, including sovereign equality, territorial integrity and political independence of States.'

Women's rights	• **Art 2 UDHR: Prohibition of discrimination** • **Art 3 ICCPR: Equal rights between men and women** • **Art 26 ICCPR: Equal protection before the law** • **Art 2 CEDAW: Prohibition of discrimination against women** • **Art 4 CEDAW: Adoption of temporary special measures** • **Art 7, para (b) CEDAW: Right to political participation** • **Art 16 CEDAW: Equality of marriage rights**
Universal Declaration of Human Rights (UDHR)	• Art 2 UDHR: Prohibition of discrimination 'Everyone is entitled to all the rights and freedoms set forth in this Declaration, without distinction of any kind, such as race, colour, sex, language, religion, political or other opinion, national or social origin, property, birth or other status. Furthermore, no distinction shall be made on the basis of the political, jurisdictional or international status of the country or territory to which a person belongs, whether it be independent, trust, non-self-governing or under any other limitation of sovereignty.'
International Covenant on Civil and Political Rights (ICCPR)	• Art 3 ICCPR: Equal rights between men and women 'The States Parties to the present Covenant undertake to ensure the equal right of men and women to the enjoyment of all civil and political rights set forth in the present Covenant.' • Art 26 ICCPR: Equal protection before the law 'All persons are equal before the law and are entitled without any discrimination to the equal protection of the law. In this respect, the law shall prohibit any discrimination and guarantee to all persons equal and effective protection against discrimination on any ground such as race, colour, sex, language, religion, political or other opinion, national or social origin, property, birth or other status.'
Convention on the Elimination of All Forms of Discrimination against Women (CEDAW)	• Art 2 CEDAW: Prohibition of discrimination against women 'States Parties condemn discrimination against women in all its forms, agree to pursue by all appropriate means and without delay a policy of eliminating discrimination against women and, to this end, undertake: (a) To embody the principle of the equality of men and women in their national constitutions or other appropriate legislation if not yet incorporated therein and to ensure, through law and other appropriate means, the practical realization of this principle; (b) To adopt appropriate legislative and other measures, including sanctions where appropriate, prohibiting all discrimination against women;

	(c) To establish legal protection of the rights of women on an equal basis with men and to ensure through competent national tribunals and other public institutions the effective protection of women against any act of discrimination; (d) To refrain from engaging in any act or practice of discrimination against women and to ensure that public authorities and institutions shall act in conformity with this obligation; (e) To take all appropriate measures to eliminate discrimination against women by any person, organization or enterprise; (f) To take all appropriate measures, including legislation, to modify or abolish existing laws, regulations, customs and practices which constitute discrimination against women; (g) To repeal all national penal provisions which constitute discrimination against women.' • Art 4 CEDAW: Adoption of temporary special measures '1. Adoption by States Parties of temporary special measures aimed at accelerating de facto equality between men and women shall not be considered discrimination as defined in the present Convention, but shall in no way entail as a consequence the maintenance of unequal or separate standards; these measures shall be discontinued when the objectives of equality of opportunity and treatment have been achieved. 2. Adoption by States Parties of special measures, including those measures contained in the present Convention, aimed at protecting maternity shall not be considered discriminatory.' • Art 7, para (b) CEDAW: Right to political participation 'States Parties shall take all appropriate measures to eliminate discrimination against women in the political and public life of the country and, in particular, shall ensure to women, on equal terms with men, the right: (b) To participate in the formulation of government policy and the implementation thereof and to hold public office and perform all public functions at all levels of government …' • Art 16 CEDAW: Equality of marriage rights '1. States Parties shall take all appropriate measures to eliminate discrimination against women in all matters relating to marriage and family relations and in particular shall ensure, on a basis of equality of men and women: (a) The same right to enter into marriage; (b) The same right freely to choose a spouse and to enter into marriage only with their free and full consent;

	(c) The same rights and responsibilities during marriage and at its dissolution; (d) The same rights and responsibilities as parents, irrespective of their marital status, in matters relating to their children; in all cases the interests of the children shall be paramount; (e) The same rights to decide freely and responsibly on the number and spacing of their children and to have access to the information, education and means to enable them to exercise these rights; (f) The same rights and responsibilities with regard to guardianship, wardship, trusteeship and adoption of children, or similar institutions where these concepts exist in national legislation; in all cases the interests of the children shall be paramount; (g) The same personal rights as husband and wife, including the right to choose a family name, a profession and an occupation; (h) The same rights for both spouses in respect of the ownership, acquisition, management, administration, enjoyment and disposition of property, whether free of charge or for a valuable consideration. 2. The betrothal and the marriage of a child shall have no legal effect, and all necessary action, including legislation, shall be taken to specify a minimum age for marriage and to make the registration of marriages in an official registry compulsory.'

Indigenous peoples' rights	• **Art 1 UNDRIP: Collective and individual rights of indigenous people** • **Art 2 UNDRIP: Equality rights and prohibition of discrimination of indigenous people** • **Art 4 UNDRIP: Right to autonomy or self-government** • **Art 12 UNDRIP: Freedom of religion** • **Art 18 UNDRIP: Right to participate in decision-making** • **Art 23 UNDRIP: Right to development** • **Art 39 UNDRIP: Right to financial and technical assistance**
UN Declaration on the Rights of Indigenous Peoples (UNDRIP)	• Art 1 UNDRIP: Collective and individual rights of indigenous people 'Indigenous peoples have the right to the full enjoyment, as a collective or as individuals, of all human rights and fundamental freedoms as recognized in the Charter of the United Nations, the Universal Declaration of Human Rights4 and international human rights law.'

<table>
<tr>
<td></td>
<td>
<ul>
<li>Art 2 UNDRIP: Equality rights and prohibition of discrimination of indigenous people
'Indigenous peoples and individuals are free and equal to all other peoples and individuals and have the right to be free from any kind of discrimination, in the exercise of their rights, in particular that based on their indigenous origin or identity.' </li>
<li>Art 4 UNDRIP: Right to autonomy or self-government
'Indigenous peoples, in exercising their right to self-determination, have the right to autonomy or self-government in matters relating to their internal and local affairs, as well as ways and means for financing their autonomous functions.' </li>
<li>Art 12 UNDRIP: Freedom of religion
'1. Indigenous peoples have the right to manifest, practise, develop and teach their spiritual and religious traditions, customs and ceremonies; the right to maintain, protect, and have access in privacy to their religious and cultural sites; the right to the use and control of their ceremonial objects; and the right to the repatriation of their human remains.
2. States shall seek to enable the access and/or repatriation of ceremonial objects and human remains in their possession through fair, transparent and effective mechanisms developed in conjunction with indigenous peoples concerned.' </li>
<li>Art 18 UNDRIP: Right to participate in decision-making
'Indigenous peoples have the right to participate in decision-making in matters which would affect their rights, through representatives chosen by themselves in accordance with their own procedures, as well as to maintain and develop their own indigenous decision-making institutions.' </li>
<li>Art 23 UNDRIP: Right to development
'Indigenous peoples have the right to determine and develop priorities and strategies for exercising their right to development. In particular, indigenous peoples have the right to be actively involved in developing and determining health, housing and other economic and social programmes affecting them and, as far as possible, to administer such programmes through their own institutions.' </li>
<li>Art 39 UNDRIP: Right to financial and technical assistance
'Indigenous peoples have the right to have access to financial and technical assistance from States and through international cooperation, for the enjoyment of the rights contained in this Declaration.' </li>
</ul>
</td>
</tr>
</table>

Table 7 ECtHR methodology of justifying human rights restrictions in times of state transitions

Step	Legal evaluation
A.	**Differential treatment**
1.	• **Comparability:** Can the groups at stake be compared to each other? (eg compared groups are all citizens and ethnic groups)
2.	• **Treatment:** Is one group, directly or indirectly, differently threatened to the other? (eg on racial or ethnic grounds)
3.	• **Prohibition:** Is the discrimination prohibited? (eg by the ECHR, ICERD)
B.	**Objective and reasonable justification**
1.	• **Legitimate public aim:** Is there a legitimate objective for the differential treatment? (eg restoration of peace, state security)
2.	• **Objective and reasonable facts:** Are there objective and reasonable facts which support justification more than non-justification? (eg reports of the UN CERD, Venice Commission, reports of the Council of Ministers, the Parliamentary Assembly, ECRI reports, governmental reports with regard to the Framework Convention for the Protection of National Minorities)
3.	• **Proportionality:** Is there a reasonable relationship between the means employed and the aim sought to be achieved? (eg the differential treatment is necessary, as there are no alternatives which are less impacting on rights but equally efficient to achieve the target aim)
4.	• **No arbitrary differential treatment:** Is the differential treatment random? (eg in substantially same situations)

Table 8 Dimensions of the proposed conceptual model for reflections about the law of peace debate and the imperfection of peace settlements

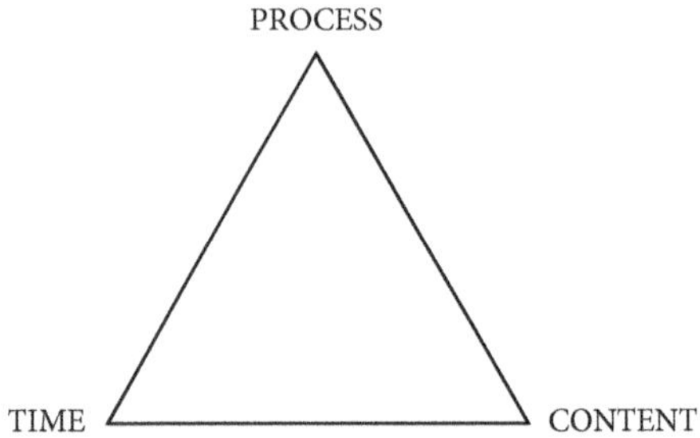

Element:	Process	Content	Time
Focus:	Who?	What?	When?
Details:	• Representation in peace negotiations • Authority of signatories • Scale of participation (inclusive or exclusive)	• Content of the peace settlement • Type of power-sharing arrangement	• Transitional or permanent solutions • Questions about phasing-out • Review mechanisms

Table 9 Dilemma of the 'imperfect peace'

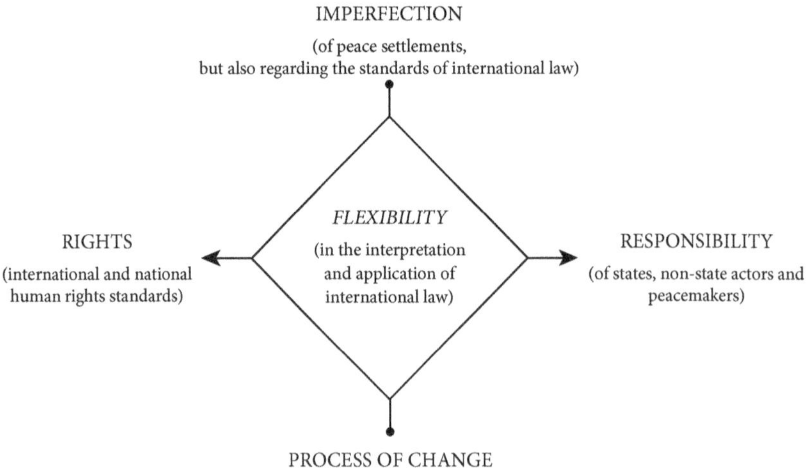

BIBLIOGRAPHY

Books, book chapters and journal articles

Addis, Adeno, 'Individualism, Communitarianism, and the Rights of Ethnic Minorities' (1991) 67 *Notre Dame Law Review* 615.

Åkermark, Athanasia Spiliopoulou, *Justifications of Minority Protection in International Law* (The Hague: Martinus Nijhoff Publishers, 1997).

Alexander, Gregory S, 'Dilemmas of Group Autonomy: Residential Associations and Community' (1989) 75 *Columbia Law Review* 1.

Alexander, Nadja, 'Mediation and the Art of Regulation' (2008) 8 *Queensland University of Technology Law and Justice Journal* 1.

Allott, Philip, 'Power Sharing in the Law of the Sea' (1983) 77 *American Journal of International Law* 1.

Al-Qattan, Najwa, 'Dhimmis in the Muslim Court: Legal Autonomy and Religious Discrimination' (1999) 31 *International Journal of Middle East Studies* 429.

Alvarez, José E, 'Do Liberal States Behave Better?: A Critique of Slaughter's Liberal Theory' (2001) 12(2) *European Journal of International Law* 183.

Aning, Kwesi and Atuobi, Samuel, 'The Neglected Economic Dimensions of ECOWAS's Negotiated Peace Accords in West Africa' (2011) 46(3) *Africa Spectrum* 27.

Arai-Takahashi, Yutaka, *The Margin of Appreciation Doctrine and the Principle of Proportionality in the Jurisprudence of the ECHR* (Antwerpen: Intersentia, 2001).

Arnardóttir, Oddný Mjöll, *Equality and Non-Discrimination under the European Convention on Human Rights* (The Hague: Martinus Nijhoff Publishers, 2003).

Aroussia, Sahla, and Vandeginstea, Stef, 'When Interests Meet Norms: The Relevance of Human Rights for Peace and Power-sharing' (2013) 17(2) *International Journal of Human Rights* 183.

Arsenian, Arda, *Confessional and Electoral Reform in Lebanon*, The Aspen Institute, Briefing Paper, July 2012.

Arthur, Paige, 'How "Transitions" Reshaped Human Rights: A Conceptual History of Transitional Justice' (2009) 31(2) *Human Rights Quarterly* 321.

Aust, Anthony, *Handbook of International Law* (Cambridge: Cambridge University Press, 2010).

——, *Modern Treaty Law and Practice* (Cambridge: Cambridge University Press, 2007).

Avritzer, Leonardo, 'The Different Designs of Public Participation in Brazil: Deliberation, Power-sharing and Public Ratification' (2012) 6(2) *Critical Policy Studies* 113.

Bailey, Betty Jane and Bailey, J Martin, *Who Are the Christians in the Middle East?* (Michigan: Eerdmans, 2010).

Baker, John H (ed), *Reports from the Lost Notebooks of Sir James Dyer* vol 109 (London: Selden Society, 1994).

Baliqi, Bekim, 'Promoting Multi-Ethnicity or Maintaining a Divided Society: Dilemmas of Power-Sharing in Kosovo' (2018) 17(1) *Journal on Ethnopolitics and Minority Issues in Europe* 49.

Barry, Brian, 'Political Accommodation and Consociational Democracy' (1975) 5 *British Journal of Political Science* 477.

Baxi, Upendra, 'Voices of Suffering, Fragmented Universality, and the Future of Human Rights' in Burns H Weston and Stephen P Marks (eds), *The Future of International Human Rights* (Ardsley, NY: Transnational Publishers, 1999) 172.

Beetham, David, *Parliament and Democracy in the Twenty-First Century* (Geneva: Inter-Parliamentary Union, 2006).

Bell, Christine, *On the Law of Peace: Peace Agreements and the Lex Pacificatoria* (Oxford: Oxford University Press, 2008).
——, 'Peace Agreements: Their Nature and Legal Status' (2006) 100(2) *American Journal of International Law* 375.
——, 'Peace Agreements and Human Rights: Implications for the UN' in Nigel D White and Dirk Klaasen (eds), *UN, Human Rights and Post-Conflict Situations* (Manchester: Manchester University Press 2005) 241.
——, *Peace Agreements and Human Rights* (Oxford: Oxford University Press, 2000).
Belmont, Katharine, Mainwaring, Scott and Reynolds, Andrew, 'Introduction: Institutional Design, Conflict Management, and Democracy in Divided Societies' in Andrew Reynolds (ed), *The Architecture of Democracy: Constitutional Design, Conflict Management, and Democracy* (Oxford: Oxford University Press, 2002) 1.
Benjamin, Walter, *Zur Kritik der Gewalt und andere Aufsätze* (Suhrkamp: Frankfurt am Main, 1990).
Benvenisti, Eyal, 'Margin of Appreciation, Consensus, and Universal Standards' (1999) 31 *International Law and Politics* 844.
Benzing, Markus, *Das Beweisrecht vor internationalen Gerichten und Schiedsgerichten in zwischenstaatlichen Streitigkeiten* (Berlin, Heidelberg: Springer Verlag, 2010).
Bercovitch, Jacob and Langley, Jeffrey, 'The Nature of the Dispute and the Effectiveness of International Mediation' (1993) 37 *Journal of Conflict Resolution* 670.
Berg, Eiki, and Ben-Porat, Guy, 'Introduction: Partition vs. Power-sharing?' (2008) 14(1) *Nations and Nationalism* 29.
Berween, Mohamed, 'Non-Muslims in the Islamic State: Majority Rule and Minority Rights' (2006) 10 *International Journal of Human Rights* 95.
Bhuta, Nehal, 'Rethinking the Universality of Human Rights' in Anver Emon, Mark Ellis and Benjamin Glahn (eds), *Islamic Law and International Human Rights Law: Searching for Common Ground?* (Oxford: Oxford University Press, 2012) 123.
Bianchi, Andrea, 'Human Rights and the Magic of Jus cogens' (2008) 19(3) *European Journal of International Law* 491.
Biden, Joseph R, Jr and Ritch, John B III, 'The Treaty Power: Upholding a Constitutional Partnership' (1989) 137(5) *University of Pennsylvania Law Review* 1529.
Bieber, Florian, *Post-War Bosnia: Ethnicity, Inequality and Public Sector Governance* (New York: Palgrave Macmillan, 2006).
——, 'Power Sharing as Ethnic Representation in Post-Conflict Societies: The Cases of Bosnia, Macedonia and Kosovo' in Alina Mungiu-Pippidi and Ivan Krastev (eds), *Nationalism after Communism: Lessons Learned* (Budapest: CEU Press, 2004) 229.
Bochsler, Daniel, 'Non-Discriminatory Rules and Ethnic Representation: The Election of the Bosnian State Presidency' (2011)10(3) *Ethnopolitics* 5.
Bogaard, Matthijs, 'Democracy and Power-Sharing in Multinational States: Thematic Introduction' (2006) 8(2) *International Journal on Multicultural Societies* 123.
——, 'The Uneasy Relationship between Empirical and Normative Types in Consociational Theory' (2000) 12(4) *Journal of Theoretical Politics* 395.
Bose, Sumantra, *Bosnia after Dayton: Nationalist Partition and International Intervention* (Oxford: Oxford University Press, 2002).
Bowett, Derek, *The Search for Peace* (London: Routledge & Kegan Paul, 1972).
Bowker, John (ed), *The Oxford Dictionary of World Religions* (Oxford: Oxford University Press, 1999).
Bowring, Bill, 'The Russian Constitutional System: Complexity and Asymmetry' in Marc Weller and Katherine Nobbs (eds), *Asymmetric Autonomy and the Settlement of Ethnic Conflicts* (Philadelphia: University of Pennsylvania Press, 2010) 48.
——, 'The Crimean Autonomy: Innovation or Anomaly?' in Marc Weller and Stefan Wolff (eds), *Autonomy, Self-Governance and Conflict Resolution: Innovative Approaches to Institutional Design in Divided Societies* (London: Routledge, 2005) 75.
Brems, Eva, *Human Rights: Universality and Diversity* (The Hague: Martinus Nijhoff, 2001).

Brooker, Penny, 'Towards a Code of Professional Conduct for Construction Mediators' (2011) 3(1) *International Journal of Law in the Built Environment* 24.

Buchanan, Allen, *Justice, Legitimacy, and Self-Determination: Moral Foundations for International Law* (Oxford: Oxford University Press, 2004).

Buergenthal, Thomas, 'The Normative and Institutional Evolution of International Human Rights' (1997) 19(4) *Human Rights Quarterly* 703.

Bunde, Tobias, 'Das Völkerrecht der Demokratien: Ambivalenzen einer liberalen Weltordnung' in Christian Tomuschat (ed), *Weltordnungsmodelle für das 21. Jahrhundert* (Baden-Baden: Nomos, 2009) 99.

Buyse, Antoine, and Hamilton, Michael, 'Conclusion' in Antoine Buyse and Michael Hamilton (eds), *Transitional Jurisprudence and the ECHR: Justice, Politics and Rights*, (Cambridge: Cambridge University Press, 2011) 286.

Byrne, Sean, 'Consociational and Civil Society Approaches in Peacebuilding in Northern Ireland' (2001) 38(3) *Journal of Peace Research* 333.

Campbell, Colm, 'Wars on Terror and Vicarious Hegemons: The UK, International Law, and the Northern Ireland Conflict' (2005) 54 *International and Comparative Law Quarterly* 337.

Cançado Trindade, Antônio Augusto, 'Co-Existence and Co-Ordination of Mechanisms of International Protection of Human Rights (At Global and Regional Levels)' (1987) 202 *Recueil des Cours* 104.

Clapham, Andrew, *Human Rights Obligations of Non-State Actors* (Oxford: Oxford University Press, 2006).

——, 'Human Rights Obligations of Non-state Actors in Conflict Situations' (2006) 88(863) *International Review of the Red Cross* 491.

Caplan, Richard, 'Assessing Dayton: The Structural Weaknesses of the General Framework Agreement for Peace in Bosnia and Herzegovina' (2000) 11(2) *Diplomacy & Statecraft* 213.

Caritat, marquis de Condorcet, Marie-Jean-Antoine-Nicolas, *Œuvres complètes de Voltaire*, vol II (Paris: Carez, Thomine et Fortic, 1822).

Cassese, Antonio, 'Terrorism is also Disrupting some Crucial Legal Categories of International Law' (2001) 12 *European Journal of International Law* 993.

Catusse, Myriam and Karam, Karam, 'Back to Parties?: Partisan Logics and Transformations of Politics in the Arab World' in Myriam Catusse and Karam Karan (eds), *Returning to Political Parties?: Partisan Logic and Political Transformations in the Arab World* (Sin el Fil: The Lebanese Center for Policy Studies, 2010) 19.

Cheng, Tai-Heng, *When International Law Works: Realistic Idealism After 9/11 and the Global Recession* (Oxford: Oxford University Press, 2012).

Chesterman, Simon, 'Ownership in Theory and in Practice: Transfer of Authority in UN Statebuilding Operations' (2007) 1(1) *Journal of Intervention and Statebuilding* 3.

Chinkin, Christine, Tomuschat, Christian and Ronzitti, Natalino, 'Panel Discussion: Has International Law Civilized Conflicts Since 1907?' in Thomas Giegerich and Ursula E Heinz (eds), *A Wiser Century?: Judicial Dispute Settlement, Disarmament and the Laws of War 100 Years After the Second Hague Peace Conference* (Berlin: Duncker&Humblot, 2009) 509.

——, 'An International Law Framework with Respect to International Peace and Security' in Marlies Glasius and Mary Kaldor (eds), *A Human Security Doctrine for Europe: Project, Principles, Practicalities: Project, Principles and Practicalities* (Oxford: Routledge, 2006) 173.

Christoffersen, Jonas, *Fair Balance: Proportionality, Subsidiarity and Primarity in the European Convention on Human Rights* (The Hague: Brill, 2009).

Cleveland, Sarah H, 'Legal Status and Rights of Undocumented Workers: Advisory Opinion OC-18/03' (2005) 99(2) *American Journal of International Law* 460.

Clinton, Bill, *My Life* (New York: Alfred A Knopf, 2004).

Cohen, John L, 'The Role of International Law in Post-Conflict Constitution-Making: Toward a Jus Post Bellum for "Interim Occupations"' (2006/07) 51 *New York Law School Law Review* 497.

Cole, Rowland JV, 'Power-sharing, Post-electoral Contestations and the Dismemberment of the Right to Democracy in Africa' (2013) 17(2) *International Journal of Human Rights* 256.

Coleman, Peter, *The Five Percent: Finding Solutions to Seemingly Impossible Conflicts* (New York: Public Affairs, 2011).
Conklin, William E, 'The Peremptory Norms of the International Community' (2012) 23(3) *European Journal of International Law* 837.
Cordell, Karl, and Wolf, Stefan (eds), *Ethnic Conflict* (Cambridge: Polity Press, 2010).
Corten, Olivier and Klein, Pierre, 'Agreements between States and Non-State Entities Rooted in the International Legal Order?' in Enzo Cannizzaro (ed), *The Law of Treaties Beyond the Vienna Convention* (Oxford: Oxford University Press, 2011) 4.
—— (eds), *The Vienna Conventions on the Law of Treaties* (Oxford: Oxford University Press, 2011).
Crawford, James, 'State Practice and International Law in Relation to Unilateral Secession' in Anne Bayefsky (ed), *Self-Determination in International Law: Quebec and Lessons Learned* (Cambridge: Kluwer Law International, 2000) 60.
Delvin, Patrick, *The Judge* (Oxford: Oxford University Press, 1979).
Demos, Vasilikie, 'Maintenance and Loss of Traditional Gender Boundaries in Two Greek Orthodox Communities' (1989) 16(1) *Journal of the Hellenic Diaspora* 77.
Derouen, Karl Jr, Lea, Jenna and Wallensteen, Peter, 'The Duration of Civil War Peace Agreements' (2009) 26(4) *Conflict Management and Peace Science* 367.
Dickinson, Edwin D, *Law and Peace* (Philadelphia: University of Pennsylvania Press, 1951).
Dinstein, Yoram, *War, Aggression and Self-Defence* (Cambridge: Cambridge University Press, 2011) 41.
Disquisitio Iuris Publici De Bonis Ecclesiasticis Eorumque, Ex Alieno Territorio Debitis, Reditibus, Inter Protestantes Imperii Status Controversis (Francofurti: Ilsnerus, 1687).
Doering-Manteuffel, Anselm, *Vom Wiener Kongreß zur Pariser Konferenz: England, die deutsche Frage und das Mächtesystem 1815–1856* (Göttingen, Zürich: Vandenhoeck und Ruprecht, 1991).
Donohue, Laura K, 'Temporary Permanence: The Constitutional Entrenchment of Emergency Legislation' (1999) 1 *Stanford Journal of Legal Studies* 60.
Dudai, Ron, and McEvoy, Kieran, 'Thinking Critically about Armed Groups and Human Rights Praxis' (2012) 4(1) *Journal of Human Rights Practice* 1.
Dunn, David J, *The First Fifty Years of Peace Research: A Survey and Interpretation* (Aldershot, Hampshire: Ashgate, 2005).
Dworkin, Ronald, *Taking Rights Seriously* (Cambridge, MA: Harvard University Press, 1977).
Edel, Frédéric, *The Prohibition of Discrimination Under the European Convention on Human Rights* (Strasbourg: Council of Europe, 2010).
Edeson, William, 'The Role of Technical Bodies' in Rüdiger Wolfrum and Volker Röben (eds), *Developments of International Law in Treaty Making* (Berlin: Springer, 2005) 63.
Eide, Asbjørn, 'In Search of Constructive Alternatives to Secession' in Christian Tomuschat (ed), *Modern Law of Self-Determination* (Martinus Nijhoff: Dordrecht, 1993) 139.
Eissen, Marc-André, 'The Principle of Proportionality in the Case-Law of the European Court of Human Rights' in Ronald St J Macdonald, Franz Matscher and Herbert Petzold (eds), *The European System for the Protection of Human Rights* (Dordrecht, Boston: Martinus Nijhoff Publishers, 1993) 125.
El-Khazen, Farid, *Prospects for Lebanon: Lebanon's First Postwar Parliamentary Election, 1992* (London: IB Tauris, 2007).
'Embassies Reserved for Confessions' (2010) 92 *The Monthly* 5.
Emon, Anver M, 'Religious Minorities and Islamic Law: Accommodation and the Limits of Tolerance' in Anver Emon, Mark Ellis and Benjamin Glahn (eds), *Islamic Law and International Human Rights Law: Searching for Common Ground?* (Oxford: Oxford University Press, 2012) 323.
Figa-Talamanca, Niccoló, 'The Role of NATO in the Peace Agreements for Bosnia and Herzegovina' (1996) 7 *European Journal of International Law* 164.
Forlati, Serena, 'Coercion as a Ground Affecting the Validity of Peace Treaties' in Enzo Cannizzaro (ed), *The Law of Treaties Beyond the Vienna Convention* (Oxford: Oxford University Press, 2011) 320.
Fox, Gregory H, 'The Right of Political Participation in International Law' in Gregory H Fox and Brad R Roth (eds), *Democratic Governance and International Law* (Cambridge: Cambridge University Press, 2000) 50.

—— and Brad R Roth, 'Introduction: The Spread of Liberal Democracy and its Implications for International Law' in Gregory H Fox and Brad R Roth (eds), *Democratic Governance and International Law* (Cambridge: Cambridge University Press, 2000) 1.

—— and Nolte, Georg, 'Intolerant Democracies' (1995) 36(1) *Harvard International Law Journal* 48.

Franck, Thomas, 'Postmodern Tribalism and the Right to Secession' in Catherine Brölmann, René Lefeber and Marjoleine Zieck (eds), *Peoples and Minorities in International Law* (Boston: Brill, 1993) 13.

——, 'Why Federations Fail' in Thomas Franck (ed), *Why Federations Fail: An Inquiry into the Requisites for Successful Federalism* (New York: New York University Press, 1968) 213.

Freeman, Mark, *Necessary Evils: Amnesties and the Search for Justice* (Cambridge: Cambridge University Press, 2011).

Friedman, Gary J, and Himmelstein, Jack, *Challenging Conflict: Mediation Through Understanding* (Cambridge, MA: American Bar Association, Harvard Law School Program of Negotiation, 2008).

Gaeta, Paola, 'The Dayton Agreements and International Law' (1996) 7 *European Journal of International Law* 147.

Gans, Herbert J, 'Symbolic Ethnicity and Symbolic Religiosity: Towards a Comparison of Ethnic and Religious Acculturation' (1994) 17(4) *Ethnic and Racial Studies* 577.

Greer, Steven C, *The Margin of Appreciation: Interpretation and Discretion under the European Convention on Human Rights* (Strasbourg: Council of Europe, 2000).

Ghosn, Faten and Khoury, Amal, 'Lebanon after the Civil War:Peace or the Illusion of Peace?' (2011) 65(3) *Middle East Journal* 381.

Gilbert, Geoff, Warbrick, Colin and McGoldrick, Dominic, 'The Northern Ireland Peace Agreement, Minority Rights and Self-Determination' (1998) 47(4) *International and Comparative Law Quarterly* 943.

Glassmyer, Katherine, and Sambanis, Nicholas, 'Rebel-Military Integration and Civil War Termination' (2008) 45(3) *Journal of Peace Research* 365.

Grotius, Hugo, *The Rights of War and Peace: Including the Law of Nature and of Nations*, first published in 1624, Jean Barbeyrac (ed) (Indianapolis: Liberty Fund, 2005).

Gunn, T Jeremy, 'Deconstructing Proportionality in Limitations Analysis' (2005) 19 *Emory International Law Review* 471.

Hamilton, Michael, and Buyse, Antoine, 'Introduction' in Michael Hamilton and Antoine Buyse (eds), *Transitional Jurisprudence and the ECHR: Justice, Politics and Rights* (Cambridge: Cambridge University Press, 2011) 1.

Hannikainen, Lauri, *Peremptory Norms (Jus cogens) in International Law: Historical Development, Criteria, Present Status* (Helsinki: Finnish Lawyers' Publishing Company, 1988).

Hannum, Hurst, 'Peace Versus Justice: Creating Rights as Well as Order Out of Chaos' (2006) 13(4) *International Peacekeeping* 582.

Hart, HLA, *The Concept of Law* (Oxford: Clarendon Press, 1961).

Hartzell, Caroline, 'Structuring the Peace: Negotiated Settlements and the Construction of Conflict Management Institutions' in T David Mason et al (eds), *Conflict Prevention and Peacebuilding in Post-War Societies: Sustaining the Peace* (London: Routledge, 2006) 31.

—— and Hoddie, Matthew, 'Institutionalizing Peace: Power Sharing and Post-Civil War Conflict Management' (2003) 47(2) *American Journal of Political Science* 319.

——, 'Explaining the Stability of Intrastate Wars' (1999) 43 *Journal of Conflict Resolution* 318.

Henkin, Louis, *How Nations Behave: Law and Foreign Policy* (New York: Columbia University Press, 1979).

Higgins, Rosalyn, *Problems and Process: International Law and How We Use It* (Oxford: Clarendon Press, 1994).

Hillman, Ben, 'Power-sharing and Political Party Engineering in Conflict-prone Societies: The Indonesian Experiment in Aceh' (2012) 12(2) *Conflict, Security & Development* 149.

Hrair Dekmejian, Richard, 'Consociational Democracy in Crisis: The Case of Lebanon' (1978) 10(2) *Comparative Politics* 254.

Holmqvist, Caroline, 'Engaging Non-state Actors in Post Conflicts Settings' in Alan Bryden and Heiner Hänggi (eds), *Security Governance and Post-conflict Peacebuilding* (Berlin: Geneva Centre for the Democratic Control of Armed Forces, Lit Verlag, 2005) 45.

Horowitz, Donald, 'Conciliatory Institutions and Constitutional Process in Post-Conflict States' (2008) 49(4) *William & Mary Law Review* 1213.

——, 'Constitutional Design: Proposals Versus Processes' in Andrew Reynolds (ed), *The Architecture of Democracy: Constitutional Design, Conflict Management, and Democracy* (Oxford: Oxford University Press, 2002) 15.

——, *A Democratic South Africa? Constitutional Engineering in a Divided Society* (Berkeley and Los Angeles: University of California Press, 1991).

——, *Ethnic Groups in Conflict. Theories, Patterns and Politics* (Berkeley: University of California Press, 1985).

Humphrey, Michael, *Islam, Multiculturalism and Transnationalism* (London: IB Tauris, 1998).

Huntington, Samuel P, *The Third Wave: Democratization in the Late 20th Century* (Norman: University of Oklahoma Press, 1991).

Hussey, Joan M, *The Orthodox Church in the Byzantine Empire* (Oxford: Oxford University Press, 2010).

Inalcik, Halil, *The Ottoman Empire: The Classical Age, 1300–1600* (London: Phoenix Press, 1973).

Jackson-Preece, Jennifer, 'The Role of Human and Minority Rights in Complex Power-sharing' in Marc Weller, Barbara Metzger and Niall Johnson (eds), *Settling Self-Determination Disputes: Complex Power-Sharing in Theory and Practice* (Cambridge: University of Cambridge, 2008) 627.

Jørgensen, Nina, 'The Responsibility to Protect and the Obligations of States and Organizations under the Law of International Responsibility' in André Nollkaemper and Julian Hoffman (eds), *The Responsibility to Protect: From Principle to Practice* (Amsterdam: Amsterdam University Press, 2012) 125.

Joseph, Sarah, 'Rights of Political Participation' in David Harris and Sarah Josesph (eds), *The International Convenant on Civil and Political Rights and United Kingdom Law* (Oxford: Oxford University Press, 1995) 534.

Joyner, Christopher C, *International Law in the 21st Century: Rules for Global Governance* (Oxford: Rowman & Littlefield Publishers, 2005).

Jung, Jai Kwan, 'Power-sharing and Democracy Promotion in Post-Civil War Peace-Building' (2012) 19(3) *Democratization* 486.

Kaldor, Mary, 'From Just War to Just Peace' in Monica Den Boer and Jaap De Wilde (eds), *The Viability of Human Security*, eds. (Amsterdam: Amsterdam University Press, 2008) 21.

Kant, Immanuel, 'Zum Ewigen Frieden: Ein philosophischer Entwurf' in Wilhelm Weischedel (ed), *Immanuel Kant: Werke in Zwölf Bänden* Bd 11 (Frankfurt am Main: Suhrkamp Verlag, 1977).

Kapur, Ratna, 'Unveiling Equality: Disciplining the "Other" Woman through Human Rights Discourse' in Anver Emon, Mark Ellis and Benjamin Glahn (eds), *Islamic Law and International Human Rights Law: Searching for Common Ground?* (Oxford: Oxford University Press, 2012) 265.

Karam, Karam, 'Post-Syria Lebanon: Internal and External Determinants of a Crisis' (2006) 41(2) *The International Spectator* 51.

Keane, David, and Castellino, Joshua, 'Transcending Sectarianism through Minority Rights in Iraq' (2012) 5(3) *International Journal of Contemporary Iraqi Studies* 387.

Keeton, Robert E, *Judging* (St Paul, Minn: West Publishing Co, 1990).

Kelman, Herbert C, 'Building Trust among Enemies: The Central Challenge for International Conflict Resolution' (2005) 29(6) *International Journal of Intercultural Relations* 639.

Kennedy, David, *Of War and Law* (Princeton: Princeton University Press, 2006).

Kirchhoff, Lars, *Constructive Interventions: Paradigms, Process and Practice of International Mediation* (The Hague: Kluwer Law International, 2008).

Kokott, Juliane, *The Burden of Proof in Comparative and International Human Rights Law: Civil and Common Law Approaches with Special Reference to the American and German Legal Systems* (The Hague: Kluwer Law International, 1998).

Koskenniemi, Martti, *The Politics of International Law* (Oxford: Hart Publishing, 2011).

——, 'The Politics of International Law' (1990) 1(4) *European Journal of International Law* 4.
——, *From Apology to Utopia: The Structure of International Legal Argument* (Helsinki: Lakimiesliiton Kustannus Finnish Lawyers' Publishing Company, 1989).
Kramer, Matthew, *Objectivity and the Rule of Law* (Cambridge: Cambridge University Press, 2007).
Lang, Andrej, '"Modus operandi," "Lex pacificatoria" and the ICJ's appraisal of the Lusaka Ceasefire Agreement in the Armed Activities on the Territory of the Congo Case More than just Latin Lessons: The Role of Peace Agreements in International Conflict Resolution' (2007) 2 *Institute for International Law and Justice Emerging Scholars Paper, New York University* 22.
Latham, Judith, 'Roma of the former Yugoslavia' (1999) 27(2) *Nationalities Papers* 205.
Layton, Robert, 'The Effect of Measures Short of War on Treaties' (1962) 30(1) *University of Chicago Law Review* 96.
Lauterpacht, Hersch, *International Law: The Collected Papers* vol 2, Elihu Lauterpacht (ed) (Cambridge: Cambridge University Press, 2004).
——, *The Function of Law in the International Community* (Oxford: Oxford University Press, 2003).
Lavender, Nicolas, 'The Problem of the Margin of Appreciation' (1997) 4 *European Human Rights Law Review* 382.
Lazar, Seth, 'Skepticism about Jus post bellum' in Larry May and Andrew Forcehimes (eds), *Morality, Jus Post Bellum, and International Law* (Cambridge: Cambridge University Press, 2012) 207.
Lederach, John Paul, *The Moral Imagination: The Art and Soul of Building Peace* (Oxford: Oxford University Press, 2004).
Leonardya, Uwe, 'Federation and Länder in German Foreign Relations: Power-sharing in Treaty-making and European Affairs' (1992) 1(3) *German Politics* 119.
Lesaffer, Randall, 'Book Review: Christine Bell, On the Law of Peace: Peace Agreements and the Lex Pacificatoria' (2011) 24 *Leiden Journal of International Law* 522.
——, *Peace Treaties and International Law in European History: From the Late Middle Ages to World War One* (Cambridge: Cambridge University Press, 2006).
Lester, Lord of Herne Hill, 'Universality Versus Subsidiarity: A Reply' (1998) 1 *European Human Rights Law Review* 75.
Letsas, George, 'Two Concepts of the Margin of Appreciation' (2006) 26 *Oxford Journal of Legal Studies* 705.
Levitt, Jeremy I, *Illegal Peace in Africa: An Inquiry into the Legality of Power Sharing with Warlords, Rebels, and Junta* (Cambridge: Cambridge University Press, 2012).
——, 'An Inquiry into the Legality of Power-Sharing with Warlords and Rebels in Africa' (2006) 27(2) *MJIL* 495.
Linder, Wolf, *Swiss Democracy: Possible Solutions to Conflict in Multicultural Societies* (London: Palgrave Macmillan, 2010).
Lijphart, Arend, *Thinking about Democracy: Power Sharing and Majority Rule in Theory and Practice* (London: Routledge, 2008).
——, 'The Wave of Power-sharing Democracy' in Andrew Reynolds (ed), *The Architecture of Democracy: Constitutional Design, Conflict Management and Democracy* (Oxford: Oxford University Press, 2002) 37.
——, 'Definitions, Evidence, and Policy: A Response to Matthijs Bogaards' Critique' (2000) 12(4) *Journal of Theoretical Politics* 425.
—— and Waisman, Carlos H (eds), *Institutional Design in New Democracies* (Boulder: Westview, 1996).
——, 'The Framework Document on Northern Ireland and the Theory of Power-Sharing' (1996) 31(3) *Government and Opposition* 267.
——, *Power-Sharing in South Africa* (Berkeley: Institute of International Studies University of California, 1985).
——, *Democracies: Patterns of Majoritarian and Consensus Government in Twenty-one Countries* (New Haven: Yale University Press, 1984).
——, *Democracy in Plural Societies: A Comparative Exploration* (New Haven: Yale University Press, 1977).

——, 'Consociational Democracy' (1969) 21 *World Politics* 216.
——, *The Politics of Accommodation: Pluralism and Democracy in the Netherlands* (Berkeley: University of California Press, 1968).
Loucaides, Loukis G, 'Reflections of a Former European Court of Human Rights Judge on his Experiences as a Judge' (2010) 1 *Roma Rights* 64.
Lucas, George R, 'From Jus ad Bellum to Jus ad Pacem: Re-thinking Just-War Criteria for the Use of Military Force of Humanitarian Ends' in Deen K Chatterjee and Don E Scheid (eds), *Ethics And Foreign Intervention* (Cambridge: Cambridge University Press, 2003) 74.
Lustick, Ian, 'Stability in Deeply Divided Societies: Consociationalism Versus Control' (1979) 31(3) *World Politics* 325.
Mahoney, Paul, 'Judicial Activism and Judicial Self-Restraint in the European Court of Human Rights: Two Sides of the Same Coin' (1990) 11 *Human Rights Law Journal* 57.
Makdisi, Ussama, 'After 1860: Debating Religion, Reform, and Nationalism in the Ottoman Empire' (2002) 34 *International Journal of Middle East Studies* 601.
——, 'Corrupting the Sublime Sultanate: The Revolt of Tanyus Shahin in Nineteenth-Century Ottoman Lebanon' (2000) 42(1) *Comparative Studies in Society and History* 180.
Manirakizaa, Pacifique, 'The African Commission on Human and Peoples' Rights' Perspective on Power-sharing Arrangements' (2013) 17(2) *International Journal of Human Rights* 238.
——, 'Insecurity Implications of Unconstitutional Changes of Government in Africa: From Military to Constitutional Coups' (2016) 17(2) *Journal of Military and Strategic Studies* 86.
Marko, Joseph, 'The New Kosovo Constitution in a Regional Comparative Perspective' (2008) 33(4) *Review of Central and East European Law* 437.
——, 'Constitutional Reform in Bosnia and Herzegovina' (2005/06) 5 *European Yearbook of Minority Issues* 207.
Markusse, Jan, 'Power-sharing and "Consociational Democracy" in South Tyrol' (1997) 43(1) *GeoJournal* 77.
May, Larry, *After War Ends: A Philosophical Perspective* (Cambridge, Cambridge University Press, 2012).
McBride, Jeremy, 'Proportionality and the European Convention on Human Rights' in Evelyn Ellis (ed), *The Principle of Proportionality in the Laws* (Oxford: Hart Publishing, 1999) 23.
McCrudden, Christopher, 'International and European Norms Regarding National Legal Remedies for Racial Inequality' in Sandra Fredman, Philip Alston and Gráinne de Búrca (eds), *Discrimination and Human Rights: The Case of Racism* (Oxford: Oxford University Press, 2001) 251.
McDougal, Myres S, 'Peace and War: Factual Continuum with Multiple Legal Consequences' (1955) 49 *American Journal of International Law* 63.
McGarry, John and O'Leary, Brendan, 'Iraq's Constitution of 2005: Liberal Consociation as Political Prescription' (2007) 5(4) *International Journal of Constitutional Law* 670.
Mehler, Andreas, 'Introduction: Power-Sharing in Africa' (2009) 44(3) *Africa Spectrum* 2.
——, *Not Always in the People's Interest: Power-sharing Arrangements in African Peace Agreements*, GIGA Working Papers No 83, July 2006.
Mehmeti, Ermira, 'Implementation of the Ohrid Framework Agreement' in *Power-Sharing and the Implementation of the Ohrid Framework Agreement* (Skopje: Friedrich Ebert Stiftung, 2008).
Mendez, Ruben P, 'Peace as a Global Public Good' in Inge Kaul, Isabelle Grunberg and Marc A Stern (eds), *Global Public Goods: International Cooperation in the 21st Century* (Oxford: Oxford University Press, 1999) 382.
Milanovic, Marko, 'Peacemaking or Discrimination: Bosnia's Dayton Constitution before the European Court of Human Rights' (2009) June *European Journal of International Law Reports* 1.
Miller, Russell, 'Paradoxes of Personality: Transnational Corporations, Non-Governmental Organizations and Human Rights in International Law' in Russell Miller and Rebecca Bratspies (eds), *Progress in International Law* (The Hague: Martinus Nijhoff Publishers, 2008) 381.
Mitchell, Matthew I, 'Power-sharing and Peace in Côte d'Ivoire: Past Examples and Future Prospects' (2012) 12(2) *Conflict, Security and Development* 171.

Moeckli, Daniel, 'Equality and Non-Discrimination' in Daniel Moeckli, Sangeeta Shah, and Sandesh Sivakumaran (eds), *International Human Rights Law*, eds. (Oxford: Oxford University Press, 2010) 189.

Morgan, Diane, 'Why "Perpetual Peace" is Almost a Pleonasm' (2013) 25(1) *Peace Review: A Journal of Social Justice* 9.

Morris, Jeremy, *The Church in the Modern Age: The History of the Christian Church* (London: IB Tauris, 2007).

Mulder, Louise, 'How Positive Can Equality Measures Be?' in Titia Loenen and Peter R Rodrigues (eds), *Non-Discrimination Law: Comparative Perspectives* (The Hague: Kluwer Law International, 1999) 65.

Müller, Wolfgang C and Strom, Kaare, 'Coalition Governance in Western Europe: An Introduction' in Wolfgang C Müller and Kaare Strom (eds), *Coalition Governance in Western Europe* (Oxford: Oxford University Press, 2003) 1.

'Myth #16: The Post of the Parliament Speaker is historically and constitutionally reserved to the Shi'a' (2008) 75 *The Monthly* 25.

Nagle, John, 'Beyond Ethnic Entrenchment and Amelioration: An Analysis of Non-sectarian Social Movements and Lebanon's Consociationalism' (2018) 41(7) *Ethnic and Racial Studies* 1370.

Nan, Susan Allen, Mampilly, Zachariah Cherian and Bartoli, Andrea (eds), *Peacemaking: From Practice to Theory* (Westport, CT: Praeger, 2011).

Nemitz, Jan Christoph, 'The Legal Status of the Republika Srpska' (1997) 43 *Osteuropa Recht* 89.

Ni Aolain, Fionnuala, 'The Fractured Soul of the Dayton Peace Agreement: A Legal Analysis' (1998) 19 *Michigan Journal of International Law* 957.

Nolte, Georg, 'Session and External Intervention' in Marcelo G Kohen (ed), *Secession: International Law Perspectives* (Cambridge: Cambridge University Press, 2006) 65.

——, *Eingreifen auf Einladung* (Berlin: Springer, 1999).

——, 'General Principles of German and European Administrative Law: A Comparison in Historical Perspective' (1994) 57(2) *Modern Law Review* 191.

Nordlinger, Eric A, *Conflict Regulation in Divided Societies*, Occasional Papers, No 29, Center for International Affairs (Cambridge, MA: Harvard University, 1972).

Noortmann, Math, and Ryngaer, Cedric, 'Introduction: Non-State Actors: International Law's Problematic Case' in Math Noortmann and Cedric Ryngaer (eds), *Non-State Actor Dynamics in International Law: From Law-Takers to Law-Makers* (Farnham, Burlington: Ashgate, 2010) 1.

Nowak, Manfred (ed), *UN Covenant on Civil and Political Rights: CCPR Commentary* (Kehl: NP Engel, 2005).

Nystuen, Gro, *Achieving Peace or Protecting Human Rights: Conflicts between Norms Regarding Ethnic Discrimination in the Dayton Peace Agreement* (Leiden: Martinus Nijhoff Publishers, 2005).

O'Connell, Mary Ellen, 'Jus cogens: International Law's Higher Ethical Norms' in Donald Earl Childress, III (ed), *The Role of Ethics in International Law* (Cambridge: Cambridge University Press, 2011) 78.

O'Flaherty, Michael, 'The Concluding Observations of United Nations Human Rights Treaty Bodies' (2006) 6(1) *Human Rights Law Review* 27.

Ogilvie, Paul Morgan, *International Waterways* (New York: MacMillan, 1920).

Okey, Robin, *Taming Balkan Nationalism: The Habsburg 'Civilizing' Mission in Bosnia, 1878–1914* (Oxford: Oxford University Press, 2007).

O'Leary, Brendan, 'Debating Consociational Politics: Normative and Explanatory Arguments' in Sid Noel (ed), *From Power Sharing to Democracy: Post-conflict Institutions in Ethnically Divided Societies* (Montreal: McGill-Queen's University Press, 2005) 3.

——, *The British-Irish Agreement: Power-Sharing Plus* (London: London School of Economics, 1998).

Oppenheim, Lassa FL, *International Law: A Treatise*, Ronald F Roxburgh (ed) (Clark, New Jersey: The Lawbook Exchange, 2005).

Orakhelashvili, Alexander, 'The Impact of Peremptory Norms on the Interpretation and Application of United Nations Security Council Resolutions' (2005) 16(1) *European Journal of International Law* 59.

Orend, Brian, 'Jus Post Bellum: A Just War Theory Perspective' in Carsten Stahn and Jann K Kleffner (eds), *Towards a Law of Transition from Conflict to Peace* (The Hague: T.M.C. Asser Press, 2008) 31.
Österdahl, Inger and van Zadel, Esther, 'What Will Jus Post Bellum Mean?: Of New Wine and Old Bottles' (2009) 14(2) *Journal of Conflict and Security Law* 207.
Packer, John, 'Making International Law Matter in Preventing Ethnic Conflict: A Practitioner's Perspective' (1999–2000) 32 *New York University Journal of International Law and Politics* 715.
Pajic, Zoran, 'A Critical Appraisal of Human Rights Provisions of the Dayton Constitution of Bosnia and Herzegovina' (1998) 20 *Human Rights Quarterly* 125.
Pandey, Tulshi Ram, 'Culture and Politics of Caste in the Himalayan Kingdom' (2005) 9 *OPSA* 65.
Parlett, Kate, *The Individual in the International Legal System: Continuity and Change in International Law* (Cambridge: Cambridge University Press, 2010).
Petrasek, David, 'A Road Less Travelled: International Human Rights Advocacy and Armed Groups' (2012) 4(1) *Journal of Human Rights Practice* 128.
Picard, Elizabeth, 'Nation-Building and Minority Rights in the Middle East' in Anh Nga Longva and Anne Sofie Roald (eds), *Religious Minorities in the Middle East: Domination, Self-empowerment, Accommodation* (Leiden: Brill, 2012) 230.
Picone, Paolo, 'The Distinction between Jus Cogens and Obligations Erga Omnes' in Enzo Cannizzaro (ed), *The Law of Treaties Beyond the Vienna Convention* (Oxford: Oxford University Press, 2011).
Pollicino, Oreste, 'The New Relationship between National and the European Courts after the Enlargement of Europe: Towards a Unitary Theory of Jurisprudential Supranational Law?' (2010) 29(1) *Yearbook of European Law* 65.
Potter, Pitman B, 'The Doctrine of Servitudes in International Law' (1915) 9(3) *American Journal of International Law* 627.
Popovic, Dragoljub, 'Prevailing of Judicial Activism over Self-Restraint in the Jurisprudence of the European Court of Human Rights' (2008-2009) 42(3) *Creighton Law Review* 361.
Prins, Gwyn, 'Conditions for Jus in Pace in the Face of the Future' in Charles Reed and David Ryall (eds), *The Price of Peace Just War in the Twenty-First Century* (Cambridge: Cambridge University Press, 2007) 236.
Prütting, Hanns, *Gegenwartsprobleme der Beweislast* (München: CH Beck Verlag, 1983).
Pufendorf, Samuel, *De Jure Naturae et Gentium Libri Octo*, first published 1673, Frank Gardner Moore (ed) (New York: Oceana Publications Inc, 1964).
Pugh, Michael, 'Challenges of Post-Conflict Intercession: Three Issues in International Politics' Carsten Stahn and Jann K Kleffner (eds), *Towards a Law of Transition from Conflict to Peace* (The Hague: TMC Asser Press, 2008) 115.
Rao, M Govinda and Singh, Nirvikar, *Asymmetric Federalism in India*, UC Santa Cruz International Economics Working Paper Series No 04-08, April 2004.
Rasilla del Moral, Ignacio de la, 'The Increasingly Marginal Appreciation of the Margin of Appreciation Doctrine' (2006) 7(6) *German Law Journal* 621.
Ratner, Steven R, 'Does International Law Matter in Preventing Ethnic Conflict?' (1999–2000) 32 *New York University Journal of International Law and Politics* 591.
Raue, Julia, *Der Europarat als Verfassungsgestalter seiner Neuen Mitgliedsstaaten: Vom Beobachter zum Reformer in Osteuropa* (Zürich: Schulthess, 2005).
Rawls, John, *A Theory of Justice* (Cambridge, MA: Harvard University Press, 1971).
Roberts, Anthea, 'Legality vs. Legitimacy: Can Uses of Force be Illegal but Justified?' in Philip Alston and Euan MacDonald (eds), *Human Rights, Intervention, and the Use of Force* (Oxford: Oxford University Press, 2008) 179.
Rowe, Peter, 'The Application of the European Convention on Human Rights during an International Armed Conflict' in Richard Burchill, Nigel D White and Justin Morris (eds), *International Conflict and Security Law: Essays in Memory of Hilaire McCoubrey* (Cambridge: Cambridge University Press, 2005) 186.
Rehman, Javaid, *The Weaknesses in the International Protection of Minority Rights* (The Hague: Kluwer Law International, 2000).

Reid, Karen, *A Practitioner's Guide to the European Convention on Human Rights* (London: Thomson/Sweet & Maxwell, 2008).
Reid Sarkees, Meredith, Wayman, Frank Whelon and Singer, J David, 'Inter-State, Intra-State, and Extra-State Wars: A Comprehensive Look at their Distribution over Time, 1816–1997' (2003) 47(1) *International Studies Quarterly* 49.
Reynold, Frederic, *The Judge as Lawmaker* (London: MacGibbon & Kee, 1967).
Riehm, Thomas, *Abwägungsentscheidungen in der Praktischen Rechtsanwendung: Argumentation, Beweis, Wertung* (München: Verlag CH Beck, 2006).
Roeder, Philip G and Rothchild, Donald S, 'Dilemmas of State-Building in Divided Societies' in Philip G Roeder and Donald S Rothchild (eds), *Sustainable Peace: Power and Democracy after Civil Wars* (Ithaca, NY: Cornell University Press, 2005) 5.
Rosiny, Stephan, 'Power Sharing in Syria: Lessons from Lebanon's Taif Experience' (2013) 20(3) *Middle East Policy* 41.
Ross, Alf, *On Law and Justice* (Berkeley: University of California Press, 1959).
Rothwell, Donald R, Kaye, Stuart, A-Khavari, Afshin and Davis, Ruth (eds), *International Law: Cases and Materials With Australian Perspectives* (Cambridge: Cambridge University Press, 2010).
Sadurski, Wojciech, 'Partnering with Strasbourg: Constitutionalisation of the European Court of Human Rights, the Accession of Central and East European States to the Council of Europe, and the Idea of Pilot Judgments' (2009) 9(3) *Human Rights Law Review* 397.
Salem, Paul, *Electoral Law Reform in Lebanon: The Experience and Recommendations of the National Commission*, Arab Reform Brief No 10, Arab Reform Initiative, 2006.
Salibi, Kamal S, *The Modern History of Lebanon* (Delmar, New York: Caravan Books, 1965).
Sandifer, Durward V, *Evidence Before International Tribunals* (Charlottesville: University Press of Virginia, 1975).
Saul, Ben, 'Criminality and Terrorism' in Ana María Salinas de Frias, Katja Samuel and Nigel White (eds), *Counter-Terrorism: International Law and Practice* (Oxford: Oxford University Press, 2012) 133.
Saxer, Urs, *Die internationale Steuerung der Selbstbestimmung und der Staatsentstehung* (Heidelberg: Springer, 2000).
Schauer, Frederick F, *Thinking Like a Lawyer: A New Introduction to Legal Reasoning* (Cambridge, MA: Harvard University Press, 2009).
Schendelen, Rinus van, 'The Views of Arend Lijphart and Collected Criticisms' (1984) 19(1) *Acta Politica* 19.
Schorm-Bernschütz, Rebecca, *Die Tatsachenfeststellung im Verfahren vor dem Europäischen Gerichtshof für Menschenrechte* (Münster: LIT Verlag, 2004).
Schwerdtfeger, Johannes, 'Zu Theorien und Methoden in der Friedensforschung' in Bernhard Moltmann (ed), *Perspektiven der Friedensforschung* (Baden-Baden: Nomos, 1988) 48.
Scourby, Alice, 'Three Generations of Greek Americans: A Study in Ethnicity' (1980) 14 *International Migration Review* 43.
Sebastián, Sofia, *Leaving Dayton Behind: Constitutional Reform in Bosnia and Herzegovina*, FRIDE, Working Paper No 46, November 2007.
Seiderman, Ian D, *Hierarchy in International Law: The Human Rights Dimension* (Antwerp: Intersentia, 2001).
Sen, Amartya, *The Idea of Justice* (London: Allen Lane, 2009).
Shany, Yuval, 'Toward a General Margin of Appreciation Doctrine in International Law?' (2005) 16(5) *European Journal of International Law* 907.
'Sharing the Lebanese Government Apparatus' (2010) 100 *The Monthly* 5.
Sheeran, Scott P, 'International Law, Peace Agreements and Self-Determination: The Case of the Sudan' (2011) 60(2) *International and Comparative Law Quarterly* 423.
Shields, Vanessa E, 'Political Reform in Lebanon: Has the Cedar Revolution Failed?' (2008) 14(4) *Journal of Legislative Studies* 474.
Simma, Bruno (ed), *The Charter of the United Nations: A Commentary* vol I (Oxford: Oxford University Press, 2002).

—— and Andreas T Müller, 'Exercise and Limits of Jurisdiction' in James Crawford and Martti Koskenniemi (eds), *The Cambridge Companion to International Law*, eds. (Cambridge: Cambridge University Press, 2012) 148.

Siorat, Lucien, *Le Problème des Lacunes en Droit International* (Paris: LGDJ, 1958).

Sisk, Timothy D, 'Peacebuilding as Democratization: Findings and Recommendations' in Anna K Jarstad and Timothy D Sisk (eds), *From War to Democracy: Dilemmas of Peacebuilding* (Cambridge: Cambridge University Press, 2008) 239.

Slaughter, Anne-Marie, Tulumello, Andrew S and Wood, Stepan, 'International Law and International Relations Theory: A New Generation of Interdisciplinary Scholarship' (1998) 92(3) *American Journal of International Law* 367.

——, 'Pushing the Limits of the Liberal Peace: Ethnic Conflict and the "Ideal Polity"' in David Wippman (ed), *International Law and Ethnic Conflict* (Ithaca, NY: Cornell University Press, 1998) 128.

Sloan, James, 'The Dayton Peace Agreement: Human Rights Guarantees and their Implementation' (1996) 7, *European Journal of International Law* 245.

Slye, Ronald C, 'The Dayton Peace Agreement: Constitutionalism and Ethnicity' (1996) 21 *Yale Journal of International Law* 459.

Somer, Jonathan, 'Engaging Armed Non-State Actors to Protect Children from the Effects of Armed Conflict: When the Stick Doesn't Cut the Mustard' (2012) 4(1) *Journal of Human Rights Practice* 106.

Sottiaux, Stefan and Van der Schyff, Gerhard, 'Methods of International Human Rights Adjudication: Towards a More Structured Decision-Making Process for the European Court of Human Rights' (2008) 31(1) *Hastings International and Comparative Law Review* 115.

Spiliopoulou Akermark, Athanasia, *Justifications of Minority Protection in International Law* (The Hague: Springer, 1997).

Stahn, Carsten and Kleffner, Jann K (eds), *Towards a Law of Transition from Conflict to Peace* (The Hague: TMC Asser Press, 2008).

——, 'The Future of Jus Post Bellum' in Carsten Stahn and Jann K Kleffner (eds), *Towards a Law of Transition from Conflict to Peace* (The Hague: TMC Asser Press, 2008) 231.

——, 'Jus Post Bellum: Mapping the Discipline(s)' in Carsten Stahn and Jann K Kleffner (eds), *Towards a Law of Transition from Conflict to Peace* (The Hague: TMC Asser Press, 2008) 103–104.

——, 'Responsibility to Protect: Political Rhetoric or Emerging Legal Norm?' (2007) 101(1) *American Journal of International Law* 99.

——, '"Jus ad bellum", "Jus in bello"... "Jus post bellum"?: Rethinking the Conception of the Law of Armed Force' (2006) 17 *European Journal of International Law* 926.

Stavros, Tsakyrakis, *Proportionality: An Assault on Human Rights?* Jean Monnet Working Paper No 9 (2008).

Steinberg, Richard H, and Zasloff, Jonathan M, 'Power and International Law' (2006) 100(1) *American Journal of International Law* 64.

Steiner, Henry J, 'Ideals and Counter-Ideals in the Struggle over Autonomy Regimes for Minorities' (1991) 66 *Notre Dame Law Review* 1539.

Sterio, Milena, *The Right to Self-determination under International Law: "Selfistans", Secession, and the Rule of the Great Powers* (London: Routledge, 2012).

Sugar, Peter F, *Southeastern Europe under Ottoman Rule: 1354–1804* (Seattle: University of Washington Press, 1977).

Sweeney, James A, 'Margins of Appreciation: Cultural Relativity and the European Court of Human Rights in the Post-Cold War Era' (2005) 54 *International and Comparative Law Quarterly* 459.

Szasz, Paul C, 'The Quest for a Bosnian Constitution: Legal Aspects of Constitutional Proposals Relating to Bosnia' (1995) 19 *Fordham Law Journal* 363.

Teitel, Ruti, *Humanity's Law* (Oxford: Oxford University Press, 2011).

——, 'Transitional Jurisprudence: The Role of Law in Political Transformation' (1997) 106 *Yale Law Journal* 2009.

Tesón, Fernando R, 'Ethnicity, Human Rights, and Self-Determination' in David Wippman (ed), *International Law and Ethnic Conflict* (Ithaca, NY: Cornell University Press, 1998) 86.

Thomas, Ward, *The Ethics of Destruction: Norms and Force in International Relations* (Ithaca, NY: Cornell University Press, 1999).
Thornberry, Patrick, *International Law and Rights of Minorities* (Oxford: Oxford University Press, 1993).
Toros, Harmonie, '"We Don't Negotiate with Terrorists!": Legitimacy and Complexity in Terrorist Conflicts' (2008) 39(4) *Security Dialogue* 407.
Tomuschat, Christian, *Human Rights: Between Idealism and Realism* (Oxford: Oxford University Press, 2008).
——, 'Reconceptualizing the Debate on Jus Cogens and Obligations Erga Omnes: Concluding Observations' in Christian Tomuschat and Jean Marc Thouvenin (eds), *The Fundamental Rules of the International Legal Order: Jus Cogens And Obligations Erga Omnes* (The Hague: Martinus Nijhoff Publishers, 2006) 425.
——, 'Secession and Self-determination' in Marcelo G Kohen (ed), *Secession: International Law Perspectives* (Cambridge: Cambridge University Press, 2006) 23.
——, 'Obligations Arising for States Without or Against Their Will' (1993) 241(IV) *Recueil des Cours* 209.
Traboulsi, Fawwaz, *A History of Modern Lebanon* (London: Pluto Press, 2007).
Triggs, Gillian, 'The Rights of "Peoples" and Individual Rights: Conflict or Harmony?' in James Crawford (ed), *The Rights of Peoples* (Oxford: Oxford University Press, 1988) 141.
Turnera, Mark, 'Autonomous Regions and the Contribution of International Relations to Peace and Development: Mindanao, Bougainville and Aceh' (2007) 6(1) *Ethnopolitics* 89.
Van Vollenhoven, Cornelis, *The Law of Peace* (London: MacMillian and Co, 1936).
Varennes, Fernand de, 'Political Participation and Power-sharing in Ethnic Peace Settlements' in Marc Weller and Katherine Nobbs (eds), *Political Participation of Minorities: A Commentary on International Standards and Practice* (Oxford: Oxford University Press, 2010) 453.
Vattel, Emmerich de, *The Law of Nations or the Principles of Natural Law*, first published 1758, Joseph Chitty and Edward D Ingraham (eds) (Philadelphia: T& JW Johnson, 1854).
Verhoeven, Joe, *Droit International Public* (Bruxelles: Larcier, 2001).
Viergang, Egbert Willem, *The Concept of Discrimination in International Law: With Special Reference to Human Rights* (The Hague: Martinus Nijhoff Publishers, 1973).
Villán Durán, Carlos, *International Law for Humankind: Towards a New Jus Gentium* (The Hague: Martinus Nijhoff Publishers, 2010).
Vitzthum, Wolfgang (ed), *Völkerrecht* (Berlin: Walter de Gruyter, 2007).
Waart, Paul de, 'The Inter-Relationship Between the Right to Life and the Right to Peace' in Bertrand G Ramcharan (ed), *The Right to Life in International Law* (The Hague: Martinus Nijhoff Publishers, 1985) 90.
Wakely, Lindsey E, 'From Constituent Peoples to Constituents: Europe Solidifies Fundamental Political Rights for Minority Groups in Sejdic v. Bosnia' (2010) 36(1) *North Carolina Journal of International Law & Commercial Regulation* 253.
Wall, Illan Rua, 'On the Threshold of Law: A Review of "On the Law of Peace" by Christine Bell' (2008) *Irish Yearbook of International Law* 210.
Walzer, Michael, *Spheres of Justice: A Defense of Pluralism and Equality* (New York: Basic Books, 1983).
——, *Just and Unjust Wars: A Moral Argument with Historical Illustrations* (New York: Basic Books, 1977).
Watts, Ronald, 'Models of Federal Power Sharing' (2001) 53(167) *International Social Science Journal* 23.
Webber, Grégoire CN, *The Negotiable Constitution: On the Limitation of Rights* (Cambridge: Cambridge University Press, 2009).
Weller, Marc, 'Introduction' in Marc Weller and Katherine Nobbs (eds), *Asymmetric Autonomy and the Settlement of Ethnic Conflicts* (Philadelphia: University of Pennsylvania Press, 2010) 7.
——, 'Settling Self-determination Conflicts: An Introduction' in Marc Weller, Barbara Metzger and Niall Johnson (eds), *Settling Self-Determination Disputes: Complex Power-sharing in Theory and Practice* (Leiden: Brill, 2008).

——, *Escaping the Self-Determination Trap* (Leiden: Brill, 2008).
—— and Wolff, Stefan, 'Bosnia and Herzegovina Ten Years after Dayton: Lessons for Internationalized State Building' (2006) 5(1) *Ethnopolitics* 1.
Wenzel, Nicola, *Das Spannungsverhältnis zwischen Gruppenschutz und Individualschutz im Völkerrecht* (Berlin: Springer, 2008).
'When Law is the Elephant in the Room' (2003) 18(2) *Tikkun Magazine* 40.
Wheaton, Henry, *Elements of International Law* (New York: Baker, Voorhis & Co, 1916).
Wippman, David (ed), *International Law and Ethnic Conflict* (Ithaca, NY: Cornell University Press, 1998).
——, 'Introduction: Ethnic Claims and International Law' in David Wippman (ed), *International Law and Ethnic Conflict* (Ithaca, NY: Cornell University Press, 1998) 2.
——, 'Practical and Legal Constraints on Internal Power Sharing' in David Wippman (ed), *International Law and Ethnic Conflict* (Ithaca, NY: Cornell University Press, 1998) 211.
——, 'The Evolution and Implementation of Minority Rights' (1997) 66(2) *Fordham Law Review* 597.
——, 'International Law and Ethnic Conflict on Cyprus' (1996) 31 *Texas International Law Journal* 141.
Wolfrum, Rüdiger, 'International Courts and Tribunals, Evidence', *Max Planck Encyclopedia of Public International Law (Online)* [retrieved 26 April 2013].
Yarwood, Lisa, *State Accountability under International Law: Holding States Accountable for a Breach of Jus cogens Norms* (New York: Routledge, 2011).
Yasuaki, Onuma (ed), *A Normative Approach to War: Peace, War, and Justice in Hugo Grotius* (Oxford: Clarendon Press, 1993).
Yee, Sienho, 'The New Constitution of Bosnia and Herzegovina' (1996) 7 *European Journal of International Law* 176.
Zahar, Marie-Joelle, 'Power Sharing in Lebanon: Foreign Protectors, Domestic Peace, and Democratic Failure' in Donald Rotschild and Philip Roeder (eds), *Sustainable Peace: Power and Democracy after Civil Wars* (Ithaca: Cornell University Press, 2005) 219.
Zartman, I William, 'The Timing of Peace Initiatives: Hurting Stalemates and Ripe Moments' (2001) 1(1) *The Global Review of Ethnopolitics* 8.
Zemanek, Karl, 'The Metamorphosis of Jus cogens: From an Institution of Treaty Law to the Bedrock of the International Legal Order?' in Enzo Cannizzaro (ed), *The Law of Treaties Beyond the Vienna Convention* (Oxford: Oxford University Press, 2011) 381.
Zisser, Eyal, *Lebanon: The Challenge of Independence* (London: IB Tauris Publishers, 2000).

News articles (chronological)

'Central African Republic: Amnesty and power-sharing at the center of peace talks', *African Daily Voice*, 29 January 2019.
'US and Taliban edge Toward Deal to End America's Longest War', *The New York Times*, 26 January 2019.
'Milorad Dodik: Republika Srpska is fully prepared for Secession from Bosnia and Herzegovina', *Sarajevo Times*, 25 January 2019.
'Charbel Insists Civil Marriage Couple Keep Sects', *The Daily Star (Lebanon)*, 26 April 2013.
Abu-Nasr, Donna, and Nadeem Hamid, 'Lebanon's Premier Resigns After Dispute on Electoral Law', *Bloomberg*, 23 March 2013.
Latifi, Ali M, 'Taliban Talks in Doha Drag on Endlessly', *Al Jazeera English*, 26 February 2013.
'Ministers, Judges Discuss Legalization of Civil Marriage', *The Daily Star (Lebanon)*, 22 February 2013.
'Nepal Exercising Partyocracy', *The Himalayan*, 14 February 2013.
'Lebanon's Sleiman Calls for Legalizing Civil Marriage', *The Daily Star (Lebanon)*, 23 January 2013.
'Mikati Says Debate on Civil Marriage Useless in Face of Political Paralysis', *The Daily Star (Lebanon)*, 23 January 2013.
'Lebanon Committee Focusing on Boutros Electoral Law', *YaLibnan*, 22 January 2013.
'Lebanon's First Request for Civil Marriage Rejected: Interior Minister', *Al Arabiya News*, 21 January 2013.

Al-Husseini, Arwa, 'Lebanon's First Civil Marriage', *NOW Lebanon*, 18 January 2013.
'USA: Egypt Needs to Do More on Religious Tolerance', *The Huffington Post*, 17 January 2013.
'Miqati Urges Politicians to be Reasonable: Says Electoral Law Takes Lebanon to Shores of Safety', *Naharnet*, 16 January 2013.
'Is Another Conflict Looming in the Balkans?', *Al Jazeera English*, 6 January 2013.
Hyatt, Justin, 'The Secular Fret in New Tunisia', *IPS News Agency*, 26 November 2012.
Burch, Jonathon, 'Turkish Police Fire Tear Gas at Banned Secularist March', *Reuters*, 29 October 2012.
Dabestani, Arash, et al., 'Is Turkey's Secular System in Danger?', *BBC News*, 24 October 2012.
'Thousands of Tunisian Secularists Protest against Islamist Rulers', *The Daily Star (Lebanon)*, 23 October 2012.
Al-Shibeeb, Dina, 'Prominent Yemeni Novelist Defends Minority Rights in Arab World', *Al Arabiya News*, 18 September 2012.
'Greece Bailout Crisis: President Seeks Unity Government', *BBC News*, 12 May 2012.
'Lebanese Protest Against Confessionalism', *AFP*, 6 May 2012.
Borger, Julian, 'Bosnian War 20 Years on: Peace Holds but Conflict Continues to Haunt', *The Guardian*, 4 April 2012.
Khouri, Rami G., 'The Islamist-Secular Battle is Under Way', *The Daily Star (Lebanon)*, 31 March 2012.
Amara, Tarek, 'Tunisian Protesters Reject Calls for Islamic State', *Al Arabiya News*, 20 March 2012.
Emma Gatten, 'Activists Reawaken Anti-Sectarianism Campaign', *The Daily Star (Lebanon)*, 27 February 2012.
Gatten, Emma, 'Anti-sectarian Spring Ended as Summer Began', *The Daily Star (Lebanon)*, 2 November 2011.
Dhumieres, Marie, 'Civil Marriages on the Rise Amongst Lebanese', *The Daily Star (Lebanon)*, 7 September 2011.
'Bosnia Edges Closer to State Government Deal', *Balkan Insight*, 28 July 2011.
'UN Welcomes South Sudan as 193rd Member State', *UN News*, 14 July 2011.
Brooke Anderson, 'Anti-sectarian Protesters Revamp Movement', *The Daily Star (Lebanon)*, 26 June 2011.
Sikimic, Simona, 'Laique Demonstrators Call for Secular State', *The Daily Star (Lebanon)*, 16 May 2011.
Moussaoui, Rana, 'Lebanon Youths Revolt Against Confessional System', *AFP*, 23 February 2011.
Mainali, Shyam Prasad, 'Boundaries in Federalism', *The Himalayan*, 5 January 2011.
Galey, Patrick, 'Thousands March in Beirut to Promote Secularism in Politics', *The Daily Star (Lebanon)*, 26 April 2010.
'Lebanese Stage First Pro-secular Demonstration', *Al Arabiya News*, 25 April 2010.
'Lebanese March in Beirut to Demand Secularism', *BBC News*, 25 April 2010.
'Interview with Dervan Sejdic', *Movimiento Por la Paz Balkans E-Newsletter*, 12 April 2010.
Rathfelder, Erich, 'Fünf Minute mit Jakob Finci: Über Menschenrechte, Gleichheit und einen gewonnenen Prozess', *Jüdische Allgemeine*, 14 January 2010.
Sandić-Hadžihasanović, Gordana, 'Strazbur Osudio BiH Zbog Diskriminacije Roma i Jevreja', *Radio Free Europe/Radio Liberty*, 22 December 2009.
Ladki, Nadim, 'Lebanon's Hariri Forms Unity Government with Hezbollah', *Reuters*, 9 November 2009.
'Doha Agreement Achieved its Aims', *The Daily Star (Lebanon)*, 26 June 2009.
Muir, Jim, 'Lebanon Deal Holds Prospect of Peace', *BBC News*, 21 May 2008.
'Lebanon Dialogue Committee Agreed to Adopt 1960 Electoral Law', *Yalibnan*, 18 May 2008.
'A New Constitution for Bosnia', *PBS NewsHour*, 22 November 2005.

INDEX